MNUMHER... ...HCS
AND PRESSURE GROUPS

With many thanks for your valuable help with the TWA campaign — and all best wishes

Arthur

With thanks to all who have supported and helped me –
including Lady Luck.

PEOPLE, POLITICS AND PRESSURE GROUPS

MEMOIRS OF A LOBBYIST

Arthur Butler

First published in Great Britain in 2010 by
Picnic Publishing
PO Box 5222
Hove BN52 9LP
www.picnic-publishing.co.uk

ISBN 9780955861369

10 9 8 7 6 5 4 3 2 1

A CIP catalogue record for this book is available from the British Library.

Set in Garamond by SoapBox
Printed and bound in Great Britain by CPI Anthony Rowe, Chippenham, Wiltshire

CONTENTS

PROLOGUE

Shaving on the morning of Wednesday, March 3rd 2010, my thoughts turned to the deaths in recent weeks of two men with whom I had enjoyed friendly professional dealings. One was Trevor Lloyd-Hughes, who reported for *The Liverpool Daily Post* when I was on *The News Chronicle*. We shared information and contacts in the Parliamentary Press Gallery before he went on to become a successful press secretary to Prime Minister Harold Wilson. The other was Norman Payne, respected former chairman of BAA. I pondered on which of my old associates would be next to feature in the obituary columns. Into my mind came Michael Foot. He had appeared so frail at his 90th birthday party, six years earlier. Despite this presage, it shocked me when Michael died later that day. I was much saddened at the loss of this great radical and supreme parliamentarian. For over forty years I had enjoyed his lively company, while yet opposing so many of his far left policies.

On one thing, we did see eye-to-eye – a shared contempt for Tony Blair. For Michael's ninetieth birthday I had sent him a postcard savagely lampooning the shallow opportunist. I thought it would make him chuckle. I wondered how he would have regarded the fulsome tribute Blair was quick to pay.

Ian Aitkin, writing in *The Guardian* as a former political editor, recalled how, in 1963, Michael had almost been killed in a car accident while his beloved wife Jill Craigie was driving. Ian, then on the *Daily Express*, had written 'a hurried and anguished obituary' of his close friend – but it was to be half a century before it was needed.

Of the fifteen founder members of the Leslie Hale Luncheon Club, only Ian, Alf Morris, Lib Dem peer George Mackie and I remained.

INTRODUCTION

On the brink of becoming one of the most successful British newspaper editors of the second half of the 20th century, David English phoned me from his office. For just over a year, since he had become editor of the *Daily Sketch*, I had headed up his political team. We got on well and I had introduced him to Prime Minister Edward Heath. Now the proprietor Lord Rothermere decided in desperation to merge the *Sketch* with his group's then limping flagship the *Daily Mail*, and English was to run the new, combined paper. My problem was that the *Mail's* one-time successful political editor Walter Terry had been moved from his parliamentary job following an affair with Harold Wilson's private secretary Marcia Williams and was currently deputy editor. David English, however, intended to retain his *Sketch* deputy and had told Terry he could go back to his old position at the Commons. I was to be without a job.

Since the age of fourteen my ambition had been to become a journalist. To gain overseas experience I volunteered for Britain's Indian Army but, presumably on learning of this, the Attlee Government wound it up. I then chose a degree course at the London School of Economics to equip me for a newspaper career and, neglecting my set books, set out to win essay prizes and learn shorthand and typing. With the help of Desmond MacCarthy, distinguished literary critic of *The Sunday Times*, I won a place on the journalists' training scheme for graduates run by the sprawling, bureaucratic Kemsley newspaper group. I learned the reporter's craft on their Middlesbrough *Evening Gazette*. There, on polluted, industrial Teesside, appalled by the wretched living conditions, I became an active Fabian Socialist. I had been a Labour Party supporter since my schooldays, encouraged by my mother (father was at war) and two uncles, militant miners toiling in the Kent coalfield.

Back in London at the Kemsley Group's headquarters, I scooped the national press with a snatched interview with Peter Townsend, Princess Margaret's lover; saw group papers dying around me; and was rescued by the liberal campaigning *News Chronicle*. I joined its political team under Ian Trethowan; wrote in my spare time for *Forward*, a Gaitskellite weekly edited by Francis Williams; and broadcast for the BBC's World Service.

Badly managed, the Cadbury-owned *News Chronicle*, originally launched by Charles Dickens, was 'controversially' merged in 1960 with the right wing *Daily Mail*. An active member of the Labour Party, I declined a television offer and became political editor of the Co-operative movement's Sunday paper *Reynolds News*. Two years later the struggling old journal that had fought for political and social reforms since its launch in 1850 to support the Chartists, was transformed into a pathetic short-lived tabloid the *Sunday Citizen*. Two famous radical papers had sunk within two years with me aboard. Deeply depressed, I gave my notice to the *Citizen* although I had no other job lined up.

I was then recruited in January 1963 by Lord Beaverbrook to the political team of his rumbustious *Daily Express*. A year or two later his lordship died and the paper's circulation began to fall. After six years, frustrated by lack of promotion, I joined the *Daily Sketch* as political editor. A year later, David English, equally frustrated on the *Express*, joined the *Sketch* as editor. The following year, like the *News Chronicle*, it was gobbled up by the *Daily Mail*.

English was embarrassed by having to make me redundant and came up with a helpful suggestion. He told me on the phone that a public relations firm, Partnerplan, owned by a former journalist friend of his, David Wynne-Morgan, needed someone with parliamentary experience to help with a campaign for the City of Cardiff. Would I be interested?

Three national newspapers had died under me in just over a decade. On each one I had enjoyed success and produced more than my share of exclusives. I had never been out of work for more than a few days. Yet I sensed that, surely, my luck must be running out in the shrinking newspaper world. Amongst my journalist friends I had earned the reputation of being the jinx of Fleet Street. At the age of forty-two I decided it was time to start a new career. At times I had toyed with the thought of trying my hand at public affairs consultancy. As I had worked for Liberal, Labour and Tory newspapers, I had a wide range of political friends. I hoped I could put my contacts book to good use. I phoned Partnerplan.

CHAPTER ONE

Local Government Hero

Multi-millionaire Paul Getty phoned a friendly Fleet Street journalist one day in the 1960s and invited him to tea at the Ritz. There he enquired how much he would need to start a public relations company. The journalist came up with the figure of £3,000 and with that Getty made out a cheque for that amount, saying: 'Start one. I'll be your first client. Just keep me out of the papers'.

It was 1971. The journalist was David Wynne-Morgan and, having made an appointment, I was about to meet him for the first time at his office in Fleet Street. I found the narrow front door entrance near the corner of Bouverie Street.

Wynne-Morgan, a muscular forty-year old with a lived-in face, rose from behind his desk in an upper floor room and with a friendly smile offered me his hand. The son of an army colonel, to his disappointment he had been deemed unfit for National Service due to a hand injury but, nevertheless, had played squash for Wales for several years in the 1950s. He had also been through two wives by then. He had been a successful, if risk-tasking, gossip columnist in Fleet Street, working as William Hickey for the *Daily Express* over a three year period from 1954-57 after spending some time on the rival *Daily Mail*. What I did not realise then was that his second marriage had been to the fashion model Sandra Paul, who had been the wife of Robin Douglas-Home, elder brother of my *Daily Express* colleague Charlie. By then Sandra had moved on to husband number three and Wynne-Morgan's third wife-to-be – an attractive girl called Karin Stines – was working in the office as a junior executive.

Over cups of coffee he outlined the Cardiff problem and as he did so my confidence and enthusiasm dipped. I had assumed that if the Welsh city was opposing the Heath Government's 1971 local government reform proposals it must be under Labour Party control. I had foreseen a Tory versus Labour battle with me rounding up the likes of Jim Callaghan and

George Thomas, local MPs, to help defeat the Government's plan. To my dismay, Wynne-Morgan explained that the Government was supported by the Labour Party as it proposed handing over the Tory controlled Welsh capital to the surrounding Labour-controlled area for local government purposes.

With a weak smile I conceded that this posed an unusually difficult challenge. Moreover, I had no experience of lobbying and PR operations and assumed Wynne-Morgan was aware of this. However, if he was prepared to employ me, I was prepared to have a go. We shook hands on it. My new life as a public affairs consultant would begin if Cardiff City Council decided to employ the Partnerplan team.

Faced with redundancy, I had been considering following up a suggestion from my friend Gerald Thomas, director of the famous series of *Carry On* films. Over dinner one evening he had asked me to give some thought to writing a script for a *Carry on Fleet Street* production. I had enjoyed the bawdy comedies from the very first *Carry On Sergeant* that livened up a dull night in the mess at an army reserve camp. But before I could try my hand at a screenplay on the other British institution of sleaze, the Press, I was swept into my new world of public affairs consultancy. I regretted that I never gave it a go as it would surely have been fun to get involved with his laugh-a-line team. As for Gerald, for some forty years he directed with the stamp of his personality the longest, most successful series of funny feature films in the history of cinema.

The Cardiff council's problem was that the Secretary of State for Wales, the Rt. Hon. Peter Thomas, had proposed in a consultation document that the city should be downgraded to the status of a district council. It was to be swallowed up by a new county of East Glamorgan – an authority bound to be Labour controlled. This would take over responsibility for major planning decisions, highways and traffic, education and personal social services. Despite his oratory and charm, the handsome Mr Thomas failed to persuade the city council that Cardiff would benefit from his proposals. We were summoned to a meeting in the City Hall by Cardiff's chief executive and town clerk, the urbane Mr Stuart Lloyd-Jones.

At Paddington station, en route to the meeting, I met Partnerplan's vice chairman David Powell, for the first time. A Welsh ex-journalist his contacts had given the company the opportunity to pitch for the Cardiff business. It soon emerged that he was intensely interested in politics and that his own were left wing. My friendship with Michael Foot impressed him. On that day out to the Welsh capital we forged a lifetime friendship – one that was soon to influence the course of my own career in public affairs.

Thanks to the presentation skills of the two Davids, Partnerplan was awarded the account and a £15,000 fighting fund was to be raised by the city. I had never been involved before in a pitch for new business and was full of admiration for my colleagues' smooth talking. As for my contribution, the vetting committee was impressed by my record as a political journalist – but were apparently given further confidence by my background as an LSE graduate and a decorated Army Emergency Reserve officer.

I was to be employed full-time on the campaign, my task being to help stoke up a great outcry not only in Cardiff but also in Wales generally. I was then to ensure that MPs were made aware of public feeling and encouraged to challenge the Government's plan in Parliament. I was to be assisted in the first part of the task by a successful local fund-raiser and event organiser in the shape of a former naval officer, Commander Ted Williams. The bulky beer-swigging Ted was to be campaign manager based in Cardiff. An independent thirty-four strong action committee under the chairmanship of Sir David Davies, the much respected former Welsh Tourist Office chief, was to front the operation and give broad guidance.

With the Labour Party disassociating itself from the city's campaign and supporting the Government's plan, my task was then made more difficult by Whitehall's unreasonable early deadline of the end of May for comments by local authorities on its White Paper. A decision by the city's action committee then came as a great help. It was to make the campaign a Welsh national issue by adopting the slogan *Keep Cardiff a Real Capital.*

Events were moving quickly. By a lucky coincidence the Conservative Party's annual Central Council meeting was due to open in Cardiff on April 1ˢᵗ – 'an appropriate Government Fools' Day', as one Welsh wag put it. As ministers and delegates arrived, they were handed pamphlets by local young Conservatives headed *Our Welsh Capital is in Danger* and demanding a fair deal in local government. Welsh Secretary Peter Thomas, who was also Tory Party chairman, must have been irritated as he took his seat on the platform. Then the tone got worse as Michael Roberts, Conservative MP for Cardiff North, strode to the rostrum to warn that if new local government proposals failed to recognise the special position of Cardiff as the capital city of Wales, there would be 'a mighty democratic and determined roar of protest'.

I had never dealt with the outspoken Mr Roberts but now I made it my business to get alongside him without delay. We were to become close friends and he too would soon have an important, helpful effect on my career.

In mobilising grass-roots support throughout Wales for the city, I was greatly assisted by David Powell. He was one of the most experienced and creative PR consultants in the local government field at that time and had previously done some work for Cardiff and the Corporation of the City of London. To get the largest possible number of people involved, a great petition was organised to be presented to Peter Thomas. Posters in English and Welsh spread like an orange and black swarm across the countryside, supported by car stickers in the same campaign colours, leaflets, buttonhole badges, a four-page broadsheet and advertisements. I interviewed supportive local citizens to provide articles for the press. One of these was the prominent and 'pushy' Cardiff businessman and financier Sir Julian Hodge, chairman of the Hodge group of companies. A key figure in the Welsh 'Tafia', he had helped local MPs James Callaghan and George Thomas with their personal finances and with the backing of a grateful Jim, had received a knighthood in 1970. When I entered his office I was struck by the number of photographs on display of himself with one-time Chancellor of the Exchequer Callaghan. He was clearly out to impress visitors with this link and soon told me that they were on very friendly terms. Some of his controversial business operations however, had led him to be regarded with suspicion by the Bank of England and London financial institutions.

Lacking support from Labour, I turned successfully for help to the Liberal Party and Welsh Nationalists. I had got to know the courteous and likeable Emlyn Hooson in 1962 when he won Montgomery for the Liberals, a by-election I had covered for *Reynolds News*. Now, as leader of the Welsh Liberal Party, he spoke up for Cardiff in a Commons debate on Welsh affairs. Michael Roberts, much liked and respected, was supported in the same debate by a number of Tory friends such as John Stradling Thomas (Monmouthshire) and Geraint Morgan (Denbigh).

Earlier in the campaign, in a Lords debate, Lord Brooke of Cumnor, a former Tory Minister for Wales and Secretary of State for Housing and Local Government, was persuaded to speak out strongly in support of Cardiff's case. To prepare the ground for the fight at Westminster I helped to organise a reception at the Commons to enable Lord Mayor Fergie Jones and members of the action committee to meet MPs and peers. Well over thirty parliamentarians attended. *The Daily Telegraph* and *The Guardian* were among papers that reported the event. *The Telegraph* also carried a letter I drafted for Michael Roberts. The *South Wales Spectator* reported: 'No other city or town in the UK has waged a more comprehensive and highly organised campaign against local government changes'. That was true – but the outcome would not be known until November when the Government was due to publish the bill implementing its proposals. Meanwhile, Peter Thomas was warned that on October 1st he would be presented with the biggest petition ever organised in Wales. Over 100,000 people signed the document calling on him to abandon his plan to demote the capital city. Great was the jubilation in Cardiff and Partnerplan's office when the Local Government Re-organisation bill was published. Instead of being merged into a giant East Glamorgan authority, the city was to be the centre on which a new South Glamorgan county would be based.

We had won. As a columnist in the *Financial Times* commented on November 5th 1971:

> 'The apparently prosaic announcement by Mr Peter Thomas MP, Secretary of State for Wales, that in the forthcoming re-organisation of local government, Glamorgan is to be split into three rather than two new counties is in fact the culmination of a novel and perhaps precedent-setting political public relations campaign run by the City of Cardiff…
>
> 'The Cardiff council voted £15,000 to fight the proposal that they should be merged into a large new county and hired a London public relations company, Partnerplan, to conduct the campaign… Cardiff's example of professional political lobbying will not, I imagine, be lost on interest groups all over the country'.

Campaign, the journal of the advertising and PR world, commented:

> 'Cardiff won its fight because Partnerplan articulated and assembled those reasons of expediency which enabled the Government to change its mind. It is just the kind of professional worldliness that is currently rare in the PR world'.

Under the headline 'Dominant Cardiff – saved by PR', the *Municipal Journal* reported:

'So within another two and half years all the county boroughs in England and Wales will have disappeared – with the impressive exception of Cardiff, that is. How was the city's victory achieved? The answer appears to be, a little surprisingly, by aggressive public relations'.

The *Western Mail* described the victory as:

'A clever, even cunning affair' and wrote that I had provided political experience and collaborated with Michael Roberts in winning substantial support in the Commons. Ann Clwyd, later to become an MP, wrote in the *New Statesman:* 'Former *Daily Sketch* political correspondent Arthur Butler skilfully master-minded the campaign…'

To have triumphed over such enormous odds in such a short time was certainly a remarkable achievement. It had been accomplished by successfully mobilising grass-roots support and linking this with media work and parliamentary lobbying. The publicity given to the success of the campaign gave a much-needed boost to the reputation of the PR industry. Too many clients had been ripped off by cynical, high-spending charlatans describing themselves as PR consultants with contacts in high places. Cardiff had proved that good PR could produce results quickly and at no great cost.

Soon after, other local authorities were beating a trail to Partnerplan's front door. The first was Luton, next came Pembrokeshire. Then I took a call from Essex County Council which gave me a special kick as that was the county that had provided my secondary school education. I regarded myself as an Essex lad. Local Government Minister Peter Walker had been persuaded by some Tory snobs around Colchester, who disliked having an Essex address, that this ancient town and a large area of land should be transferred to the more up-market county of Suffolk. At a meeting in the county council offices at Chelmsford, it was quickly agreed that Partnerplan should direct a campaign to keep England's oldest chartered town in the county to which it had belonged for so long. My tactics followed closely those of the Cardiff campaign, playing up the historic role of the town within the county.

This time my staunch Tory MP collaborator was a bluff, bustling, World War II infantry field officer, Bernard Braine, a human steamroller who had represented South East Essex since 1955. Despite his name, he was not noted for great cerebral activity but he had served in government as a Parliamentary Secretary for Pensions, Commonwealth Relations and Health, and was a respected and popular member of the Commons. It was a great pleasure to work with him and he, in turn, was grateful for the publicity I got for him by drafting press releases and letters to such newspapers as *The Daily Telegraph*. With Bernard entering the lists, Secretary of State Peter Walker backed off and Colchester was allowed to remain in Essex.

If the phone call from Essex County Council had personal resonance for me, then the one that came from Middlesbrough had me even more motivated. Peter Walker's plans for local government reform for Teesside were not acceptable to the gritty town where I had served my apprenticeship as a journalist on the *Evening Gazette*, owned by the Kemsley newspaper group. By good fortune I had been in the Commons when Walker, under pressure, conceded that he was prepared to listen to public opinion on the issue. When I mentioned this on the phone to the town clerk he was impressed that I was already in touch with the issue and invited me to give a presentation to Middlesbrough town council the following week. I accepted and told him, that the last time I attended the town council meeting it was to report on it for the *Evening Gazette* some twenty years before. What a turn of the wheel.

I flew north with David Wynne-Morgan. With the Cardiff and Colchester victories it was easy to convince the council that Partnerplan's proven ability to mobilise grass-roots support, could provide proof that local public opinion favoured a new county straddling both sides of the Tees with Middlesbrough as its administrative centre. At the meeting, I spoke from the rostrum, and on the Labour benches I recognised some friendly faces of men who had attended Teesside Fabian Society meetings that I had organised as secretary. Invited to the Mayor's parlour for a cup of tea, I then played a card I had been holding back. By luck, I had recently visited nearby Stockton-on-Tees to discuss an aspect of the local government reform proposals. There I had discovered that this historic little town, together with others in the area, was opposed to becoming part of a new county that had Teesside in the title. The connotation of heavy industry and its pollution offended their sensibilities. They preferred the name *Cleveland County* – inspired by the nearby Cleveland Hills.

As the Mayor began to talk about a campaign for Teesside County, I coughed and revealed that my soundings had shown that it would be difficult to get the essential support of the surrounding rural areas if Middlesbrough insisted on sticking to that name. I suggested that we would gather support more quickly if we decided to adopt the name Cleveland County. Such was Partnerplan's reputation that over another brew, the key council members and officers in the room decided that Cleveland County it would be. We were off to our third major victory.

In view of the distance from London, I needed a local man to act as campaign manager. I visited the *Evening Gazette* office to enquire about some of the key people who had taught me the trade of journalism twenty years before. I learned that Sidney Jackson, the shrewd one-time leader writer, lived in retirement in the area and that evening I tracked him down. Under the title *Unite to Fight for Cleveland County*, the campaign was launched with pipe-puffing Sid as on the ground point person.

It was a good slogan but compared to the battles of Cardiff and Colchester, it was more difficult to stir the hearts of local people on an issue that involved a new authority and matters of administration and efficiency. Nevertheless, we drummed up significant support - and Peter Walker had to admit that he for one was impressed. Cleveland County was transformed from a slogan into a geographical administrative fact of life.

Asked to comment on Partnerplan's employment, Alderman Pearson told the *Evening Gazette*, 'We are very impressed with them. They are really professional'.

The *Local Government Chronicle* reported on March 17th: 'Behind last week's decision by Graham Page, Minister for Local Government and Development that there will, after all, be a new county based on Teesside – it will now be called Cleveland – lies yet another success for Partnerplan'. Referring to the previous successes in Cardiff and Essex, the writer concluded: 'The victory in Teesside seems to me an even more remarkable one'.

Partnerplan's achievements were the talk of local government and a steady stream of authorities approached the firm for assistance – but time was running out. One city which admitted that it had probably left matters too late was Plymouth. It had been over-cautious in approaching us because of a previous bad experience with the world of public relations and had decided never again to employ PR consultants. I told the city council that it was so late in the day that it would be very difficult to influence the outcome. But I did promise that Partnerplan would orchestrate an eye-catching campaign which would leave the Government in no doubt about the city's views. As the councillors had been criticised by local people and organisations for not fighting the Government's plans, this assurance came as some relief to them. With a clear understanding on the touchy subject of expenses, the campaign was launched. It was proposed that Sir Francis Drake's drum should be taken to Downing Street in the hope that its symbolic beat would scatter Plymouth's Whitehall foes. Alas, it was not to be. But despite this, Partnerplan had restored a great city's faith in PR. We were thanked warmly for our efforts.

Soon after surviving the local government attack, Cardiff faced a serious new threat. The British Steel Corporation announced that it intended to close their Cardiff East Moors plant. As there were already doubts about the long-term future of GKN's local steel rod making mill, the city council feared that the local economy could be seriously harmed. Now Partnerplan was asked to draw up a campaign to save the British Steel works, and this time the task was made easier for me as all the local politicians were united in wanting to prevent the closure. I worked with David Powell in producing leaflets and stickers, and organising a deputation of local MPs, councillors and trade unionists to the Welsh Office and BSC headquarters in London. We hired a double-decker bus to drive around Westminster, and on a rainy day MPs Jim Callaghan, George Thomas and Michael Roberts led the deputation with me holding an umbrella over them as they ran in and out of the bus to deliver their views.

Meanwhile Michael Roberts, feted as a local hero in Cardiff, had bounced back into my life in another role. He had been elected secretary of the Tory backbench Transport Committee and in that capacity had met representatives of the British Road Federation (BRF) and the Roads Campaign Council (RCC) – two highly professional lobbying organisations campaigning for the completion of a strategic motorway network for Britain. Faced by vociferous anti-motorway groups and an influential railway lobby with deep roots into the Labour Party through the railway trade unions, they were looking for new men and new ideas to help them. Michael told them about the success of our Cardiff campaign in mobilising grass roots opinion and channelling it into the media and Parliament. I received a call from Robert Phillipson, the sharp brained, no-nonsense director of the BRF with an invitation to submit proposals for giving a much-needed boost to the motorway campaign.

At a meeting in his office I was surprised to encounter a man I had known by sight for years and whom I assumed held an official post in Parliament.

With his black jacket and striped trousers, sober tie and stiff appearance he could certainly have passed for an officer of one of the Houses. He was, in fact, Lt. Commander Christopher Powell RN (retired), one of the earliest – and certainly the most successful – professional lobbyists to haunt the corridors of Westminster. He strongly disliked the word 'lobbyist' and described himself as a 'parliamentary consultant'. Trained to be a naval officer, he joined forces in 1929 with Charles Watney, a former political editor of the *Daily Mail,* to set up a parliamentary information and consultancy business – the first of its kind – trading under the name of Watney & Powell. They also provided a secretarial service to help Tory MPs deal with constituents' letters.

In the Second World War, Powell was director of censorship at the Ministry of Information and following the death of Charles Watney in 1948, carried on running the business, still under their joint names. One of his clients was the Inter Parliamentary Union that had an office in the Commons from which he worked as secretary. Unfortunately for 'The Commander' as he was known, he was discovered using the office for work on behalf of other clients and was ejected in disgrace. Soon after, he was involved in further trouble as someone reported him to the Speaker when he was seen trying to stop a friendly MP from entering a standing committee to vote on a private member's bill. The fact that he had these two entries in the 'Black Book' no doubt accounted for the fact that his name never appeared in the Honours' List for services to Parliament.

Robert Phillipson invited him to my presentation meeting out of courtesy, as he supplied the BRF with parliamentary information, helped with the tabling of questions, and advised on procedure and legislation. As he confined his efforts to the parliamentary arena, however, he could not assist the BRF in the task of mobilising grass roots support for motorway building around the country – so I was given the job. I was to be consultant to the most formidable lobby in Britain, comprising the road construction industry, the motor industry, the oil industry and three major road-user organisations – the AA, the RAC and the Road Hauliers' Association.

My direct employer was to be the Roads Campaign Council. I was instructed to report to Sir George Middleton, chairman of the BRF and chief executive of the British Industry Roads Campaign – a fund-raising operation. This gentlemanly former ambassador who had spent a key part of his career in the Middle East, occupied expensive offices in Mayfair together with the secretary of the Roads Campaign Council, a salty ex-submariner Lieut. Commander Arthur Pitt DSO. Pitt's main job was to liaise with the All-Party Roads Study Group in the House of Commons. He organised monthly meetings at which MPs would be lectured on road construction issues before being well wined and dined in St. Stephen's Tavern opposite the Houses of Parliament. He won his DSO in 1944 as captain of the submarine Taku, having done a lot of damage to enemy shipping in the Mediterranean and Norwegian seas.

After the war he served for a time with MI6, which no doubt accounted for his rather conspiratorial style and habit of occasionally putting his hand to his mouth during a conversation. His lively sense of humour made him good company.

His boss, the courteous Sir George, was a cosmopolitan character and gifted linguist who spoke seven languages. His work in the Consular and Diplomatic Service had taken him to countries as varied as Romania, Argentina, Egypt, Iran and Poland. In Washington, he had been a bridge partner to the diplomat who spied for Moscow – Donald Maclean. On leaving government service, he picked up a string of directorships and joined the PR firm of Michael Rice that had profitable business in the Middle East.

Convivial cigar-smoking Sir George had a penchant for good living and a substantial expense account from the BRF to entertain captains of industry who were seen as potential donors to the roads campaign. The problem was that, having paid for costly lunches at the Dorchester Hotel, Savoy Grill or other favoured watering holes, he was too gentlemanly a chap to ask his guests for donations to bolster the roads' campaign's dwindling funds. This state of affairs could not continue. The BRF decided to end Sir George's operation, close down his expensive suite of offices and find somewhere to switch Arthur Pitt before his imminent retirement. It was agreed that I should replace him as secretary of the Roads Campaign Council and All-Party Roads Study Group (APRSG) and that Arthur should have a desk at Partnerplan.

The APRSG, founded in 1956, was one of the oldest such groups linked to industry and met regularly in Parliament. Its Tory joint chairman John Osborn MP was just handing over to Peter Fry, MP for Wellingborough, and the Labour joint chairman was Alan Fitch MP for Wigan, a former coal miner who had been an effective Party Whip for some eight years. Well liked and respected, he was an important political figure in the North West. The group was in need of a shot in the arm as the aggressive tactics of the conservationist anti-roads lobby had started to deter backbenchers from joining. Hard-playing rugby enthusiast Peter Fry was going to help me turn the tide.

Meanwhile, another major new client for Partnerplan was looming. One of its clients was a cigar company based near Ipswich which was part of the Imperial Tobacco Group. Wynne-Morgan decided it would be useful to introduce me to the managing director, a member of the well-known Bonham Carter family. Over lunch, the conversation turned to the industry's growing problem in dealing with the smoking and health issue. A voluntary agreement had been signed between the Government and the tobacco industry under which advertising was slowly being reduced and advertising slogans toned down. Anti-smoking crusaders were far from satisfied and had decided to try to get legislative action through private members' bills in Parliament. Secretary of State for Health, Sir Keith Joseph, was on record as saying that legislation regarding cigarettes was 'a significant and dangerous diminution of corporate and personal freedom'. He was not convinced that a ban on advertising would reduce consumption. Way back in the 1950s the Government had secretly backed off from dealing with the issue when it was first claimed by medical authorities that a direct link existed between heavy smoking and lung cancer.

In January 1971 I had reported for the *Daily Sketch* on the publication of a report by the Royal College of Physicians on smoking and health. Under the headline *You Have Been Warned*, I wrote that the most high-powered inquiry ever held into smoking in Britain had given a grim warning of the deadly dangers involved. I forecast that the Government's first move would be to bring pressure on manufacturers to print a health caution on cigarette packets – as in America. Sir Keith Joseph had given tobacco firms only a few months to agree to print such warnings – and threatened legislation if they failed to do so. I added, however, that Sir Gerald Nabarro MP, in a private member's bill, was already proposing that manufacturers should be forced to print the following strongly worded notice on packets: 'Danger. These cigarettes can harm your health. Cigarettes are known to cause lung cancer, bronchitis and heart disease'.

By chance, I had witnessed a development in the Commons which made me suspect that Sir Keith Joseph was playing a double game. Editor David English had allowed me to start getting involved with my new PR career while still working out my notice with the *Daily Sketch*. I had gone to the Press Gallery one Friday afternoon when a member of the 10 Downing

Street press office hurried along the main corridor drawing attention to the fact that Nabarro's bill had been given a second reading without debate and 'on the nod'. The industry had been led to believe that the Government, abiding by the voluntary agreement, would make arrangements for the Whips to kill off the measure by shouting 'NO!' when its title was called.

Foolishly, Imperial Tobacco's parliamentary consultants had failed to ensure that a friendly MP attended to take the necessary action if the Whips failed to do so. The measure, entitled the *Tobacco (and Snuff) (Health Hazards)* bill, had been introduced by Nabarro, the flamboyant Tory MP for Kidderminster, using a special procedure known as the 'ten minute rule' and not the normal ballot system that would have provided an allotment of time if he had won a high enough place. Why had Downing Street drawn attention to the bill's surprise progress? I suspected that Sir Keith had arranged for the Whips to let it through and, rather than involve his own press office, had asked 10 Downing Street to alert the media. He had done so in order to frighten the tobacco industry into being more co-operative in the next round of talks under the voluntary agreement.

I told Bonham Carter what I had discovered and he said he would bring me to the attention of the chairman's office at Imperial Tobacco. A few days later I received a phone call from a Dr. Herbert Bentley, Imperial's director of research, who was also responsible for some of the company's public affairs operations. He invited me to dinner at the Hyde Park Hotel and by the end of the meal had offered me a consultancy with the company. Voice and Vision, the lobbying firm that had been employed by the industry, was informed that its services were no longer required. At one time it had been a leading operator in the then small field of public affairs consultancy and I had witnessed its operations in Parliament on behalf of the Central African Federation.

David Wynne-Morgan, delighted at my success in winning another major client, made me a director and put me in charge of a new subsidiary he launched under the title Partnerplan Public Affairs. My close relationship with the tobacco industry was getting underway and was to last for some thirty-four years.

Despite Sir Keith Joseph's surreptitious assistance to Nabarro, my task in killing off the bill was to prove not too difficult. There had been a few previous and unsuccessful attempts to curb tobacco marketing by private members bills, notably by my Labour Co-op MP friend, the persistent anti-smoker Laurie Pavitt. Thanks to Nabarro and Joseph, such a bill had at last made progress and reached committee stage in the Commons. The timing of the bill was helpful to the minister who was involved in negotiations with the industry about the printing of such warnings on packets. His double-dealing paid off and faced with the Nabarro threat, the industry agreed to his proposal. On March 16th 1971, he announced a successful outcome to the talks and asked the self-important Nabarro to withdraw his bill as its purpose had been achieved on a voluntary basis. But the MP refused, arguing that a legal basis for action was to be preferred to a voluntary arrangement. His bill then passed through the committee stage as Nabarro had been able to choose a lot of the MPs sitting on it, but by the time it reached the next hurdle I had been able to prepare strong opposition. On my advice, Imperial wrote to MPs with constituency links to its factories; to others with relevant trade union links; and to those known to take a stand on the issue of the liberty of the individual. Other tobacco companies followed Imperial's lead. When the bill reached the stage where the small committee reported its progress back to the full House, the industry's forces were prepared and marshalled. They kept the debate going over three days until Nabarro's allotted time expired. The bill was dead.

Nabarro was correct to point out that those who opposed his measure represented constituencies with links to the tobacco industry. Of the twelve MPs who spoke against the bill at the report stage, six could claim such links, and that they had been intent on protecting the jobs of their constituents. Moreover, only five MPs could be mustered to speak in support of the measure.

What made my task so easy was that swaggering moustachioed Nabarro had few friends in the Commons. On the Tory benches, weighed down by former officers of all three services, he behaved like an overbearing, cocky member of the sergeants' mess. When I told some of my friendly knights of the shires about the bill problem they assured me that there was no way 'that cad' would get it through. Nabarro, in fact, was rightly suspected of leaking the private discussions of the Tory backbenchers 1922 Committee meetings to Lobby journalists. As for Labour MPs, he was deeply loathed by the Left and only a few dedicated anti-smokers were prepared to help him.

The defeat of the Nabarro bill was a severe blow to the anti-smoking lobby. It failed, however, to learn the lesson about the difficulty of succeeding with private members' legislation in the face of well-organised resistance and continued to encourage supporters to introduce bills. Their next target was the advertising and sponsorship of cigarettes and the next seven bills aimed to ban such activities. They all failed to make progress.

A co-sponsor of the Nabarro bill was a newcomer to the Commons named Gerard Folliott Vaughan, a psychiatrist and consultant at Guy's Hospital. Tall and personable, with a smooth bedside manner, he had been serving on the London County Council and GLC since 1955 and narrowly won Reading from Labour in 1970. I was introduced to him by David Powell, who knew him well and considered him 'a bit tricky'. I took him to lunch at Locket's restaurant in Westminster where he asked my advice on whether he should accept a post in the Tory Whips' Office. He thought it would make it impossible for him to continue doing his work on the GLC. I advised him to accept the Whip's post on the grounds that if he had parliamentary ambitions it would be a bad career move to refuse this, admittedly lowly, government job. He took my advice and became a Whip, thus beginning a bumpy career in government.

Imperial was the largest and most successful of the five big players in the UK tobacco industry. The others were another British based firm Gallaher which, like Imperial, manufactured and marketed in the UK; British American Tobacco (BAT), which had a factory in Southampton and whose products were all exported abroad; and the foreign owned companies Rothmans and Philip Morris. The industry employed over 40,000 people at the time I was taken on, and the introduction of more efficient cigarette machines was to be the main cause of a steady reduction in the workforce rather than the continual increase in taxation on cigarettes or the activities of the anti-smoking crusaders. Initially the industry denied there was a link between smoking and health but by the time I got involved it had followed lawyers' advice and adopted the 'tight rope' formula, declaring that it was not qualified to make medical judgements.

Any guilt I felt about helping to organise the death of a health measure was quickly assuaged by the opportunity then provided to help the interests of the disabled. I was meeting Labour MP Alf Morris regularly and knew that he was disappointed that far too many people suffering from disabilities, and those trying to help them, were not aware of the assistance available under the important 'new deal' private member's bill he had put through Parliament in 1969-70 – The *Chronically Sick and Disabled Persons* Act.

Then Alf had an idea. Would I write a book about the battle to get the bill into law and the many ways in which the new Act could make life easier for disabled people? Without hesitation I accepted his offer – but added one condition. That he would write the foreword and have his name on the book as joint author with me. Knowing Alf's popularity with the press, my condition was aimed at ensuring that the book would receive maximum coverage. Alf agreed and added that he knew that Lord Longford's publishing firm, Sidgwick and Jackson, would be pleased to handle the book.

I had embarked on a project that was to greatly increase my awareness of the problems of disability - and to bring me into contact with some of the remarkable people campaigning for a better deal for the millions suffering from some form of disability. These included Duncan Guthrie, director of the Central Council for the Disabled and Peter Large, chairman of the Joint Committee on Mobility for the Disabled. Peter had been a civil engineer employed by Shell International Petroleum when he was struck down by polio in 1962. Confined to a wheelchair and able to move his head and arms only slightly, he decided to devote the remainder of his life to campaigning on behalf of the disabled. For forty years he was to do so with great effect, working tirelessly to improve their rights in the fields of mobility, social security and protection from discrimination. Active on the political front, he helped Alf draft sections of his bill and was now pleased to assist me in compiling the history of its passage through Parliament.

Working five days a week on behalf of a growing number of Partnerplan's demanding clients, I devoted most of my spare time for a year to completing the book.

I seriously under-estimated the number of people I would need to interview and the amount of detailed information I would have to absorb. But at last I could pass the finished manuscript to Alf with a request for a suitable title. In a speech made during the course of his bill's passage through Parliament, he had once bitterly criticised the authorities for 'dragging their feet' when it came to making proper provision for the chronically sick and disabled – dragging their feet in providing help for those who often had 'no feet to drag'.

It sounded right in the speech but when Alf suggested that *No Feet to Drag* would be a good title for the book, I was not too sure. Lord Longford and his team accepted it without a blink. The dust cover of the book would feature a photograph of a five-year-old boy, a victim of spina bifida, bravely attempting to play football with both legs in callipers and supported by a pair of crutches. When my copy arrived in September, I was pleased with the look of it. Then I flicked through the first few pages and discovered to my everlasting embarrassment that my list of acknowledgements to the many people who had generously assisted me had carelessly been omitted.

Alf and I were grateful to Lord Longford and his firm for publishing the book. His Lordship had become chairman of Sidgwick and Jackson in 1970, two years after resigning from the Wilson Government over its decision to postpone raising the school leaving age. Other Cabinet ministers found it difficult to take him seriously.

A press conference and drinks reception to launch the book had to be arranged. As a number of parliamentarians were to be invited, the publishers chose St. Stephen's Tavern opposite the House of Commons as the venue. More embarrassment. The room reserved for the function was at the top of the building and, there being no lift, it could be reached only by clambering up several flights of narrow stairs. The fact that a lot of disabled people would be attending had been overlooked. I helped to manhandle three wheelchairs to the top – one containing Peter Large. Having a weak back I feared I would be disabled myself. I survived and in mid-September received a letter from Peter thanking me for helping him and his wife attend the press conference. He wrote: 'Writing the book itself was a sufficient labour. For anyone having to physically carry a disabled person in a wheelchair up three floors was an added labour that no co-author should have to face. Both feats, however, demonstrate a very real and practical approach to the problem of disability'.

Harold Wilson, leader of the Opposition, found time to attend and received thanks from Alf for arranging the parliamentary timetable in such a way that his bill was enabled to become law before Parliament was dissolved in the run up to the 1970 General Election.

In an afterword last chapter to the book, Alf wrote: 'There is still much to do if we are to turn precept and law into administrative practice and full social provision. The problem still facing us is a vast one requiring every organisation, statutory and voluntary alike, to discuss their priorities…'

Within a few years he was to play a leading role in tackling the problem as the first ever Minister for the Disabled, empowered to look at the totality of the needs of disabled people and how all relevant government departments could help. By then the successful publication of the book and the considerable publicity it received had produced the desired result.

Public demand for action to implement Alf's Act had grown swiftly, putting Whitehall under considerable pressure.

Alf's popularity with the press ensured that *No Feet to Drag* received wide coverage and sympathetic reviews in newspapers all over Britain. Typical of the good coverage was a review by Des Wilson in *The Observer* who wrote: 'If anyone doubts the urgency of an increase in the national contribution to the cost of providing local services for the disabled they should read this book… a damning, moving report on the priorities of these fellow citizens'.

If Harold Wilson had given support to the book, he was to be less than helpful to my next venture – the Europe-America Conference. I received a call from former Labour MP Alan Lee Williams who, having lost his Hornchurch seat in 1970 had become director of the British Atlantic Committee. A bright and breezy backbencher when in the Commons, I knew him to be an expert on defence matters and one of Parliament's strongest supporters of NATO and the Anglo-American Alliance. Would I be interested in handling the press relations for an important international conference to be held in March 1973 in Amsterdam? I told Alan I would, and he invited me to lunch at the National Liberal Club to discuss it - and to meet a certain Joseph Godson who was co-ordinating the conference.

Over a rather frugal meal, Alan and Godson explained it would be the largest non-governmental gathering of prominent Americans and Europeans ever brought together to discuss trans-Atlantic relations. It would provide the forum for discussion on the need to ensure a continuing close relationship between Western Europe and America on economic and security issues, in the light of Britain having joined the European Economic Community. There was mounting impatience in Washington with Western Europe. It seemed to a growing number of Americans that Western Europe had ambitions to become the USA's trade rival whilst sheltering under the American nuclear shield as a subsidised ally. As I was showing my enthusiasm for this grandiose project, I was told that there was very little money for administering the conference. I said I would have to get the agreement of my colleagues – but was sure they would want me to get involved. David Wynne-Morgan slumped when I mentioned the proposed fee but it was agreed that it would be good for the reputation of the company to be associated with such a prestigious operation. We were on our way to Amsterdam.

It was to be convened in March 1973 by Professor Walter Hallstein, President of the International European Movement. He would welcome the delegates and the hundred or so guests from the diplomatic corps and media. At the opening session, the speakers would include HRH Prince Bernhardt of the Netherlands, Governor Nelson Rockefeller of New York, the Rt. Hon. Roy Jenkins MP and Professor Raymond Aron of France. Former Cabinet ministers Michael Stewart MP and Reginald Maudling MP would be part of the British delegation.

I pushed ahead with encouraging friends and colleagues from the political and diplomatic press corps to sign up, promising them good hospitality and a night out in naughty Amsterdam. I was therefore surprised and concerned to learn that Harold Wilson had been going round the Commons tearoom trying to persuade MPs not to attend. He alleged that the conference was the brainchild of Washington's notorious Central Intelligence Agency – the CIA. My immediate reaction was to dismiss the allegation as a typical Wilson paranoid fairytale. On this occasion, however, the suspicious little man was near the truth.

Joe Godson, I was to discover, was one of the most influential and successful officials working on behalf of the CIA in Britain after the Second World War. A one-time left-wing trade unionist, he became Labour attaché at the American Embassy in London in the 1950s. Such was his success at infiltrating the upper echelons of the Labour Party that the CIA decided to use his services. One of his closest, most fruitful contacts was ex-miner Sam Watson, who, as secretary of the powerful Durham Miners' Association, wielded considerable influence in the Labour movement. He sat on Labour's National Executive Committee and its International sub-committee and was part of a Labour Party delegation to Moscow and China led by Clem Attlee in 1954. Right-wing on defence and a staunch supporter of the American Alliance and NATO, Watson was in Godson's pocket to the degree that the US Embassy provided him with a rent free flat in London.

I liked Joe Godson (who returned to London from America in the 1970s to assist CIA projects) and we remained friends until his death. Nevertheless, I was irritated at having been 'misled' by him into assisting Uncle Sam's spooks – and for peanuts.

My fee rankled even more when I witnessed huge amounts of money lavished on entertainment. The Conference opened with a costly floating dinner party – one of the biggest ever held. Eleven boats with some forty people each drifted through the city to the accompaniment of piped music and running commentaries. Some three hundred politicians, industrialists, academics and trade union leaders, with one hundred and fifty media representatives taking part in the cruise, tucked into a three-course meal washed down with a selection of great European wines. They had come from the European Union countries, North America, Canada, Norway - and Japan.

About thirty British parliamentarians took part including Douglas Houghton, chairman of the Parliamentary Labour Party. Peter Kirk, leader of his Party's delegation to the European Parliament, and Winston Churchill, grandson of the great old man, represented the Tories. Jeremy Thorpe led the Liberal Party delegation. It had been hoped that Denis Healey, Shadow Chancellor, would attend but he and a few other Labour MPs decided not to take part, perhaps influenced by Harold Wilson's intervention.

Prince Bernhardt of the Netherlands opened the Conference and handed over to Professor Hallstein. A key factor in the US Government's interest in the Conference emerged on the second day: the world oil crisis and the fact that America could no longer produce enough oil and gas to meet its energy needs. It was moving towards ever-greater dependence on Middle Eastern suppliers to fuel its factories, vehicles and homes.

This became clear when Walter J. Levy, President Nixon's special advisor on energy problems, addressed the Conference. There was an urgent need, he argued, for co-ordinated planning by America, its Atlantic partners and Japan to design a new Atlantic-Japanese energy policy to achieve optimum energy security for the free world. This was the reason for Washington's plan that the Conference should support the setting up of a permanent body to improve communications between the US, Europe and Japan. That was why Japan, a major importer of oil, had been invited to the Europe-America Conference. Joe Godson had not informed me of that. Now it was clear. Washington hoped that if it could get together with the EEC and Japan to produce a common energy policy, it could prevent the Middle East oil producers from blackmailing the industrialised nations. The balance of power had shifted dramatically from the consumer countries to the producer nations, situated mostly around the Persian Gulf and North Africa. The role of the international oil companies was also changing from being in control to becoming buyers, competing as best they could. So that was why the directors of multi-national corporations such as Shell Oil had given up precious time to attend.

The political implications of the oil states' awareness of their power were seen by some to be even more serious than the economic. What would be the effect on Israel when it was surrounded by oil-rich states able to exert pressure on North America? In December 1972, General George Lincoln, former Director of the US Office of Emergency Preparedness, warned that the energy crisis would replace the Cold War as perhaps the most urgent problem North America faced in years ahead.

Apart from the oil crisis, the Conference covered the military balance, East-West relations and international economic policies. Overshadowing everything was the nagging worry that an impatient USA would desert Europe and move into isolation.

The Conference ended on March 28th in discord and confusion. The final resolution was described as meaningless by disappointed British MPs and other delegates. Chairman Professor Hallstein had annoyed participants by refusing amendments aimed at putting real substance into the document. Not only did the Conference fail to calm the troubled waters between Europe and America, but it revealed - according to Professor Eugene Rostow, a former US Under Secretary of State - that the differences of perception between the two were even deeper than had been thought as Europe struggled with so many of its internal problems. The original idea of setting up a permanent body or pressure group to improve communications between the US, Europe and Japan disappeared from the final resolution. Indeed, Japan was not even mentioned.

Some of the toughest words, however, were uttered at the final lunch meeting by George Ball, former US Under Secretary of State, who complained that the Europeans were becoming 'Both parochial and isolationist'. He added that the United States had become 'Frankly disillusioned with Europe'. Behind the scenes tempers reached such a pitch that a portable typewriter was thrown at a British official in the secretariat office. Such disarray and acrimony was unexpected, coming after two days of presentations in what had been an academic atmosphere of civilised exchanges. On the surface it had been so much like a university seminar that some of my chums on the popular press were looking glum – despite a tour of the city's raunchy nightlife and one of the most famous red light districts in the world.

As a result of the deep differences that emerged, the final resolution relied on bromide terms such as the expressed hope for an open and frank discussion between America and the EEC on problems of substance within a suitable framework.

Sir Frank Roberts, President of the British Atlantic Committee, faced with reports of gloom and doom, tried to strike an optimistic note, denying rumours that the Conference had been US financed. He claimed that the £50,000 cost had been wholly met by the British Government and British and continental business. The final verbal punch-up cheered up the hacks of the popular press. 'That's more like a story, Arthur', said Victor Knight of the *Daily Mirror*, patting me on the back. I returned a not entirely convincing smile.

Partnerplan's next international assignment might have brought my new career to an early and sticky end. We received a phone call from the owner of a laundrette in the Midlands asking us to meet his brother who wished to employ us in connection with the campaign to set up a separate Sikh state. When the tall turbaned figure appeared for the meeting, he looked like a character from a Buchan or Kipling novel. His fierce, bearded face was scarred and in place of a right hand – lost in a fight – he flaunted a lethal looking hook.

He explained that he was planning an uprising of the Sikhs in India and, in advance, wanted the case for an independent Sikh state put to the British public through the media. No problem. Through our press contacts we got some articles on the foreign news pages of several national papers. Encouraged by this, our client came in for more advice on how to advance his cause. It was decided that he should draw up a draft constitution for his new state. We needed a model and as Britain had no written constitution I undertook to get a copy of the American one from the US Embassy.

When I returned from my mission, the man who would be ruler of the new Sikh state had moved on to another meeting, but the two Davids had news for me. Our client had asked them to arrange for me to act as his PR man on the ground when the Sikh war of independence began. They told him they were sure I would be honoured to do so. After all, I had once volunteered for the Indian Army of the British Raj, just before it was closed to British officers on the eve of India's independence, so was obviously keen to see some action there. Our client, however, did not return and we then received another call from his brother who owned the laundrette, who paid the bills. The operation was indefinitely postponed. We heard no more. For the second time in my life, my passage to India had been aborted.

Having successfully launched Partnerplan Public Affairs with me as managing director, it was decided to produce a smart brochure to market the new subsidiary. In it, I offered a specialised service aimed at providing clients with early warning of government actions and parliamentary developments; advice and assistance in lobbying at Westminster and influencing government decisions; and practical programmes for mobilising public sympathy and support.

We circulated the brochure widely to companies, trade associations and local authorities. Then a letter arrived from the chairman of a professional association of public relations consultants, complaining about the use of the word 'lobbying'. In pompous terms it suggested the brochure should be withdrawn. We were astounded. How could anyone be so out of touch and ignorant of our parliamentary history? Lobbying had played an honourable role in our democratic system for centuries. We replied to the author to that effect, and added significantly that so long as lobbying was conducted openly and above-board, no one need be ashamed to use the word. I already had evidence that some PR consultants were employing MPs to push their clients' interests surreptitiously and provide their employers with free parliamentary documents and information from private committee meetings.

Imperial Tobacco had a rule that it could employ only one PR company at a time. To get my services, therefore, it informed its PR consultancy F J Lyons that it must pay a fee to Partnerplan for which it would be reimbursed. Lyons was not pleased to receive this instruction as it employed Tory backbencher Sir John Langford-Holt to provide political advice and information.

Sir John was a friend of the managing director Christopher Bosanquet (cousin of newsreader Reggie), and his main contribution appeared to be the provision of his daily allocation of parliamentary documents which arrived at the F.J. Lyons' office addressed to him. He had been MP for Shrewsbury since 1945 but not very active in the Commons chamber so I had not got to know him when I was a parliamentary journalist. I remembered him mostly for his appearance of languid lassitude as he lolled back on the green benches and for the brightly coloured socks he displayed when his feet were up on the bench in front. As I now got to know him, I found the wealthy ex-wartime Fleet Air Arm officer very good company.

Imperial were charged for his services and shortly after I became a consultant to the company I suggested it would be in their interest to appoint a Labour MP for the sake of political balance. I was asked to recommend a suitable backbencher, drew up a list of three and took it to Labour's Chief Whip Bob Mellish. I knew that many Labour MPs objected to members of the parliamentary party taking on such work and that the tobacco industry was one of the least popular manufacturing sectors. No one had ever consulted Bob on such an appointment before and he was suitably impressed. I told him I wanted the appointment to be above board and asked him to pick the name he thought would be best for the job. I knew that Bob would be pleased to be given this patronage and that whomever he picked would be strengthened by his support. He chose James Wellbeloved, MP for Erith and Crayford, my own first choice.

Alert and blessed with highly sensitive antennae, James would provide first class feedback on parliamentary developments affecting the tobacco industry, and his below deck matelot humour would enliven our meetings. He had been a valuable parliamentary private secretary to the Minister of Defence, then Foreign Secretary from 1967 to 1970, becoming an Opposition Whip in 1972. Educated at South East London Technical College, he had then served as a boy seaman and, like his friend Alan Lee Williams, was interested in defence and NATO affairs. He quickly made himself useful to Imperial Tobacco and it was a feather in my cap that I had recruited him.

The tobacco industry had been under attack for using animals in research to improve cigarettes and some of the criticism had been ill-informed. I persuaded Dr Herbert Bentley, in his role as Imperial's director of research, to permit me to organise press visits for health and science correspondents to the Huntingdon Research Centre. Herbert accompanied the journalists and his open, straightforward style won him their respect and made the visits worthwhile for all concerned. I also organised briefing lunches for him with my old colleagues in the Parliamentary Press Gallery and for groups of leader writers from national newspapers. My efforts were appreciated – and I was to win even more regard by a lucky development that took me across the frontier into the world of art sponsorship.

Throughout the 1970s, education was the issue dominating the chatter at our Dulwich dinner parties where my family was now living. As I had enjoyed a good State education and had faith in the system established by RAB Butler's Education Act, I had not intended to send our daughter Caroline to a fee-paying school. While I did not advocate abolishing public schools I did not want my child to attend one. When it came to decision time, however, the situation had changed. The comprehensive school experiment was well underway and in our area of Dulwich the local example was, in my opinion, appalling, with a reputation for serious indiscipline and poor education standards. The local fee-paying establishment, James Allen's Girls' School (JAGS), in contrast, had a good reputation and so my wife Evelyn and I decided, reluctantly, that Caroline should be enrolled there. It was a good choice as she did exceptionally well and enjoyed her time there.

Thanks to my daughter, I became friendly with one of the most colourful go-getting innovators in English cultural life in the second half of the twentieth century. Caroline's closest school friend, Vanessa, was the daughter of John Campbell Bonner Letts, a well-read cricket-loving literary and museum impresario who, after an early career in advertising and publishing, had taken a gamble in 1971 with two partners in buying the Folio Society.

Set up in 1947 to produce fine editions of the classics, it was going through something of a slump, quality was suffering and I had cancelled my subscription. Over dinner one evening, John persuaded me to rejoin and spoke of his plan to produce a give-away book for members, on the Roman city of Pompeii and its destruction. He had gone to Naples to research it and had interviewed the curator of the city's museum which housed many of the artefacts and remains dug-up from the nearby ruins. He was told that the museum was soon to close for renovations, so he had asked about the possibility of borrowing some of the exhibits for a show in London. The curator was interested and on his return to London, John started the search for a sponsor. That evening at our house in Dulwich he asked if I could help him find one.

The following week, I raised the subject with Colin Knowles, Imperial's new Public Affairs manager. He was looking for prestigious projects for the company to sponsor. He was immediately enthusiastic and soon after, the company chairman Anthony Garrett gave the go-ahead for the project. The great Pompeii Exhibition opened at the Royal Academy in London in November 1976.

It was a great success and became the first sponsored event at the Royal Academy to make a profit. The precocious duo Caroline and Vanessa told anyone who would listen - which included the camera team from the evening news - the exhibition would never have happened had it not been for them. Members of the anti-smoking lobby jeered that a city-smothered in ash was ideal subject matter for a tobacco company. Bernard Levin, whom I had invited, was more helpful. In an enthusiastic review that appeared across five columns of *The Times* he wrote that the catalogue – 'a sumptuous and wonderfully informative volume' – reminded readers that:

'No event in history perhaps has caught so sharply the human imagination or been held so firmly in our memory as the overwhelming of this modest provincial town'.

Imperial, having made an unexpected profit on the exhibition, used some of the funds to establish an annual portrait award in 1980 in association with the National Portrait Gallery.

As for the ever-busy John Letts, by the time the exhibition was launched he had increased his work for the arts by setting up National Heritage. Established to raise standards in small museums around the country – and eventually on the continent – it organised the prestigious annual Museum of the Year award with the *Illustrated London News* as its first sponsor. I succeeded in involving Imperial Tobacco in the support of small museums, and the company agreed to put in money to match a sum pledged by the Pilgrim Trust. At that time I was active on the committee of the Friends of the Dulwich Picture Gallery, the superb collection of old master paintings housed in an architectural masterpiece designed by Sir John Soane. Second only in excellence to London's National Gallery, it is the oldest public art gallery in Britain and particularly important for seventeenth and eighteenth century works. Owned by Dulwich College, it was desperately short of money and some of the paintings were deteriorating at an alarming rate. Delighted by my assistance in getting funds for his small museums operation, John Letts demonstrated his gratitude in a practical way by recommending that the gallery should receive a grant via National Heritage.

John went on to found the Trollope Society, as no complete edition of Trollope's works had been published by then. In 2002 I was invited to Bristol for the opening of his British Empire and Commonwealth Museum. He had struggled for years to bring this about and with the financial assistance of the Bahamas-based businessman Sir Jack 'Union Jack' Hayward, had eventually succeeded.

As Imperial became more deeply involved in arts sponsorship, anti-smoking MPs created a growing clamour for a ban on such activities. Our small team of PR consultants began to turn to finding ways of consolidating and unifying corporate sponsorship operations. It was agreed that a new organisation was required to fly the flag for such operations and so, with Imperial taking the initiative and providing the backbone, the Association for Business Sponsorship of the Arts (ABSA) was set up in 1975.

It needed a strong and influential chairman, someone not too fussy about working closely with the tobacco giant behind the scenes. That giant of a man, the wily fixer and contact man Lord Goodman, who had been made chairman of the Arts Council in 1965, was the obvious choice. To our delight he agreed to take on the task.

With Goodman in place we felt confident that we had set up a formidable bulwark to protect our operations. The likelihood of the Government backing the ban-tobacco-sponsorship campaign had been greatly reduced. To cement Imperial's influence within the organisation, the company's highly successful Public Affairs Manager, Colin Knowles, was appointed as the first secretary of ABSA. With Goodman as chairman, there is no doubt that some companies joined to get closer to this man of influence.

On the local government front, work continued to flow into Partnerplan following its series of achievements in connection with Peter Walker's bill. Worcestershire County Council employed us to publicise the launch of its structure plan and then we became involved with a number of disputes arising from Boundary Commission recommendations. Across Fleet Street from Partnerplan's office was the King and Keys, a popular public house much used by members of *The Daily Telegraph* staff. One evening while enjoying an after work pint, I found myself standing next to someone I had not seen since my days at the London School of Economics. It was Alfred Sherman whose contributions to LSE student union debates I had enjoyed, and whose writings on East European affairs in the 1950s I had also admired.

The son of a Jewish Labour councillor in Hackney in the East End of London, Alfred had become a Communist as a young man and fought in the Republican Army in the Spanish Civil War as a machine gunner. He had left the Communist Party in 1948 – the year I entered the LSE, where he earned himself a reputation as a formidable debater. As he did not know me, I introduced myself at the bar. When I told him that I had recently been involved in a number of major local government affairs initiatives, he was immediately interested as he reported on just that for *The Daily Telegraph* and knew about Partnerplan's activities. To my surprise, he then said that he would like to move out of journalism into local government related public relations, and believed he could make a useful contribution.

In order to cope with our many campaigns, we had been taking on people on short-term contracts and were currently looking for a new recruit. I told him I might be able to take him on and the following day confirmed that he could join us. He soon learned the ropes. His writing skill was a great asset and I enjoyed working with him. He could be abrupt and abrasive, however, in dealing with anyone slow on the uptake. Diplomacy was not his strong point. I involved him in some of the BRF work too and director Robert Phillipson was much impressed by his intellect.

In my regular visits to the King and Keys, I rubbed shoulders with some of *The Telegraph's* other journalists, including bright young leader writers such as Colin Welch and John O'Sullivan. They did not share my regard for Edward Heath – especially after he lost two elections to Wilson in 1974. My visits to the pub also renewed my acquaintance with Prime Minister Macmillan's former 'information' minister, the amiable William Deedes. He had become editor of *The Telegraph* at the end of 1974, to the surprise of Fleet Street's pundits who expected the job to go to either Welch or City Editor Kenneth Fleet. Deedes's regular golfing outings with Denis Thatcher during Margaret's reign were to provide political satirists with much humorous material over the years.

A serious test of my commitment to my new career came in the autumn of 1972. Due to Prime Minister Heath's determination, Britain joined the European Economic Community and my old friend George Thomson accepted the post of one of our first EC Commissioners. George was MP for Dundee East and I had known him since 1956 when I worked in my spare time for the re-launched Socialist weekly paper *Forward*. It was launched as a pro-Gaitskell journal to compete against the Bevanite weekly *Tribune*. We had become close friends and I was very pleased when Prime Minister Harold Wilson appointed him Foreign Office Minister of State in 1964, eventually promoting him to Commonwealth Secretary and Deputy Foreign Secretary.

In April he had joined Roy Jenkins and Harold Lever in resigning from Labour's front bench in protest at the Shadow Cabinet's decision to hold a national referendum on whether Britain should stay in the Common Market when Labour returned to power. George, in fact, having been dubious when Wilson, as Prime Minister, had appointed him the Government's Mr Europe, had become a staunch European and had taken on the chairmanship of the Labour Committee for Europe. Heath had made a good choice and George, in accepting the post, had to resign as MP for Dundee East, which he had represented in Parliament since 1952. As soon as I heard the news on the radio I phoned to congratulate him. As he lived near my Dulwich home, I suggested that to avoid the media who were surely about to descend on his front door, he and his wife Grace should come round to us. They happily accepted.

Soon after, George was in touch with a flattering offer. Would I take on the job of handling his media relations in Brussels with a seat in his cabinet? I thanked him and asked for a little time to consider the proposal which, if accepted, would change my life dramatically. My main problem was that I had only recently signed contracts with the British Road Federation and Imperial Tobacco and felt indebted to them for showing confidence in me. Another problem was my poor French. I thought I would not be able to give George the support he needed in a situation where France could be expected to offer only sluggish co-operation.

George was disappointed when I told him I had decided, reluctantly, to decline his offer. When I mentioned the linguistic reason he brushed that aside saying that he would be doing a crash course and I could do the same. I pointed out that if he too was weak at parlez-vous then it was vital he had someone around him with a mastery of French to offer support in the difficult early days. I was worried I would let him down. George looked elsewhere and found someone in the Labour movement who was sufficiently fluent.

The following year, as assistant secretary of the Roads Campaign Council, I travelled to Brussels with the All-Party Roads Study Group, to learn about the EEC's approach to motorway development and to inspect some of Belgium's major road construction projects. To my delight, George Thomson accepted our invitation to be guest of honour at one of our dinners in the Belgian capital. It was the last overseas study tour organised by Arthur Pitt before his retirement, and in taking part I began to understand why the RCC was known as the 'Roads Champagne Council'. We were put up in an expensive hotel just off the city's historic great square and we were led by the RCC's chairman, a convivial top motor agent named Jack Williams. He enjoyed wining and dining MP members of the APRSG after a day of lectures and visits to construction sites. He did so in grand style, and like Sir George Middleton, was a connoisseur of wines and cigars. A big character with a fund of good stories, Jack was very popular with the parliamentarians.

On taking over from Arthur Pitt as RCC secretary, I moved quickly to involve key MPs more closely in planning the programme for the APRSG. This was appreciated by the joint chairmen Peter Fry and Alan Fitch. Previously, invitations to meetings had been sent out on RCC notepaper, so I produced APRSG stationery carrying the joint chairmen's names, which soon encouraged more MPs to attend our gatherings.

Anthony Crosland was Shadow Environment Minister and with Fitch's support, I persuaded him to attend a meeting and dinner of the group. He had won the support of the conservationists by sharply attacking the Government's plan for an airport at Maplin on the Essex coastline. But he had come into conflict with the active environmentalist lobby over what he regarded as their ill-conceived opposition to progress and their lack of understanding of the needs of ordinary people. Determined to improve housing and encourage modern factory building, he was an advocate of economic growth. And, as I saw it, an essential element of that was an extensive motorway system.

However, during the after-dinner discussion in the upstairs room at St. Stephen's Tavern, when the port had been passed several times, I pushed him further than he wished to go on the motorway aspect of his grand design. Red in the face and slightly slurred, Crosland snapped that he had not come to the occasion 'to be bullied by Arthur Butler'. I had pushed my luck too far and apologised.

A lot of bad and ugly development had been taking place in and around Britain's towns and cities. Crosland himself had complained that, 'Greedy men, abetted by a complacent government, are prowling over Britain and devastating it'. My environmentalist co-director at Partnerplan, David Powell, and some of his friends in local government, had become concerned by the trend. Development companies were persuading local planning committees to accept unsightly, badly designed blocks of flats, offices and stores in return for the gift of a new swimming pool or some other amenity for the area. Shoddy developers were making a killing.

David had come to the conclusion that a group of dedicated specialist consultants covering planning, finance and public relations could get local authorities out of the grasp of the cowboys and had started to talk to possible associates about a joint venture. In his view, traditional methods of handling local government business were no longer adequate, especially in the fields of marketing and development finance. In his spare time he had been in discussion with Guinness Mahon, the merchant bankers, and a firm of economic planning specialists, Economic Consultants. David decided that Partnerplan, as run by Wynne-Morgan, was not involved closely enough with high finance or planning and that he would have to bring in a more suitable company. He was recommended to try to involve John Addey who was running the fastest growing city PR firm.

John Addey's long list of clients included some of the big names in banking, industry and commerce and he had a reputation as a successful, if ruthless, operator in takeover battles. Earlier in his career he had been in flamboyant partnership with Wynne-Morgan, but they had had different ambitions and decided to split up. He had set up his own company, John Addey Associates, in 1970 with the financial assistance of the city-orientated PR and advertising company Charles Barker that retained a half-share in the business.

Addey and David Powell impressed each other at their first meeting. The way was open for David to leave Partnerplan and start his new local government venture. He wanted me to move with him, and Addey had shown interest in my record. Although I liked Wynne-Morgan, who was a generous and agreeable boss, both Powell and I had disapproved of some of his more glamorous PR operations in the South of Spain and East Africa, which we believed to be a drain on the company's limited resources.

I agreed to meet Addey, together with David, in April 1973, for a talk about the possibility of joining him to develop a public affairs sector for his agency. The office was situated in Wardrobe Court down a maze of narrow lanes on the riverside by St. Paul's Cathedral. Despite the subdued lighting in his comfortable office, I noticed the tasteful prints and old master watercolours. On one wall hung the gold disk of a unique recorded appeal made by his friend Sir Anthony Burney, chairman of Debenhams. At Addey's suggestion, it had been sent to shareholders and helped fight off a take-over bid by United Drapery Stores.

Addey, in expensive monogrammed shirt and flashing an elegant gold bracelet watch, oozed charm and success. The meeting went well and he seemed keen to take me on but, outside, I told David I was not happy. There was something about it all that made me uneasy. Disappointed by my reaction, David offered to find a respectable merchant banker who would vouch for Mr. Addey's integrity. I agreed that if he did so, I would seriously consider moving with him to Wardrobe Chambers. I quickly received the assurance I needed and in my naiveté, believing that merchant bankers were men of sound judgment, I accepted.

David Wynne-Morgan was naturally angry when I told him I would be leaving after my three-month notice period. David Powell had already given his notice and would be off a month before me. Major General Nigel St. John Gribbon - who had recently retired as head of intelligence for NATO – had joined the company to learn the art of public affairs consultancy and Wynne-Morgan decided to make the courteous ex-soldier chairman of Partnerplan Public Affairs.

He then recruited Nicholas Ridley, Tory MP for Cirencester and Tewkesbury, to replace me as managing director. A passionate advocate of the free market, the languid and cultured Old Etonian had been serving as a junior minister in the Department of Trade and Industry when he had a serious policy clash about Edward Heath's U-turn over the control of the economy. Heath decided Ridley must be moved, and knowing of his skill as a water colourist – he was a grandson of Lutyens – offered him the post of Minister for the Arts. Ridley refused and left the Government.

An aristocratic friend of Wynne-Morgan and the younger son of the third Viscount Ridley, he joined Partnerplan Public Affairs and, as a chain-smoker, was no doubt pleased that Imperial Tobacco was one of our clients. Like the British Road Federation and Roads Campaign Council, however, Imperial would decide to follow me to the Addey stable. Alfred Sherman would also move to Wardrobe Chambers, but for a few weeks, with Ridley aboard, Partnerplan had under its roof two of the most important architects of what would become known as Thatcherism. Ridley had a reputation for prickliness – and was understandably twitchy about my hope of taking my main clients with me – but we did not fall out as I explained the workings of the company. He could be blunt and outspoken and was known to despise cant and humbug. Adopting the straight talking style he preferred, I told him through the haze of tobacco smoke that he should be prepared to see a sharp fall in clients and income when I left. He seemed not to take my warning seriously.

I left him as he opened another packet of cigarettes – he smoked four packs a day – and went in search of Wynne-Morgan. I told him that Wilfred Sendall had just been sacked as political editor of the *Daily Express* and might be interested in joining Partnerplan as a consultant. Sendall joined Partnerplan and I was flattered to be replaced by three people – Gribbon, Ridley and Sendall. I was not an experienced businessman but it looked like commercial madness. Gribbon and Ridley, however, did not stay long. The former left to set up his own successful public affairs consultancy, Salingbury, and Ridley, enjoying the freedom to criticise Heath's handling of economic affairs, switched all of his considerable talents to the political arena.

After Ted Heath's defeat in the 1974 General Election, Ridley was to become leader of the anti-Heath faction, backing first Sir Keith Joseph for leader and then, reluctantly, Margaret Thatcher. A consistent advocate of the free market, he claimed to have been a Thatcherite before her. In due course he was to become one of her most influential Cabinet ministers, serving as Secretary of State for Transport, the Environment and Trade and Industry.

Two other members of Heath's Government had resigned – but for reasons salacious rather than policy-driven. Lord Lambton, the darkly good-looking, elegant second son of the Fifth Earl of Durham had been appointed Under Secretary of State for Defence (RAF). As a political journalist, I had often talked to him in the Lobby and admired his intelligence, straight talking and expertise on defence issues. I was surprised, however, when he was given a Government post as I had assumed that this wealthy aristocrat valued his independence and enjoyed a racy private life. Because of an eye problem, he invariably wore dark glasses, and this habit, when added to his handsome Latin looks and raffish style, contributed to an appearance of upper-class decadence.

I was not surprised when in April 1973 he was photographed by a newspaper while smoking cannabis in bed with two prostitutes. Norma Levy was one of the two women involved – and one of fifteen farmed out by a society madam. My old friend from *News Chronicle* and *Daily Express* days, Brian Vine, had been involved in the spectacular sting. Following up this disclosure, Scotland Yard detectives came across a note in one of the girls' flats that appeared to indicate the involvement of another, more senior, client from within the Government. It read 'Jellicoe' with a number and time of day. The police called on the much decorated World War II hero Earl George Jellicoe, First Sea Lord. With the equivalent of 'fair cop Guv', he abruptly resigned, owning up to liaisons with call girls.

Jellicoe, a straightforward man, would have been well advised not to confess so quickly. The note the police had found did not refer to him at all. It was about an appointment the prostitute had with someone who lived in a flat in the *Jellicoe* block of Dolphin Square, an upmarket residence on the Embankment near the House of Lords. I was to be closely involved in due course with the efforts of his friends to reinstate George Jellicoe, a justly well-liked man. Meanwhile, David Wynne-Morgan had pulled off what he regarded as a journalistic coup. As I was leaving Partnerplan's office for the last time, we passed on the stairs. 'Arthur', he said, 'you've made a big mistake in leaving', adding triumphantly, 'I'm going to write Norma Levy's biography!'

If I needed convincing that I had made the right move, Wynne-Morgan's news did the trick. How could he believe that writing the life story of a notorious prostitute who had helped to bring down two Government ministers would help Partnerplan Public Affairs to win and hold respectable clients? His pride in being linked as a journalist with this grubby affair seemed to me a serious misjudgement. His world was inhabited by good-looking society women and much of his effort went into smart club projects. Since 1963 he had handled the public relations for Annabel's, high society's favourite nightclub, launched in that year by his close friend Mark Birley. In 1966 he had married Sandra Paul, whose marriage to Robin Douglas-Home had ended a year earlier. A year after their separation, Robin, deeply in debt and drinking way too much, killed himself with an overdose of sleeping pills on the eve of entering a clinic.

Soon after I joined Partnerplan I phoned his brother Charlie about a coming meeting of the 'Leslie Hale luncheon club' of which I was the founder and organising secretary. Ex Labour MP Leslie Hale, a solicitor by profession and my neighbour in Dulwich, had earned the reputation of being the wittiest, fastest talking member of the Commons. Following his resignation from Parliament in 1968 in disgust after the Wilson Government killed off his private member's bill to have byssinosis recognised as an industrial disease – of importance to the cotton workers of his Oldham constituents - he became lonely and depressed. To help restore his good humour I began to arrange lunches for him with some of his old, mostly left-wing, friends at the Gay Hussar restaurant in Soho. These were such a success that they developed into a convivial club that met monthly in an upstairs private room.

When I told Charlie I had joined David Wynne-Morgan's company there was an icy silence at the other end of the line. I did not know at that time about my employer's marriage to Sandra, which had ended some years before when she found it too difficult to balance her work as a top model with her husband's hectic social life. Charlie unfairly blamed Wynne-Morgan for taking Sandra from the womanising Robin and contributing to his suicide at the age of 36 in 1968. In due course I explained to Charlie that I had not known about the link to Sandra. Before I arrived at Partnerplan she had already left Wynne-Morgan to marry Nigel Grandfield, one of his clients who worked in advertising. That marriage was not going well when the future Tory politician Michael Howard, then a barrister, arrived on the scene in 1975 and gave Sandra her fourth wedding in sixteen years.

On leaving Partnerplan I whisked away Alfred Sherman, who had been doing good work on local government campaigns, and my assistant Mary Rice. I was grateful to David Wynne-Morgan for giving me a start in my new career. I had enjoyed some good times at Partnerplan and learned useful lessons. Now it was time to apply them in a wider field of operations.

CHAPTER TWO
Something in the City

Sipping champagne from a silver goblet and surrounded by expensive antiques in a set of rooms once occupied by Lord Byron, I was enjoying a short teach-in from John Addey, the golden boy of City public relations. He had invited me in for a quiet chat on the eve of joining his company as a director and head of his new public affairs department. He lived in fine style in Albany, the exclusive Georgian block of chambers set back from Piccadilly, where, nearly ten years earlier, I had been entertained to lunch by Edward Heath. His address, fittingly, was Byron's Chambers and in his spare time he was secretary of the Byron Society.

He had risen in spectacular fashion to dominate the shadowy world of the City of London's financial public relations practitioners. As the managing director and front man of John Addey Associates, he operated at boardroom level, at times directly advising company chairmen on how to fight off unwanted bids or to launch a take-over. At a lower level, much of the work of his company consisted of helping to prepare and distribute company announcements, a humdrum task easy for ex-journalists for which high fees were charged. The list of Addey's clients included some of the best known names in banking and industry and the company had played a key role in several recent takeover battles involving such organisations as Trust House Forte.

As I was making my move from Partnerplan, Michael Roberts again opened up the way for some new business for me. A Welsh Tory friend had told him that officials at the Spanish Embassy in London believed that Spain need to become more acceptable to western democracies in the last few years of dictator Franco's life. Tristan Garel-Jones, married to a Spaniard and fluent in Spanish, was a merchant banker with political ambitions. He became personal assistant to the Tory Party chairman in 1974, entered Parliament in 1979 for Watford and after a spell as Margaret Thatcher's Chief Whip, served as Minister of State for the Foreign Office from 1990-93. Michael had been introduced by Garel-Jones to a young diplomat at the Spanish Embassy, Antonio de Oyarzábal, who was US-orientated and married to the daughter of an American statesman. Oyarzábal believed that since Franco had only a few years left, the time was ripe for a campaign to soften up Western politicians to accept a new, hopefully democratic, Spain. He was especially keen to get at leaders in the Labour movement who had bitterly opposed Franco's Spain since the end of the Civil War. He had made known that he was looking for someone who had good links with Labour and could act as the go-between. Michael, knowing my Labour background, had helpfully suggested that I might be the right man.

A meeting was arranged at the Commons and from the start I liked the young Antonio. He had a frank, pleasant manner – and his faith that Spain was on the brink of a breakthrough to democracy was moving. Although I had no time for the reactionary Franco regime, it seemed to me that the policy of Western states of keeping Spain at arm's length had not succeeded in speeding up progress to democracy. In particular, I despised the manner in which Harold Wilson used the Spanish bogey man to win a cheap cheer at the Labour Party Conference whenever he was in trouble with the delegates. I had holidayed in Spain several times– Sitges, Barcelona and Majorca – and believed that the proud, hard-working and long-suffering Spanish people deserved a more constructive approach to their problems than that offered by Wilson and the Labour old guard.

I advised Antonio, however, that it would be very difficult to make progress within the Labour movement by a direct approach. Moreover, unlike Antonio, I feared that when Franco died, the right wing in Spain would be so scared of a left wing uprising that, far from loosening the reins, they would tighten them. I also had a personal problem. It was important to keep my channels open to the Labour movement and if it became known that I was the Spanish Embassy's PR consultant in London, the Left would not want to deal with me. However, I offered to advise them on improving public relations and suggested a programme of cultural and sporting links to create a better, more sympathetic, understanding of the Spanish people.

Antonio proposed a meeting with the Ambassador and arranged a lunch in June 1973 at his club – Boodles, in St. James'. Michael Roberts attended and the Ambassador was accompanied by Francisco Mayans, the Embassy's Counsellor for Information and Press Relations. I was impressed by the

Ambassador who had a lively personality which I was sure could be used to much greater advantage in press relations. Soon afterwards, I was called to the embassy to discuss details of a PR programme.

Spain's Prime Minister, Admiral Luis Carrero Blanco, had just been assassinated in a car bomb attack in Madrid and I was not optimistic about an early advance to democracy. At the meeting, I met Carlos Mendo, the recently appointed Press Counsellor, who had been a journalist in Madrid and was not in the mould of the professional diplomat. As we talked, it became clear that they wanted me to do some direct political lobbying and were less interested in cultural activities, such as mounting an exhibition of the golden age of Spanish painting.

After the meeting, I grew increasingly worried about the prospect of lobbying, and not only in respect of my own position. I had persuaded Reg Prentice MP, a member of Labour's Shadow Cabinet, to become a director of the company being set up by John Addey Associates, to assist local authorities with development plans. Reg had been increasingly outspoken in his criticisms of the extreme Left and I knew that they were after his scalp. If it were to become known that he was associated with a company handling Spain's PR in London, they would destroy him. Moreover, within my office team, Labour supporters David Powell and Mary Rice were twitchy at the prospect of a Spanish contract.

Embarrassed, I wrote a long letter to Mendo regretting that I could not take on the work, but outlining a PR programme that again included an exhibition at the Royal Academy of great Spanish painting. I also offered to help find someone with good Labour contacts who might be prepared to assist them. In January 1974 I took Antonio to a lunch organised by the Diplomatic Writers' Group in honour of Prime Minister Heath at the Royal Commonwealth Society. The country was in a state of economic crisis - a three-day week and the miners were on strike and challenging the Government. The air was full of speculation about an early general election but Heath dodged a question on this at the lunch. By the time it was held on 28th February on the theme *Who Governs Britain?* Heath had left it too late. Labour won – but by only five more seats than the Tories and lacking an overall Commons majority.

At the lunch Antonio begged me to think again about the consultancy and I promised to do my utmost to find a suitable replacement. I had some luck. A fellow director at Wardrobe Chambers was a former Guards officer named Philip Woolley, employed mainly as a contact man, business getter and organiser of excellent parties. To my surprise, he revealed one day that his brother-in-law was the well-known PR man and adviser to the Labour Party on election tactics, Dennis Lyons. I knew enough about his scruffy reputation to suspect that the fat and bearded Lyons might not be too worried about working for the Spanish despite the enormous embarrassment it would create for the Labour Party if it were to be revealed that they shared a PR consultant with Franco's embassy in London. I made contact and following another good lunch with Antonio at Boodles in April, Lyons informed me that he had come to an agreement with the Spaniards.

At a Diplomatic Writers' Group lunch at the Waldorf Hotel in the autumn, the Spanish Ambassador confirmed to me privately that Lyons had been working for the embassy for some months and thanked me for my assistance. At the Labour Party Conference following the February General Election, Wilson had again taken a side-swipe at Franco's Spain. Near the front of the hall, his bulky PR adviser Lyons showed no reaction at this attack on his other employer, and that year, Wilson made him a life peer. In October 1975, the satirical magazine *Private Eye* revealed Lyons' link with the Spanish Government, in a devastating profile of Lyons, adding: 'Naturally he denied this, but according to the Spanish ambassador in London it was true and Lyons received an annual fee of £14,000 for his work on behalf of the Spanish Institute. When questioned about this, Lyons, apart from denying the contract, also says that Franco "was not as bad as he was painted"'.

In due course I was proud to learn that the Spanish Embassy, following my recommendation, had got agreement for a major exhibition of Spanish painting to be held in London. It took place in 1976, the same year as that dealing with Pompeii – so I had played a role in the staging of two major exhibitions within twelve months. Franco died in his bed in November 1975, ending thirty-six years of intolerant, authoritarian rule. Within ten years, democracy had been securely established in Spain through a successful revival of the monarchy.

In the Addey office, there was relief in my small team that we had not taken on the Spanish Embassy work. Despite his role as a republican machine-gunner in the Spanish Civil War, Alfred Sherman had not got involved in our arguments. Now he was on the right wing of the Tory Party and as he did not conceal his opinions, this caused unease in our left wing corner of Wardrobe Chambers. He had proved himself a useful part-time member of the team, however, and when we were struggling to produce a name for our new local government project it was Alfred with a typical flash of inspiration who solved the problem. 'Why not call it LOGOS – for Local Government Services?' he suggested. 'Logos', from the Greek for 'word' or 'reason': what a good idea. We adopted the suggestion – and soon the name was to become well known in local government circles.

Alfred also helped out with other work and with growing interest in the latest attempt to construct a tunnel under the English Channel, I was asked to assist with a British Road Federation tour of inspection. He was put in charge of a group of members of the All-Party Roads Study Group who were being escorted by the BRF to visit the tunnel diggings at Sangatte on the French coast. He returned full of praise for the hospitality showered on them by the French and if I could have foreseen how deeply involved I was to become with the Channel Tunnel, I would have taken part myself.

There was not enough work, however, to provide Alfred with the salary he was worth, although he was supplementing it as a freelance writer in the field of polemical journalism. Unbeknown to me at the time, Alfred had visited Health Minister Keith Joseph in the dying days of the Heath Government to tell him in forthright terms where it had gone wrong with economic policy. He first met Joseph in the 1960s when he interviewed him as a journalist specialising in local government and council housing issues. Joseph was then Housing Minister in the Macmillan Government and I had become involved with him when he made an ambiguous statement in the Commons that I had brought to the notice of his department. Instead of leaving it to a civil servant to clarify, he rushed to the Press Gallery to clear up the matter, wringing his hands with anxiety – and thanking me profusely. The son of a wealthy Jewish businessman and baronet, he had been educated at Harrow and Oxford, possessed a fine intellect and was a Fellow of All Souls. He did not always find it easy to make his mind up, however, and his agonising over decisions, coupled with his intense ideological thinking, earned him the title 'the mad monk'.

Soon after Heath's General Election defeat, Joseph invited Alfred to his Chelsea home for a discussion on policy issues. Joseph was disappointed to the point of anger by the Heath Government's failure in economic policy. Frustrated and searching for a workable alternative, he had been impressed by Alfred's argument that in economic policy 'Keynesianism was dead' and only monetarism could produce stability and growth without inflation. Passed over for the post of Shadow Chancellor, Joseph had asked for a

Party policy role but, in giving him this, Heath ruled out a review of economic policy. Seeking a greater understanding of economics, Joseph at first sought out the help of the Institute of Economic Affairs, directed by the extrovert, pipe-smoking Ralph Harris, a lively character I was to get to know later through my work for the tobacco industry.

Joseph, encouraged by Alfred, decided to set up his own think-tank, the Centre for Policy Studies. With Heath's blessing it was launched with the ostensible aim of studying how the market system worked in other economies around the world. Joseph was chairman, Margaret Thatcher a director and there was to be a director of studies. I first heard of the think-tank not from Alf Sherman but from John Addey, some of whose wealthy friends were being asked to help fund it. Knowing of Alf's link with Joseph and worried about our ability to continue employing him, I tentatively suggested that he might think of working full time at such a centre. No doubt the thought was already in Alf's busy mind. He agreed to be Joseph's director of studies and we parted friends and continued to keep in touch.

Addey heard of the think-tank partly because of his own very real interest in politics. He had first come to public notice when, as a young Tory candidate, he fought Labour leader Hugh Gaitskell in South Leeds in the 1959 General Election. Five years later he fought Huddersfield West, losing by only a narrow margin. His company secretary was the man who had been his Tory agent in Leeds – Frank Richardson. Following Alf's departure, and with business building up, I persuaded Addey, who wanted to change the company secretary arrangements, to allow Frank to join my team. As secretary of the Association of Conservative Party Agents, he was still very much in touch with Tory affairs and top people.

Membership of the Leslie Hale luncheon club continued to grow and at times it was a problem seating all who turned up in the private room upstairs at the Gay Hussar. They were very lively events and the latest to add to the laughter was Lord Willis of Chislehurst. He was better known as Ted Willis, creator of the television series *Dixon of Dock Green* about the adventures of an old-time bobby on the beat. Genial and jokey, Ted was to win entry to the Guinness Book of Records in 1979 as the writer with more TV series to his name than any other.

In 1973 Leslie Hale asked if he could bring a friend to the next lunch and because of the accommodation problem I was not overjoyed. The friend was a Labour-supporting businessman Leslie had met through the Saints and Sinners' Club. This was a convivial gathering of showbiz people, businessmen, politicians and sundry characters who enjoyed a good meal in a top hotel and contributed generously to charities. The chap Leslie introduced was Sir Desmond Brayley and, on seeing the man, I experienced an instinctive feeling of distaste. As Michael Foot shook hands with him I thought I saw the same reaction trouble him.

Brayley was heavily built and had a face that appeared to have had some experiences on the inside of a boxing ring. He looked rough and tough and his small eyes had the glint of cunning. He contributed little to conversation over lunch but at the end, in thanking us for allowing him to come, asked if he might attend again. Leslie Hale nodded and looked expectantly at the rest of us – so we said yes.

Soon after, I saw him dining with Harold Wilson in the Commons and I wondered if he was telling Wilson he had become friends with Michael Foot. He was certainly a friend of Labour MP George Wigg. Wigg had got him involved with the Labour Party and encouraged him to donate money, some of which helped to equip Wilson's private office before the 1964 General Election. In return for the cash, Wilson had given him a knighthood in the 1970 Dissolution Honours List. It was then revealed that Labour held 60,000 donated shares in Brayley's company, the Canning Town Glass Works – the only company in which the Party had a stake. After losing the 1970 General Election, Wilson was given the use of Brayley's flat in Arlington House, the luxury block of apartments in St. James'.

He liked to be known as Colonel Brayley – and his *Who's Who* entry gave the impression that this was a wartime rank. In fact, in the regular army he had never risen higher than lieutenant (temporary captain). He had joined the army at seventeen and his prowess in the boxing ring helped him rise to non-commissioned rank in the Army Physical Training Corps. With the start of World War II, he became a paratrooper, was commissioned and won the Military Cross in North Africa. On leaving the army in 1945 he found work in the glass business and in his spare time helped the local Army Cadet Corps, providing generous donations. Somehow these activities helped him to rise to the rank of Lieutenant Colonel.

The politically sophisticated members of the Leslie Hale luncheon club found the 57-year old Brayley as thick as two planks when it came to the discussion of parliamentary affairs. We were stunned, therefore, when in April 1974 he was given a life peerage by Wilson and appointed Army Under Secretary. In the House of Lords, his bumbling attempts at answering questions made him a figure of fun. On his first appearance, having read out the answer prepared by his civil servants, he went on to read out the guidance notes they had given him on how to reply to possible supplementary questions. Even Leslie Hale was reduced to a state of bewildered despair.

Then, on the eve of Wilson calling the second General Election of 1974, which he hoped would give him a workable majority, Brayley cancelled an official visit he was to have made to Mexico. There was a growing furore over £16,500 he was alleged to owe his old company, Canning Town Glass Works. He found it hard to understand when he was called to 10 Downing Street to be told that this meant he would have to leave the Government - but he resigned. Two years later, the police accused him of conspiracy to defraud the company he had built up. He was summoned to appear at Bow Street Magistrates' Court in September 1976 but before the case could proceed, the man who had been Wilson's benefactor had a heart attack and died.

Following the February 1974 General Election, the *Daily Express* decided to serialise Marcia Williams' life story. I had attended a Roads Campaign Council dinner and, returning to Dulwich via Victoria Station late at night well fortified with port, I bought a copy of the first edition of the *Express*. As I read the first instalment of the Marcia Williams story I became puzzled and annoyed. The political editor of the *Daily Express* was by then Walter Terry, the father of Marcia's children. How could the paper have decided to cover her life story without referring to this interesting fact? On leaving the train at West Dulwich station, I entered a telephone box and dialled the *Express* number. I was put through to the news desk and recognised the voice of a young man I had dealt with when employed by the paper. Disguising my voice with a high pitched Scottish accent, I said I had just read with interest the first instalment and asked, 'Can I assume that the next will reveal your political editor is the father of her two sons?'

I thought I heard a sharp intake of breath before I put down the phone and sauntered home, chuckling in my inebriated state. I assumed the editor of the *Express* knew of the connection and that, as it had not become public, had decided to risk running the articles to boost circulation. I was wrong.

In the *Express* office the alarm bells were ringing. The immediate suspicion was that the call had come from old rival the *Daily Mail*, from whom Terry had recently been poached. When *Express* editor Ian McColl was informed, he was flabbergasted. His promotion to the London office from the *Scottish Daily Express* meant he knew nothing of the Marcia-Terry affair. Although a few political journalists were aware of it, no one had ever written about it. As the old adage goes, 'In Fleet Street dog doesn't eat dog'.

As political correspondent of the *Daily Express* in the late 1960s, I had seen the love affair begin and correctly foresaw problems ahead in trying to compete with Walter. He was already pulling off too many scoops without the aid of pillow talk from Wilson's personal private secretary. I warned *Express* proprietor, Max Aitken, of the situation but he decided to take no action. Now, years later, I had acted. The moment of truth had arrived.

Walter was called in to see the editor the next morning and admitted his paternity. The immediate reaction of McColl, a strict Presbyterian, was that the *Express* must publish the truth. Terry, equally stunned by the turn of events, hurried off to phone Marcia who in turn broke the news to the harassed Wilson. The Prime Minister called Lord Goodman – the arch fixer – who was soon breathing heavily down the receiver to McColl. Once again, the gargantuan solicitor succeeded in doing the trick. McColl backed off. The *Express* did not run the story. Its reporters, however, spread the story in the pubs and bars of Fleet Street as they drank their lunch. Soon another paper – *The Times* – would belatedly break the news, discreetly burying it away in a lengthy article.

With Labour in power, Wilson began to turn the wheels for the 1975 referendum he had promised on whether Britain should remain in the Common Market. Roy Jenkins was leading the all-party *Britain in Europe* campaign, supported by my friend and LOGOS colleague Reg Prentice. Prominent in the all-party anti-Market camp were my friends Alf Morris and Tory MP Neil Marten. As the battle hotted up, they recalled from the platform that Sir Oswald Mosley, one-time leader of Britain's black-shirted fascists, had echoed the German Nazi Party by ardently advocating the idea of a European Union. It was on record because in 1971 they had asked me to interview Mosley on the issue and it had been published in the weekly journal *The Spectator*. Interested in the prospect of meeting Mosley, I had agreed to take on the job. Alf and Neil had assumed that because the Nazis and Mosley wanted a European Union, this would put a lot of Britons off the idea. I met him in a terraced house in a smart little street off the Kings' Road in Chelsea.

His fanatical demeanour and clipped delivery reminded me of Enoch Powell. Leaning forward in his chair, his eyes alight with the fire that hypnotised his followers in the pre-war London rallies, he declared: 'We need to get together with the Germans and other Europeans to make a continental system. Britain must now form part of that system – a new third force in the world'. 'A nuclear-armed third force', I asked. 'Yes', he replied, 'No one will trust Germany at present with nuclear arms. But in a united Europe she would be part of an integrated defence force – integrated almost to regimental level'.

He went on to argue that when European power was fully developed, the American presence on the continent would not be necessary. The 74-year-old, who lived in Paris and no longer maintained a home in Britain, claimed to see his role as essentially one of persuading the British people to join Europe. 'If they don't do that there may be a great crisis – and if I were asked to help at such a time it would be my duty to do so', he asserted. He continued, 'In recent history, all the messes have been made by young men while old men like Adenauer, De Gaulle and Mao have succeeded'.

His wife Diana, frail but still evincing something of her one-time good looks saw me to the door. She was his second wife, and had married the notorious womaniser in Berlin. Hitler and Goebbels, the Nazi propaganda chief, had attended the wedding, held in the greatest secrecy. Diana had met Hitler through her sister Unity, the most scatterbrained of the famous Mitford sisters, and after that often lunched with him.

Walking to the King's Road, I joined the youngsters parading outside the Chelsea gear shops and coffee bars. The Mosleys would soon be returning to their home in Paris, an elegant neo-classical villa named Temple de la Gloire. There they regularly entertained their friends the Duke and Duchess of Windsor, who flirted with the Nazis and lived in exile outside the city. I wondered what the name Mosley meant to most of these hip boulevardiers. How many would know that in the early 1930s it had been said he could have become leader of either the Tory or Labour Parties?

A glamorous and wealthy First World War veteran, he had been appalled that post-war Britain, far from being a place fit for heroes to live in, had offered many ex-servicemen only unemployment and poverty. He had been elected Tory MP for Harrow at the age of twenty-two but crossed the floor of the Commons in 1924 to join the Labour Party. A brilliant young man and a spellbinding orator, he entered a Labour Government in due course but, shocked by the ineptitude of Ramsey Macdonald's administration, resigned in 1931 in despair and frustration to form his own New Party. He hoped Tories would join him but after a series of electoral defeats, it was wound up. He then launched his Union of Fascists – the Blackshirts. Despite Mosley's support for the *Yes* campaign, the British people voted on June 5th to stay in the Common Market.

Back in the Addey office, LOGOS got off to a good start. Thanks to David Powell's effective marketing, over a dozen local authorities applied to use the services. It had been decided that in building up the business it would be an attraction if we had some prominent MPs on board as directors. I persuaded my old comrade-in-arms from the Colchester battle Sir Bernard Braine to be our Tory member and he joined Reg Prentice, our Labour representative, on the board.

The main attraction of LOGOS, however, was a special low-interest loan offered by merchant bankers Guinness Mahon to councils to help finance their development plans. The demand was greater than expected and the bank was taking time to cope with it. Then, as the economic situation deteriorated, the Treasury moved to tighten credit facilities. LOGOS was brought to the attention of the men in Whitehall. They made it known that while we were not breaking any rules our lending arrangements were not in harmony with Treasury policy. Not wishing to fall out with Whitehall, Guinness Mahon decided to call a halt to the operation but asked the Treasury if the local authority at the head of the queue could be allowed to continue with its plan. It was Brighton, which wanted to finance a much-needed new conference hall. It was agreed that the development could proceed, much to the delight of the politicians who suffered cold feet for years in the old ice rink venue for their annual party conferences. In due course, the Brighton Conference Centre was opened by Prime Minister Jim Callaghan.

There had been another important development on the local government front. The Corporation of the City of London had made it known that it intended to employ new public relations consultants and, for the first time, needed assistance on the parliamentary front. John Addey Associates ended up on a short list of two. Our competitors were employing a Tory MP – Geoffrey Johnson-Smith – and thought this would give them an edge. We had recently recruited as our chairman the lively Sir Desmond Heap, a former controller and solicitor to the City Corporation - and we feared that the Aldermen and Councillors might think it would look improper to take on a firm headed by one of their former senior officers. As it turned out, they decided that it would not be right to engage a company that employed a Member of Parliament. We won this prestigious account and the champagne corks popped in Wardrobe Chambers.

Sir Desmond joined us following John Addey's purchase of more shares in the company which had left him in a controlling position. Having lost control, the Charles Barker company happily gave up the chairmanship, which had been held by one of their senior directors, so a vacancy had to be filled. David Powell knew Sir Desmond and in view of our local government work and links with City financial institutions recommended that we should offer him the position. Sir Desmond, one of the most famous planning lawyers in Britain, was pleased to accept. In 1972 he had been elected president of the Law Society and from 1964 to 70 had been chairman of the Town Planning Committee. A small, neat man he had an infectious sense of humour and in his spare time loved singing, cycling and the theatre.

Before putting our contract-winning proposals to the Corporation, we had been told that the City wanted to improve relations with City institutions, such as the Stock Exchange, and with Members of Parliament. To bag both, I suggested organising visits for MPs to City institutions, sponsored by the Corporation. These could then be followed by lunches at the Corporation's offices for the parliamentary guests and the bodies' representatives. This simple idea was greeted with acclaim and it was promptly my job to get on and organise the events.

The main reason why the Corporation needed to improve relations with MPs – especially on the Labour benches – was that the man responsible for this area on the authority's staff had not been up to the job. Geoffrey Peacock CVO held the title of the City's Remembrancer, which involved organising ceremonies and liaison between the City, Parliament and the Lord Chamberlain's Office. As a master of protocol, he was good on ceremonies, and with enough sense to follow precedent and appear unflappable if something went wrong. But his rather pompous style made him few friends in parliament and his political naivety was a problem. This tall, imposing wartime colonel and Inner Temple lawyer was not overjoyed when the Corporation decided it needed an experienced parliamentary consultant. The need seemed all the greater when Labour won the General Election and left wing MPs began to support the campaign of the Labour-controlled Greater London Council for the abolition of the Corporation of the City of London, if needs be by a private member's bill. Wise Aldermen and members of the City's Common Council realised that Peacock was not up to coping with that challenge.

My visits to City institutions, such as Lloyd's of London and the Stock Exchange, had started well and been regarded as worthwhile by the parliamentarians taking part. I had carefully handpicked the Labour MPs from the centre and right of the Party, there had been no embarrassments and I was congratulated by members of the Corporation. Then Peacock met one of the Labour MPs – Harry Lamborn – at a Whitehall reception who said he had noticed that there were no left wingers on the visit to which he had been invited. He thought the Corporation should try and win them over and when Peacock asked Lamborn to suggest a name, one was quickly produced. Peacock, anxious not to offend the well-meaning Lamborn, insisted that his suggested name should be added to the next list of MPs to be invited – this time to visit the Bank of England.

The visit went smoothly and the Governor of the Bank hosted a spectacular lunch to round it off. Then, to my horror, the following week's issue of the left wing journal *Tribune* featured a scathing article on the front page about the operation of the Bank and the high life-style enjoyed by its officers. Peacock's chosen left-winger had been a no-holds-barred, strident opponent of the capitalist system named Brian Sedgemore. His piece oozed contempt. The Bank was furious, the Corporation deeply embarrassed and it was decided to organise no more such visits.

Peacock failed to admit that it was his fault. He was knighted in 1981 for his services to the City. Sedgemore went on to become a member of the Commons Treasury Select Committee and gave a series of Bank of England governors a searing time when they gave evidence. He described one – Robin Leigh-Pemberton - as 'a useless deadbeat'.

Some of Addey's city clients had a reputation for sailing close to the wind. One was property tycoon Eric Miller – another of Harold Wilson's rogues' gallery of friends and benefactors. Addey popped his head into my office during the 1974 General Election to announce excitedly that Miller, head of Peachey Properties, had loaned to Wilson his Bell Jet Ranger helicopter for his personal use during the campaign. Miller had also contributed funds to Wilson's office and had become a close friend of Marcia Williams. Through his friendship with Miller, Addey hoped to impress other clients – perhaps to have some influence on policy in 10 Downing Street where, after Wilson's election victory, Miller was a regular visitor. He suggested a lunch at which Miller could be introduced to some of my public affairs clients interested in government policy making. Miller received his pay off when he received a knighthood in Wilson's highly controversial resignation honours list in 1976. Addey lost no time in calling to congratulate him – but also admitted that with Wilson's departure our line into 10 Downing Street through Miller had been severed.

A year later, in September 1977, Miller, the poor boy who had become a millionaire by thirty four, was found shot in the garden of his smart Chelsea home. With the police and company creditors moving in on him, he committed suicide on Yom Kippur, the Jewish Day of Atonement. Harold Wilson, occupying a Peachey property apartment provided by Miller, declined to comment on his benefactor's death. A confidential Scotland Yard report on Miller described him as, 'A very unpleasant person who would screw anyone for a buck'.

Much of John Addey's work involved take-over bids by companies involving tight initial secrecy about who was employing him. In 1973, the Public Relations Consultants' Association set up a register in which the seventy-six members would be compelled to provide details of their pecuniary interests and names of clients. The PRCA had been set up in 1969 with the aim of raising and maintaining professional standards in consultancy practice and promoting confidence in the profession. John Addey Associates was a member company. Supporters of the proposal argued that the reputation of the business could suffer from 'undue secrecy and covert techniques'. Conversely, some financial public relations specialists, led by Addey, opposed it, arguing that they were already bound by Stock Exchange rules and that in the run-up to take-over bid operations having to reveal their identities would be detrimental to their clients' interests.

A major row erupted at the annual meeting of the PRCA in May 1974. I attended with Addey and when a motion was moved to set up the register he argued that the answer to the problem of the misuse of PR operations was for the PRCA to draw up a much stricter code of conduct. Michael Rice, chairman of the PRCA's professional practices committee, who had objected to my open use of the word 'lobbying' some years before, described Addey's arguments as 'naïve'. Rice insisted that the profession had to discipline itself before 'Somebody else decides to do it for us'. The pro-register motion was passed by twenty-eight votes to five.

Addressing the meeting, I declared that the area in most urgent need of a register was that of public affairs consultants operating in and around Parliament. I complained that some PR companies were abusing the facilities of the Commons by employing MPs to do undercover work for them and provide them with parliamentary documents free of charge. Speaking as a former political journalist, I expressed the belief that some parliamentary consultancies were doing a more important job as communicators to the worlds of business and local government than newspapers which had ceased to be papers of record and failed to provide detailed information on legislation and other parliamentary activities.

Parliament, I suggested, should be asked to recognise this and I proposed that in return for having their clients and MP employees entered in a register controlled by Parliament, consultancies that could prove that they were in regular attendance at Westminster should be granted privileges enjoyed by newspaper correspondents. Such privileges could include a daily free issue of parliamentary papers, such as the *Order Paper* and *Hansard*, easy access to the public galleries, access to a bar, such as Annie's, used by the Press, and limited access to other useful areas. Rice brushed aside my proposal and insultingly added, 'If Arthur Butler wants to know how to get into the bars at Westminster, I shall be pleased to tell him'.

Many PR firms were no doubt using the MPs on their payrolls to take them into the bars at Westminster when the need arose. I was stunned at this response from the chair. Nobody in the large audience supported my proposal and I noticed that Christopher Bosanquet, who took a highly elastic attitude towards the system through his use of Sir John Langford-Holt, looked suitably embarrassed. I avoided any dealings with the PRCA for some years after that. Fewer than half the association's members voted on the issue that Rice and his supporters claimed was so important. Some reputable PR firms did not even bother to belong to it and I could understand why.

The PRCA move to set up a register in which the clients and political connections of member firms would be listed was welcomed by Leader of the Commons Edward Short in a Commons debate on MPs' interests. Patrick McNair-Wilson, Tory MP for New Forest, employed by Michael Rice, claimed that the PR profession had taken action to establish, as near as possible, a code of practice to prevent *loose slanders* about the industry and MPs employed by it. It was to become apparent in the years that followed that many loopholes remained that might have been covered if my proposals had been adopted. In Mark Hollingsworth's well-researched and readable book on political lobbying, *MPs for Hire,* he quotes McNair-

Wilson - in his chapter *Whom Does Your MP Serve?* - as saying, 'The public does not have an automatic right to know what Members of Parliament get up to'.

At the end of the Commons debate in May 1974, MPs voted to set up a Select Committee on Members' Interests. Such is the way in which the Commons has run its affairs, members of that policing body have been allowed to be employed as consultants and directors of PR and other companies.

Overshadowing the PR profession and prompting the move for the PRCA register was the spectre of the Poulson – T. Dan Smith case. John Poulson, who built up a large, highly successful town planning and architectural business, masterminded a network of bribery and corruption to win contracts, assisted by Newcastle public relations operator Smith. If Poulson had not been made bankrupt and subjected to close questioning in the bankruptcy court, his illegal activities might never have been disclosed. He received a five-year prison sentence and PR man Smith and others were also sent to jail. Reggie Maudling, who had been chairman of Poulson's principal company, resigned from Heath's Government in July 1972 as a result of the scandal.

As consultant to Imperial Tobacco, I was invited to attend the AGM of the Imperial Group, of which the tobacco sector formed the most important and profitable part. As I walked around the edge of the gathering in a Park Lane hotel, I saw a familiar figure. Michael King had been diplomatic correspondent of the *Daily Mirror* when I was covering the Foreign Office for the *Sketch* and *Express*. He had become Public Affairs Manager for the Group and after the AGM invited me to become its political consultant. A rule that no consultant could work both for the Group and for one of its member companies was ignored in my case. A very important new addition had been added to the Addey client list. Michael was the son of Cecil King, the major publisher who built the group which owned the *Daily Mirror*. On leaving the *Mirror*, Michael worked for the CBI whose chairman had been Sir John Partridge before switching to the chairmanship of Imperial Group.

Under growing pressure from the anti-smoking activists, Imperial Tobacco decided to diversify and moved into brewing and food production to form the Group. The hope was that, as the tobacco market shrank, these new ventures would provide the bulk of the profit. It was not to be. Having bought Courage Breweries, the tobacco men discovered that it was badly managed and run down. Soon after employing me, Imperial Group made an even worse purchase – a hotel chain in America in an even worse state. Meanwhile, I was having to expand my knowledge and parliamentary contact work to cover such problems as alcoholism and factory farming. Then, through the links between the CBI, Partridge and King, I was asked to advise the employers' organisation on parliamentary developments and to cover in detail the progress of the Government's industry bill. This latter task proved to be too manpower intensive for my small team. I advised the CBI that it would be cheaper for them to employ someone directly than for me to take on an extra employee and hit them with our substantial charge-out rates. The CBI, which at that time had no internal office specialising in parliamentary and political affairs, was grateful for my advice.

Michael King, a charming, courteous and thoughtful man, had been CBI director of information until 1973 when he followed Partridge to Imperial as public affairs adviser. Tall, fair and good looking, he was rather heavily built and had suffered two heart attacks in 1968 which prompted him to abandon the daily stress of Fleet Street where he had been foreign editor of the *Daily Mirror* for over ten years.

Michael's boss Sir John Partridge had started the diversification of Imperial in the mid 1960s, transforming it from a purely tobacco-based company into a group with interests ranging from frozen foods to brewing. He was followed as chairman in 1975 by the gentlemanly Sir John Pile who continued the process with a £300 million purchase of the Howard Johnson hotel and restaurant chain in the USA. The normally calm Michael was unusually excited when he broke the news to me. The deal turned out to be a bitter disappointment for Imperial, however, as the operation needed vast sums to bring it up to standard.

Like Partridge, he had been a strongly pro-Europe business operator and was furious when the EEC changed the system of charging duty on cigarettes, giving an advantage to King-size products – an area in which Imperial was weak compared to some competitors. This set-back prompted Imperial to pay more attention to the need for constant monitoring of European Commission activities and more effective lobbying in Brussels – which was good for my business.

On the home political front, following the Tory General Election defeat, Margaret Thatcher moved into my area of operations by shadowing Environment Secretary Tony Crosland. As such, her responsibilities covered transport, housing and local government. I started at a disadvantage in my dealings with her for I had never got to know her as a Lobby journalist, partly because she had always given the impression that she was far too busy to talk. She reminded me of a breathless hen scuttling through the corridors, usually carrying a bulging bag of shopping. She was, in fact, not only a conscientious and hard-working MP but a dedicated housewife, putting her family responsibilities at the top of her priorities. As a minister, she would adjourn meetings to get to the grocer's before closing time.

Some years earlier – before Heath beat Wilson in 1970 – she had been Shadow Transport Minister and at that stage had given little encouragement to the roads lobby. In her opinion, there was a major need for more capital investment in the railways. She depressed the British Road Federation by warning that if the Government built bigger and better roads, they would soon become saturated with more vehicles and the country would be no nearer to solving the transport problem. The BRF had breathed a sigh of relief when in 1969 following Sir Edward Boyle's resignation she replaced him as Shadow Education Minister. Now she was back on the transport front – and the BRF looked to me as their political consultant to try to make her more roads friendly.

It helped that in her old Ford Anglia, she had been driving herself around London and had some sympathy for the city's motorists, so often reduced to a frustrating snail's pace. It helped further that Alfred Sherman, having worked with me for the BRF, by then had important input into Tory policy making. I arranged for the BRF director Robert Phillipson to provide Alfred with up-to-the-minute information on road needs and developments. With Alfred's assistance, I arranged for Mrs Thatcher to be guest of honour at a working lunch hosted by the Roads Campaign Council at the Royal Automobile Club. A number of Tory MPs who supported the roads lobby were also invited. I was then informed by the RAC's catering manager that, as most of the club's premises were not open to women, she would not be allowed in certain areas en route to the private dining room reserved for the function.

Foreseeing an embarrassing scene if the formidable lady were to be restricted in her movements, I told the manager that if the club was seriously suggesting bundling her into a service lift then I would hold the lunch elsewhere. The occasion was a useful one. Soon, with Alfred's well-informed encouragement, she was speaking of the importance of the car economy and the need for better roads. Moreover, to the dismay of the rail lobby, she began to make known her dislike of train travel.

Another factor in helping the shadow minister to support the calls for more and better roads was the effect of my campaign on behalf of the BRF to mobilise grass roots opinion in favour of motorways and by-passes for congested towns and villages. I had helped to set up a number of pro-motorway groups around the country and letters to local MPs were now arriving at Westminster.

Finally, there was an unplanned factor operating in our favour. Christopher Powell, long-time parliamentary adviser to the BRF, was a friend of Margaret's husband Denis. Indeed, Christopher had known Denis before he married her and, as they both had flats in the same Chelsea block, witnessed the courtship. The couple then rented for years a cottage Christopher owned on his Share Farm estate, near Goudhurst in Kent. At weekends, over drinks and dinner with the Powells, Margaret was subjected to much pro-road propaganda from Christopher and Denis, who liked expensive cars and drove them regularly along the M4 to his office at Burmah Oil HQ in Swindon.

Christopher, as founding secretary of the All-Party Channel Tunnel Committee at the House of Commons, had no doubt also influenced Margaret's views on that venture. She had congratulated the Wilson Government on its decision to support the building of the tunnel and was not best pleased when it decided that Britain must pull out of the project because of the country's economic difficulties.

Working with Keith Joseph at the Tory Centre for Policy Studies, Mrs Thatcher quickly became involved in the early stages of the Tory leadership struggle following Heath's failure to win the second General Election in 1974. As disgruntled Tory MPs discussed the need for a new leader, it quickly became clear that Keith Joseph was the front-runner for the right wing. Thatcher was pleased to support him as his informal campaign manager. Then, suddenly, Joseph destroyed his position as Heath's potential challenger by making a speech suggesting that adolescent mothers in social classes four and five were having too many children and endangering Britain's human stock. The speech had been largely written for him by Alfred Sherman and reflected Alf's lack of PR skills and sensitivity. Joseph, to his surprise and embarrassment, found himself faced with national uproar. As a naturally compassionate man, he was appalled by the impression he had created and started to apologise and complain. An angry Alf urged him to stand fast and said the fuss would blow over. But Joseph, who appeared hell-bent on earning his *mad monk* moniker, decided that he could not brazen it out and, moreover, could not now be a candidate in the looming leadership battle. On being told, Margaret Thatcher said in that case, she would run against Heath herself.

Alfred had destroyed Joseph's prospects of becoming Tory leader. Some journalists cast doubt on whether Alfred was responsible for the fatal words. Knowing him as I did, I saw his fingerprints all over the speech. Lunching with him many years later, I asked Alfred to confirm he had written it – and he did. Moreover, he argued that Joseph should have stood by the words instead of backing off in the face of the outcry.

With Margaret Thatcher's hat in the ring, Airey Neave, who in 1968 had asked my advice on whether he should challenge Heath, now stepped forward to play a decisive role in her campaign. He had at first supported the idea that Edward du Cann, former Party chairman and chairman of the 1922 Committee of all Tory MPs, should be the challenger. But when du Cann said he couldn't, for 'business reasons', Airey switched his allegiance to Thatcher and became her campaign manager. Fuelled by his intense personal dislike of Heath, Airey put enormous energy into her campaign and his skill at organisation took her first past the post. She won on the second ballot, her nearest rival being waffly, wobbly Willie Whitelaw, a Tory *Vicar of Bray* who, having been a close supporter of Heath, went on to serve as her mainstay.

At Wardrobe Chambers, my team joined me in a hearty if somewhat incredulous laugh. We could claim that if we had not encouraged our colleague Alfred to take up full-time employment with the Centre for Policy Studies, Joseph would not have made that fatal speech and he would now be Tory leader. Due to our intervention, Mrs Thatcher was Top Cat. When I told Airey the story after the event, he smiled thinly and asked,

'So are you claiming credit for the fact that Margaret is our leader?'

'Oh no, Airey!' I replied. 'I'm prepared to share the credit with you!'

Thatcher rewarded him with the job he wanted – Shadow Secretary of State for Northern Ireland. He was also her Chief of Staff. Another friend who enjoyed the joke, and who was to serve Margaret in due course, was Henry James, for years the hard working, trustworthy and popular Number Two in the 10 Downing Street press office. I had remained in touch with him after leaving journalism and was lunching with him at Burke's dining Club, co-founded by my friend Gerald Thomas. I also told him, in strict confidence, how I had broken the Marcia –Walter Terry paternity story.

As we discussed that relationship he said, 'Harold's having an affair!'

I looked incredulous. 'It's true', he went on. 'Harold's driver told me. Sometimes, when Harold accompanies Marcia as she's driven home, he tells the driver to stop on the way back and he picks up this other woman'. I gawped.

'Unbelievable!' I said.

'Isn't it just', agreed Henry.

But it was true. Years later, when I ran this by a highly respected left-wing journalist who was often at 10 Downing Street when Labour held power, he confirmed the story. Moreover, he gave me the woman's name. I knew her. The late, and normally discreet, Jane Parsons who retired in 1981 as head of the 10 Downing Street secretarial team known as the Garden Room Girls, has been reported as saying that 'Wilson liked a bit of skirt'. In due course Henry James was promoted from 10 Downing Street to become director general of the Central Office of Information.

John Addey, on the recommendation of one of his clients, had done work for Tesco, run by the Cohen family. One day in 1976 he called me into his office to say that he had been asked to visit the giant food retailer's HQ in Cheshunt and wanted me to go with him. The request came at short notice and Addey rightly sensed an impending dramatic development. He was right.

We arrived on time but were asked to wait. The secretary explained there had been a slight hitch, which we discovered later meant that Tesco Life President Sir John (Jack) Cohen had ended an argument with his son-in-law, Leslie Porter, the newly appointed chairman, by throwing a coffee pot at him. This delayed our meeting while staff cleaned up the mess. I was told that on another day, Sir Jack and Leslie were seen exchanging punches in the office lobby – not unlikely as they had both encouraged boys' club boxing.

On the week of our visit, tempers had been unusually high due to the forcing through of a major change in trading policy advocated by the young new managing director Ian MacLaurin. Tesco had been suffering dramatic losses, partly due to an oil crisis, and profits had slumped by twenty per cent. In a tour of the stores, MacLaurin realised that giving customers Green Shield Stamps was no longer encouraging them to buy. They didn't want stamps, they wanted better value. When MacLaurin proposed scrapping them he met with stiff opposition from Sir Jack and other senior board members.

Following a battle, MacLaurin won by one vote. John Addey had been called in to provide the sophisticated PR needed to successfully launch MacLaurin's *Operation Check Out* – scrapping the stamps and lowering prices. The turn-around was somewhat chaotic with delivery failures and near fights in some stores – but Tesco's turnover increased by 200 per cent. MacLaurin saw the scruffy high street shops gradually replaced by a chain of giant super-stores stocked with enough up-market produce to provide a serious challenge to Sainsburys. By 1996 it was ahead of Sainsbury's.

MacLaurin, made chairman of Tesco in 1985, foresaw that the massive growth he envisaged would require the assistance of expert consultants in the field of local government planning and political contacts. On my first visit to Cheshunt with Addey, he asked me to propose a programme involving up to the minute information on relevant Government policies, parliamentary liaison and local government contacts. Driving back to London that day we heard on the car radio that Harold Wilson had resigned as Prime Minister. Joe Haines, Wilson's press secretary, has recorded that immediately after his first General Election victory in 1974 Wilson told a small group of cronies that he intended to serve no more than two years as Prime Minister and would retire on his sixtieth birthday in 1976.

By retiring when he did, Wilson had given Callaghan a good chance of succeeding him but in the first ballot there were five other runners – Tony Benn, Tony Crosland, Michael Foot, Roy Jenkins – and my preferred choice, Denis Healey. Healey came third in the second ballot with only 38 votes. Michael Foot, my friendly fellow member of the Leslie Hale luncheon club, had come second with 133 votes compared to Callaghan's 141. Big Jim, busily cajoling and bullying behind the scenes, picked up Healey votes in the final ballot and won. My suspicion that Callaghan would not make a good Prime Minister was to be justified but I never suspected that his period in office would end in such an appalling shambles. Nevertheless, he remained personally popular with the public who, in their ignorance, saw him as a big, kindly, avuncular fellow – trustworthy and benevolent. Columnists in the popular press chose to call him 'Sunny Jim'.

Jim Wellbeloved, one of the most astute operators in the Commons, was one of Callaghan's campaign managers and when I met him on March 30th he gave me his estimate of the final result. It revealed that Callaghan was bound to win. There had, however, been some surprises. Bob Mellish, former Chief Whip, revealed that he intended to vote for that old left wing rebel Michael Foot. Jim told me that in the Callaghan Government, he would like to be Chief Whip or Deputy Chief Whip. He was appointed Under Secretary for Defence (RAF).

In view of my general lack of confidence in Callaghan, I was surprised to feel some respect for him in his handling of one major issue in the first six months of his premiership. On becoming Prime Minister in April, he had been immersed immediately in the type of economic crisis he had experienced on becoming Chancellor of the Exchequer twelve years before – a crisis caused by the weakness of sterling and an over-high borrowing requirement. Having learned some lessons in the interim, he made an important speech at the autumn Labour Party Conference in Blackpool that I was attending with clients. Some of it could have been written by Alfred Sherman.

He declared: 'We used to think you could spend your way out of recession and increase employment by cutting taxes and boosting Government spending. I tell you in all candour that that option no longer exists and that in so far as it ever did, it only worked on each occasion since the war by injecting a bigger dose of inflation into the economy, followed by a higher level of unemployment as the next step. Higher inflation followed by higher unemployment'.

He reminded his audience that Britain had just suffered the highest rate of inflation it had ever known and had not yet escaped the consequences – high unemployment. His Chancellor Denis Healey followed up by demanding from his Cabinet colleagues a tough new monetary discipline aimed at achieving monetary targets. Labour was attempting its own form of monetarism before Mrs Thatcher entered 10 Downing Street with the Milton Friedman 'bible' in her bag.

Jim Wellbeloved's appointment to the Government had affected the MP consultancy arrangement I had set up for Imperial Tobacco. He had done an excellent job for the company and when he suggested that his replacement should be Labour MP Bob Mitchell the proposal was accepted. Jim had been involved with me and other PR and political advisers on a major new initiative by the company which, had it been successful, might have transformed the smoking and health issue worldwide. In a Commons debate on the problem on 16th January 1976, Dr David Owen, then Minister of State for Health, declared, 'I have always rejected a strategy which fails to understand the problems and difficulties of the confirmed smoker and that is only composed of restrictions, warnings and education'.

He added that it was on the reduction of health hazards among smokers that the industry and Government 'could, and should, co-operate'.

Owen understood that the co-operation of the industry was vital because if, unlike Imperial, it did not invest heavily in research for safer cigarettes there would be no marked progress. Some years before, Imperial had pressed for the publication of tar content league tables to guide smokers. This initiative was welcomed by the then Health Minister Sir Keith Joseph – but implementation was delayed for five years by anti-smoking crusaders in the Health Ministry who wanted nothing less than bans and restrictions. In fact, it is not surprising that Owen should have paid acknowledgement to the industry's contribution to research, for the Government itself, which at that time was raising - annually - over £2,000 million in tax revenue from tobacco, was spending virtually nothing on research in the smoking and health field.

In particular, Imperial Tobacco had by 1978 invested over £15 million in research, development and production related to the only British-made substitute tobacco on the market – a new smoking material (NSM). In collaboration with ICI, the company had established by 1972 that a product could be manufactured and used as a tobacco substitute in ways that showed every promise of reducing the risks that had been associated by medical authorities with the smoking of cigarettes. In line with its well-established policy of co-operation with Whitehall, Imperial had talked with Sir Keith Joseph about the future of the product and he agreed that further research and development would be in line with the policy of the Health Department.

As a result, an independent committee of distinguished medical scientists was set up under Professor (later Sir) Robert Hunter, to recommend how such products should be tested and evaluated. To add to the Government's involvement and support, when Imperial built a factory at Ardeer in Scotland to produce NSM, part of the £15 million cost came from public funds in the form of a Regional Development Grant.

The Hunter Committee announced in March 1977 that there would be no objection to the manufacture and sale of cigarettes containing NSM. David Ennals, who replaced Dr Owen as Health Minister, welcomed the report as a valuable contribution to the success of the Government's strategy on smoking and health. Indeed it was, for it was a second important step beyond reducing the tar yield of cigarettes by altering the character of the tar itself. As if to reassure the Government, the Royal College of Physicians said tobacco manufacturers should be encouraged to develop tobacco substitutes.

However, far from encouraging the experiment, the Health Education Council – appointed and financed by the Government – launched an intemperate campaign aimed at discouraging people from buying the new product. It included costly full-page advertisements in the national press proclaiming that 'switching to a cigarette with tobacco substitute is like jumping from the thirty-sixth floor instead of the thirty-ninth'.

Due to that campaign, the market launch of the new product was much less successful than Imperial had hoped. After a short time, the product was withdrawn.

In an article in January 1978 in the magazine *Time and Tide*, ghosted by me, Imperial's chairman Tony Garrett bitterly complained:

> 'The substitute tobacco story is a good example of the damage done by those people employed by Whitehall or its agencies who see issues only in terms of black or white. By their crusading approach, they can delay – or even kill - important developments which it would be in the public interest to introduce. Moreover, it is my sad suspicion that publicity hungry politicians sometimes lend support to the anti-brigade in the knowledge that they are notoriously successful in capturing easy headlines'.

Garrett concluded, 'The Government must never forget that when it comes to working with industry there is no substitute for trust'.

I was personally disappointed by the failure of the substitute tobacco project for it had been my belief that once established in Europe, it would have been taken up on a great scale in the Third World where countless millions of people were beginning to smoke, did not know real tobacco, and were looking for a cheap product.

And I had a personal, family reason for deploring the activities of anti-smoking crusaders who were opposed to compromises that could have helped smokers by providing information, such as tar league tables, and products such as NSM. In June 1974, my father died from lung cancer at the age of sixty-seven, having been a heavy smoker until 1956. No son could have wished for a more supportive and generous parent. He and my mother had backed me in all my endeavours. I consoled myself with the thought that if my widowed mother needed financial support from me it would be poetic justice if some of that money were to come from my fees from the tobacco industry.

Tony Garrett had been getting increasingly fed up with what he regarded as the Government's double dealing with regard to smoking policy and on

Friday April 28th 1978, the watershed was reached in relations between the company and Whitehall. At a meeting of his public affairs advisers, which I attended in the panelled boardroom in Bristol, he announced that as a result of a series of setbacks, including the bitter disappointment over the failure of New Smoking Material, the board had decided to end all expenditure on research into smoking and health. It had been spending up to £2million a year.

I knew the company had good reason to be angry with the unhelpful attitude of the Government, especially over NSM and the breaking of a three-year agreement by the introduction of an EEC-sponsored health tax. The ending of this important research, however, seemed to me to be going too far.

Garrett, explaining his reasons, said he could 'no longer co-operate with this Government'. Trying to play for time, I chipped in to point out that there could be a general election within less than a year which the Tories might win. Would the company be prepared to review the situation if that happened? Garrett intimated that he did not expect the Tories to adopt a very different attitude from Labour. I appealed to him to have private talks with Mrs Thatcher to get an agreement under which, in return for certain assurances, the company would continue some research. Garrett was adamant. He then announced the decision to end production of substitute tobacco.

Appalled by this, I suggested that he should have a report made on the possibilities of selling NSM in overseas markets, especially the developing areas where smoking was on the increase. I pointed out that one reason NSM had not taken on in the UK was that it had been introduced at only a twenty per cent level, which was not a high enough dosage to enable Imperial to describe the cigarettes as 'safer'. I suggested that if aimed at the new smoking public of the developing countries it might be possible to sell cigarettes containing 40% or more of NSM which would entitle them to be labelled safer. I added that the World Health Organisation might be prepared to give support to such a project. Warming to my argument, I reminded him that the anti-smoking brigade was already accusing the Western tobacco companies of exporting their 'killer brands' to areas such as Africa. But Garrett did not accept my argument. He saw no point in having such a report made.

At about this time I learned that the ever-active Joe Godson had set up the Labour Committee on Transatlantic Understanding (LCTU). As

Robin Ramsay records in his published series of well-researched essays *Politics and Paranoia*, the aim of LCTU was to cream off promising British Labour politicians and trade union officials, sending them on study tours to America. In the USA they were wined and dined and fed the American Government line on such issues as the role of nuclear defence and the Soviet Communist threat. Later, this was to expand into the Trade Union Committee for European and Transatlantic Understanding chaired by my old friend Alan Lee Williams. Tony Blair, a member of CND at the time, went on one of these well-funded trips in 1986 and on his return dumped his anti-bomb line and argued the case for nuclear deterrent. Another body, 'Peace through NATO', designed to counter the influence of CND, was set up under the umbrella of TUCETU and at Lee Williams' suggestion I joined it and later arranged for members of my Parliamentary and Scientific Committee to take part in its well-organised visits to NATO research establishments in Europe.

1976 had been a bad year for one of my old Labour politician contacts caught up with the law. In August, John Stonehouse – whom I first met when we were students at the LSE - was sentenced at the Old Bailey to seven years in prison at the Old Bailey, branded a fraudster, forger, thief and liar. Way back in 1969, while serving as Minister of Posts and Telecommunications, he had told me over lunch that he did not think Labour had much hope of winning the next general election. In February that year, I returned his hospitality by taking him to the Coq d'Or where he showed great interest in the wine list.

Although he appeared to be enjoying his job, he was pessimistic about his long-term prospects of holding office. He did not tell me then, but he had decided that if Labour lost he would go into business and took steps to set up several companies in the spring of 1970. Later that year, as we waited for taxis outside the Commons, he told me proudly about one of these – Connoisseurs of Claret Ltd – which he was confident would do well as wine consumption soared in Britain. After a couple of years, however, the company suffered losses of over £45,000 and was propped up by loans from other companies under his control.

By 1972 he was telling me even more proudly about his success in setting up a new bank – the British Bangladesh Trust. Adopting his elder statesman pose, leaning forward and holding the lapels of his jacket, he claimed it would be a great help in the development of Bangladesh. By spring 1973 it had become two companies and he was involved with over twenty others, keeping them afloat by transferring money from one to another. By summer 1974, however, he had to face the fact that his rickety financial empire was on the verge of collapse.

To avoid personal ruin, he began to plan an audacious escape route involving his disappearance and the salvaging of as much money as he could to support him in his new life. He assumed the false identity of a dead man, Joseph Markham, and flew to Miami where he became involved with international confidence tricksters. At our last meeting in New Palace Yard he had given me a business card describing his operations as 'export promotion and consultancy services limited' with an address in Gillingham Street, SW1. Our paths did not cross again before I learned from the press in November 1974 that he was thought to have drowned while swimming off Miami Beach.

I sent my condolences to his wife Barbara. I need not have bothered. He faked his death to escape his creditors and ended up in Australia under a false name. He intended to start a fresh life there with his secretary and mistress Sheila Buckley. It was his bad luck that the Australian police on the look-out for a tall Englishman – the suspected murderer Lord Lucan – had Stonehouse drawn to their attention. He was arrested and extradited back to England to face charges of fraud, theft and deception.

He was released from jail in 1979 after serving less than half the seven years to which he was sentenced. While he was in prison, I met his close friend Bernard Levin travelling on the underground. Like me, Bernard had got to know Stonehouse at the LSE where they had been active members of the chess club. I asked him if he was still in touch with Stonehouse and he said he had visited him recently in jail. I thought that was kind and compassionate of Bernard and I had a twinge of conscience. In view of my dealings with Stonehouse as an MP and the occasions on which I had enjoyed his hospitality, perhaps it would have been the decent thing for me to have done. It was not too late to follow Bernard's example but I failed to do so. I never saw Stonehouse again. He died in 1988 aged 62.

Ever since his student days at the LSE, he had shown he could not be trusted with other people's money. As that was known to a lot of people in the Labour movement, it is surprising that he got as far as he did. But then, Harold Wilson, who put him into his Government, was not noted for good judgement when it came to people.

Another company to join my client list at about the same time as Tesco was Standard Telephones and Cables (STC) – the world leader in submarine telecommunications cables. Led by Kenneth Corfield, a polished and ambitious engineer, it had been under the control of the controversial International Telephone and Telegraph Company (ITT) of America for decades when it asked me to provide a service. One of the USA's most powerful multinational corporations, ITT ran into political trouble in the early 1970s. Among other accusations it was alleged that the company had offered cash to the CIA to undermine the left wing Allende regime in Chile which was threatening to nationalise ITT's business there. As copper cables were replaced by optical fibre systems, an exciting period of expansion in the world market beckoned and one of my responsibilities was to take groups of MPs to visit the company's impressive cable research station near Greenwich. The fact that Corfield employed as his public affairs manager the experienced, impresario-like Peter Earl made my work especially enjoyable.

Peter, with an eye to getting a knighthood for his boss, organised high-grade social events, including a series of glittering discussion dinners in the theatrical extravaganza of a dining suite designed by Oliver Messel at London's Dorchester Hotel. Leading politicians, business and assorted top people were invited and Reg Prentice greatly enjoyed the occasion when I took him as my guest. To provide a link with the Royal Family, Prince Michael of Kent sat on the STC board but contributed little on the occasions I attended in an advisory capacity.

At my suggestion, Bill Deedes, editor of *The Daily Telegraph*, was invited to be the guest of honour and speaker at a Dorchester dinner party in March 1976. Bill was on good form and the evening was a great success. I sat next to Imperial's chairman Tony Garrett, who was always good company and soon after offered me a fulltime job, which I declined with thanks. When Corfield retired as chairman and chief executive in 1985 – five years after receiving his knighthood – the company was facing a difficult time. It had widened its operations but less than a year after his departure, the mood at STC had changed. Heady optimism had been replaced by anxiety and falling confidence, the share price was plummeting and there were calls for drastic cost cutting. The days of high living at the Dorchester were over.

Peter Earl, elected President of the Institute of Public Relations, arranged for Margaret Thatcher to address an IPR lunch at the Dorchester in November 1977. Her flamboyant, cigar-smoking public relations adviser, Gordon Reece, was already improving her appearance and style of speech making. What a change had been wrought from the suburban housewife I had avoided tackling in the Lobby seven years before. Spelling out her broad approach for the future of Britain, she declared that to create incentive for people, Tory strategy would be less taxation, less interference and less government. Government, she argued, should focus more on the important area of private enterprise which created most of the new wealth and jobs.

Behind the scenes, a running battle was raging on policy-making between Alfred Sherman's Centre for Policy Studies and the official Conservative Research Department run by the up-and-coming Christopher Patten. Alfred complained that the CRD was trying to prevent Margaret from fulfilling her destiny as a Thatcherite. Airey Neave, her chief of staff, supported Patten which made life more difficult for Alfred, who had by then introduced Mrs Thatcher to a free market economist who was to replace him as her closest adviser on monetarist policies – Alan Walters.

To improve the efficiency of the company, the board persuaded Addey to appoint a non-executive finance director. I had played a leading role in this initiative and one bright and go-getting young director, Brian Basham, took a particular interest in what I had to say. He recommended a friend with the right experience named Michael Preston. His suggestion was accepted.

Meanwhile, in December 1975, *Private Eye* published an article that was to lead to more trouble for Addey. It alleged that financier Sir James Goldsmith had been involved in the disappearance of Lord Lucan in 1974. The peer was wanted for questioning by the police in connection with the murder of the Lucan family nanny, Sandra Rivett. In January 1976, another *Private Eye* article suggested that Goldsmith was connected with T. Dan Smith, the North-east PR and local government whizz-kid languishing in prison for corruption. The article further suggested that Goldsmith's solicitor Mr. Eric Levine was not honest.

Some forty writs were issued by Levine, many aimed at stopping further distribution of the *Eye*. Doing some digging into Levine's past, the magazine then sought information from a solicitor named Leslie Paisner and from John Addey, both of whom had dealt with Levine. But then Addey and Paisner refused to confirm that the records of their statements were accurate, and signed affidavits denying their accuracy.

Addey later claimed that pressure had been put on him to confirm the record of his statement. He also asserted that the *Eye* threatened to blackmail him with a document that mentioned a homosexual relationship. Addey, in fact, was an active homosexual and, while not disguising this in the Wardrobe Chambers circle, did not want it made public.

The *Eye*'s editor Richard Ingrams, in an affidavit, revealed that in a meeting he had with Addey in May, Addey admitted he had been threatened with a libel action by Goldsmith and Levine and claimed he had no alternative but to provide them with a statement.

'I did not realise they had so much power', he had confessed.

Two judges, after listening to how Addey lied about Levine and then claimed to have been blackmailed by *Private Eye* contributor Michael Gillard - an accusation Addey unreservedly retracted – made these observations: Lord Justice Templeman said Addey 'Was not to be believed in any particular'. Master of the Rolls Lord Denning declared, 'No one would believe a word he said'.

As the *Private Eye* affair rumbled on, Addey received an important letter from the board's financial director in July 1976. Bluntly, it warned that:

'The extreme seriousness of the present situation requires the utmost discipline and attention to areas of weakness in the company. In particular, I refer to the money borrowed by you from the company in 1975 to enable you to meet your commitment to Charles Barker Ltd. in respect of shares in the company which you were contractually bound to purchase from them. When I discovered… that you had drawn a cheque to cover your requirement I was extremely alarmed on both legal and financial grounds'.

The letter went on to point out that the loan was illegal, breaching sections of the 1948 Companies Act, which prohibited a company from lending money to a director to enable him to buy shares in that company. Finally, it stressed the absolute need for Addey to repay the 'loan' before October when the company's annual Corporation Tax account became payable.

Faced with this serious problem, the directors became increasingly alarmed. They had already confronted Addey on the issue of the distribution of clients' fees. Under pressure, he admitted that some clients he regarded as 'purely personal' and their fees went straight into his personal bank account to support his extravagant style of living. Reluctantly, the directors allowed him to get away with that, accepting that perhaps he had a special case. Indeed, one of his personal successes had involved helping to transform Vidal Sassoon from a West End hairdresser into a highly successful international business – and a large part of his personal wealth came from Sassoon shares. Tiring of Albany, he had moved at great expense to Canonbury House, a grand Georgian residence in Islington, and travelled to and from the office in a chauffeur-driven Rolls Royce.

In July, a series of board meetings, some stormy, got underway as the directors put pressure on Addey to clean up the mess. Rumours he was in trouble with his board, coupled with his involvement in the battle between Goldsmith and *Private Eye*, fascinated City journalists. They assumed, wrongly, that one was the cause of the other. There was, in fact, no leak about the real cause of the directors' revolt, partly because that would have reflected badly on the board, catching up with the mismanagement under their nose so late in the day. Indeed, if I had not drawn Brian Basham's attention to the discrepancies, Addey's illegal operations might not have been discovered.

On August 11th the respected city editor of *The Daily Telegraph*, Kenneth Fleet, led his comment column with news that a major board meeting was to be held at the offices of John Addey Associates that day. He wrongly assumed that it was to deal with the chief executive's relationship with *Private Eye*. Fleet noted that this – a revelation to many of his distinguished clients though fairly well known in the trade – was bound to cause problems for the firm. Whether those would be resolved by putting a distance between the firm and its owner-founder was a question for Chairman Sir Desmond Heap and his colleagues to decide, he concluded.

Another prominent city editor Patrick Hutber, leading his column with the Addey affair, also wrongly linked the boardroom struggle with the *Eye* – but rightly thought that as Addey held ninety per cent of the company's shares, the directors were not well placed to attempt a coup.

On another point Hutber was soon proved to have made a misjudgement. While noting that PR was an intensely personal business, he assumed that the clients were basically hiring Addey and so the result of his ejection would be the company's extinction.

Faced with the threat of resignation by his chairman Sir Desmond Heap and six directors, Addey tendered his own as Chief Executive and board member at the meeting – and this was made public in a press release. Then, with his agreement, the board reconvened the next day, chaired in Sir Desmond's absence by a respected director Alan Mole. Addey made a statement saying firstly, he hoped the money he borrowed from the company would be repaid the next day; and secondly, he was prepared to resign as a director if he believed that was in the company's best interests – but he did not believe it was.

I reported to the board that Sir Desmond felt so strongly about the association of Addey's name with the company that he would resign if Addey remained. I added that his departure would cost the company the prestigious Corporation of the City of London account. Tesco, embarrassed by the link with *Private Eye*, had already made it clear it was ending its contract with the company.

Asked whether they would still resign in the light of Addey's statement, six directors said they would – Basham, Mole, Powell, Preston, David Stirling and myself. Only two remained. Then Addey, with his ninety per cent share holding, voted himself back into control – and fired the rebels. Sir Desmond, too late to be at the final showdown, arrived in shirt, slacks and sandals to be told the news as we stood on the pavement by Wardrobe Court. Having been involved, along with David Powell, in bringing Sir Desmond into the company, I was embarrassed and apologetic. Sir Desmond, however, took it well and even sang a few words from an appropriate Gilbert and Sullivan opera – before cycling off home to his flat in the Barbican.

To the drama of the boardroom battle there had been added drama on the street – a 'bomb' alert. Had John Addey Associates decided to go out with a bang? Police sealed off a nearby lane. It proved to be a false alarm – courtesy of Brian Basham. In clearing out his office he had thrown unwanted paper into a mail bag – together with an old alarm clock – and dumped it at a local rubbish collection point. A passer-by heard ticking coming from the bag and, as IRA terrorists had been busy in London, suspected a bomb and called the authorities.

We decided to keep quiet about the financial scandal and the press continued to misinterpret the situation. It was widely reported that the directors had resigned over the *Private Eye* affair. I would not have resigned from the company over Addey's involvement in the *Eye*-Goldsmith case, and I doubt whether any of the other directors would have left immediately either, with the exception of Sir Desmond.

There was no apparent anger or bitterness as we sat around the boardroom table. I felt sad. We had been a highly successful team - key members of the City's fastest growing public relations agency. In the interests of clients, the directors who resigned continued to work out their three-month notice period. They were also hoping to take their clients with them. When I left I took all mine, including the BRF and Roads Campaign Council, Imperial Group and Imperial Tobacco, STC and the Royal Automobile Club. They related to me, not Addey. Mr Hutber had been wrong. Moreover, soon after I left I was working again for Tesco and the Corporation of London.

In the year running up to the break-up, the company had continued to enjoy great success with City clients. It had been involved in the rescue of several secondary banks, including Keyser Ullmann and United Dominions Trust and had assisted with the reconstruction of the Lowson organisation and of Barker & Dobson, the sweet manufacturer. But by August severe damage had been done to Addey's reputation. The accusation that he had broken the professional code by passing on information about clients at media functions, such as *Private Eye* lunches, was especially harmful. Having built up the largest privately owned PR firm in the business, with over fifty important clients, he went into steady decline.

In June 1979 Sir James Goldsmith was cleared by a High Court jury which found that he did not libel or slander Granada TV reporter Michael Gillard when he named him as a blackmailer. Goldsmith had claimed that Gillard had blackmailed Addey in 1976 to obtain information against his solicitor Eric Levine for use by *Private Eye*. It was explained that at the time the *Eye* was engaged in legal proceedings with Sir James who had started a criminal libel action against it. Addey had claimed Gillard had blackmailed him but in the High Court withdrew the accusation, apologised and paid Gillard £5,000 in damages.

Sir James had nevertheless repeated the blackmail allegation to the press. In evidence he revealed that Addey apologised to him for having settled the earlier action brought against him by Gillard, explaining that he had done so because he feared his business would be destroyed. Addey also felt that as his homosexuality had not been made public, it was a major matter for him.

The Goldsmith-*Private Eye* case had run for eighteen months and the swashbuckling entrepreneur was eventually persuaded to drop the libel charges against the journal in exchange for an apology. Addey, encouraged to retire as a JP and stripped of his fellowship of the Institute of Public Relations, spent his last years living quietly in London's docklands dying in 1994 aged sixty-three.

CHAPTER THREE

Wanted By the Police

News of the break-up of the John Addey board spread quickly through the media and public relations world and soon after I received a call that was to lead to a major new opportunity. The call came from Christopher Bosanquet whose PR company, F.J. Lyons, had been bought by the Charles Barker Group, the oldest advertising agency in the world, gentlemanly, discreet, blue-blooded and apparently secure. It was the same Charles Barker company that had set up John Addey in business and allowed him gradually to buy up their share-holding in his firm until, by breaking the law, he had come to own ninety per cent of the shares. Bosanquet, with whom I had worked for Imperial Tobacco, had been authorised to offer me a position in the company's public affairs and parliamentary division – and gave the impression that I would be virtually in charge of it.

The timing could not have been better. My one-time Parliamentary Press Gallery contact, Conrad Vos Bark, who had joined Barkers from the BBC some years before, had decided to retire as the company's parliamentary expert to concentrate on what he loved best: fly-fishing. At the same time, Christopher Powell, whose company Watney and Powell had been bought by Barker's, and whom I worked alongside for the British Road Federation, was looking for someone to take over his clients so he could ease his way into retirement. Barker's previously small public affairs division had been greatly expanded into Charles Barker Watney and Powell. It had also been linked to the consumer PR company Charles Barker Lyons under the chairmanship of George Pulay, the shrewd and kindly ex-journalist whom I had known on the *News Chronicle* before he became city editor of *The Times*.

Bosanquet, as managing director of Charles Barker Lyons, was anxious to enlist me to consolidate his profitable Imperial Tobacco account which he feared might be at risk if I were to join another company. I decided to play safe and head for a large, well-established operation such as Charles Barker. No company in the business had a firmer foundation – it went back to 1812.

Early in the nineteenth century, James Lawson, a printer at *The Times*, went into partnership with the young Charles Barker and persuaded his newspaper to open a city office to gather advertisements. The arrangement allowed Lawson to use reports from the newspaper in a newsletter that was circulated to the editors of provincial and continental papers. The agency supplemented this service with reports from its own team of correspondents in the City and at Westminster – thus providing the first ever parliamentary information service. News from the continent arrived by pigeon post and thanks to the company's unrivalled courier service the influential bankers Rothschilds were the first people in the City to learn of the outcome of the Battle of Waterloo in 1815. Rightly assuming that the stock market would fall when news of the battle became known, Nathan Rothschild instructed his agents to sell English bonds while they were still high and sure enough, other traders followed suit. With his superior intelligence service, of which Mr Barker was an important part, he was the first in the city to know that Wellington had beaten Napoleon, a result that would determine which currency held financial sway in Europe. Rothschild then ordered his traders to buy up British bonds, by then virtually worthless. The Rothschilds made a killing – and duly grateful to Barker and his pigeon post, continued to use Barker as part of their devastatingly effective network of monetary, diplomatic and political operations.

In encouraging me to join Charles Barker now, Bosanquet had led me to believe that I would be in charge of the parliamentary subsidiary Charles Barker Watney and Powell. When I joined, however, I agreed to be joint managing director with a competent young woman, Evie Soames, who had been running the company. As we had a very large client list, with many big names, this division of authority made sense. Evie was married to a baronet, Sir Andrew Duff Gordon, one of whose ancestors, Sir Cosmo, had survived the sinking of the Titanic.

On my arrival at the Charles Barker office in Farringdon Street, Lt. Commander Christopher Powell RN (retired) quickly moved in on me. Well advanced in years, he had been waiting for the right person to take over his list of prestigious personal clients and decided he could rely on me to do the job. Those clients included the Parliamentary and Scientific Committee, the most respected and important of the unofficial all-party specialist bodies operating at Westminster, and the Society of Motor Manufacturers and Traders (SMMT), the trade association for the British motor industry. Apart from providing clients with a daily information service, administering all-party specialist committees and lobbying generally, he specialised in piloting private members' bills through Parliament. He often drafted them himself and with help from friendly MPs had them introduced into the Commons by means other than the annual ballot for private members' legislation. Mastering the procedures of the Commons, he became so expert that at times he would get a bill through all its stages without a debate.

Powell succeeded with countless campaigns but, as a bon viveur, his favourite was that conducted for the Port Wine Trade Association. Worried about falling sales of port, they blamed this in part on high customs duties imposed on 'heavy' wines. For many years, in the months running up to each budget, Powell would take Tory or Labour MPs to lunch in the back parlours of the Port Wine Shippers to discuss the case for a cut in duty. The port wine lobby became one of the most popular in the Commons and after three years the Chancellor of the Exchequer played to the gallery and reduced the tax.

As secretary of the Franco-British Parliamentary Group, Powell had further opportunities to enjoy good food and wine – and he told the story of an extraordinary champagne lunch in Rheims. On the eve of Britain joining the Common Market, he organised a visit to the city for British parliamentarians. Lord Hore-Belisha, who introduced the Belisha Beacon to our roads in the 1930s, was chosen to lead the party. He was delighted to be asked and wrote a long high-flown speech for the occasion which he insisted on rehearsing ad nauseum to the other members of the delegation. The night before arriving in Rheims, Powell and the group stopped in Paris where Lord Hore-Belisha was photographed by the Press against a background of scantily dressed long-legged Bluebell Girls in a famous Champs Elysées cabaret club. The next day in Rheims town hall, prior to a great lunch hosted by the local champagne industry, his lordship rose to deliver his speech. Hardly had he uttered the first sentence when he fell backwards into the arms of the Mayor who gently lowered him to the ground. He was dead.

As the guests tried to recover from the shock, they were hit by more bad news – the lunch would have to be cancelled. The practical French then realised, however, that people have to eat. For the British, Sir Hugh

Linstead MP declared that Lord Hore-Belisha would have wanted them to carry on, so that is precisely what they did. Seven courses were washed down with seven different champagnes as the body of his lordship sat propped up on a chair in an anteroom.

I was particularly pleased to take over the Society of Motor Manufacturers and Traders (SMMT) account from Powell – an organisation I had become involved with already through my work for the British Road Federation and as secretary of the Roads Campaign Council and All-Party Roads Study Group. I was to provide them with a daily parliamentary information service; advise on political developments and contacts; and report to a regular PR and public affairs meeting attended by representatives of all the car manufacturers in membership at their stately home HQ in Belgravia.

In 1977 my colleague Frank Richardson and I arranged a highly successful study tour to America for the All-Party Roads Study Group that included visits to Chicago and Washington. A highlight of the trip was to be a reception at the British Embassy in Washington on the eve of the group's return to Britain. It began well, hosted in Ambassador Sir Peter Ramsbotham's magnificent official residence, on a warm evening. But as the champagne flowed I was disconcerted to notice that one of the diplomatic staff was someone I had known to be unhelpful when I worked as a journalist covering the Foreign Office.

The other guests with us were members of the Commons Select Committee on Expenditure, a more important bunch, who had just completed a fact-finding visit to the capital. The committee was ably led by a friend, the Labour MP Michael English, who represented a Nottingham seat, many of whose constituents worked in the local Imperial Tobacco cigarette factory. Michael was in a bad mood and when I asked why, he explained that he was holding a press conference at the embassy but the staff, instead of providing him with a private room, had told him to conduct it in a corner of the noisy salon where the reception was being held. This was not only impractical but insulting to such an important Commons committee.

Harry Lamborn, joint chairman of the APRSG and parliamentary private secretary to Chancellor of the Exchequer Denis Healey, then approached me with a request. As our group of MPs was due back in the Commons the following Monday, he wanted me to ask the embassy to provide information on the business of the House which had already been announced in London. I passed on the request to one of the champagne-swigging officials.

Just before we were due to leave, a small sheet of paper was produced with very general headings and no detail. It was virtually useless. I tackled the fellow that I remembered as being unhelpful in the past, only to be told that it was not possible to get any more information as the London office was closed. I asked about the all-night duty clerk, only to be told he could not deal with such a request. I told Harry Lamborn who was furious but he decided not to create a fuss that night by complaining to the Ambassador, who appeared to be an amiable old chap. Harry, like Michael English, decided to make their complaints when they returned to London.

Unbeknown to us, the reports of the embassy's inefficiency played into the hands of two important people – Foreign Secretary David Owen and the Prime Minister. In the previous February the then Foreign Secretary Tony Crosland, whom I greatly admired, suffered a severe stroke and died. Callaghan knew that Denis Healey's ambition had always been to run the Foreign Office but he left it to Healey to decide whether he should leave the Treasury at a time of economic crisis. Healey decided to soldier on as Chancellor but might in due course ask to be switched.

This meant that Callaghan needed a stop-gap Foreign Secretary who could be moved out without a fuss. The obvious choice was the young David Owen, a middle-weight politician. He had been Crosland's deputy and had no great personal following of MPs to create trouble if he had to be demoted. In 1968 Harold Wilson had given him his first step up the ladder by appointing him Parliamentary Under Secretary for the Navy on the eve of his thirtieth birthday. Perhaps Wilson had been told that Owen had been rude about him at a meeting in his Plymouth constituency, saying something to the effect that he would not want to hold office under him. Had Wilson decided to put him to the test? Owen has since admitted that he found it incredible to be offered the post as he had exchanged sharp words with Wilson and discussed with friends how to get him out of office.

Now Callaghan's Foreign Secretary – the youngest ever up until then – he was aware of the unsatisfactory state of affairs at the Washington Embassy and had recommended that the Ambassador should be replaced by Peter Jay. This suited Callaghan as Jay, a clever financial journalist, was actually his son-in-law. It was obvious, however, that if he gave this top diplomatic post to his daughter Margaret's husband, he would be accused of nepotism. With bad reports piling up about the Washington Embassy, he decided to risk the accusation and appointed Jay. Ramsbotham was bundled off to the minor post of Governor of Bermuda. In time, the highly intelligent Jay was judged to have done a good job in Washington even if the personal affairs conducted by both him and Margaret while there would see their marriage end in divorce.

My first social meeting with the other Margaret, and her husband Denis Thatcher, came in early August 1977 – thanks to Christopher Powell. He and his wife invited me to a dinner party at their country home, Share Farm, near Lamberhurst in Kent. The only other guests would be the Thatchers and the Powell's daughter, whom I would partner for the evening. Christopher had developed the estate gradually since buying the property around the outbreak of World War II. It was a fine warm summer evening when I arrived and the estate, fringed with borders of flowers, was looking its best.

Christopher explained that the Thatchers had rented a cottage on his estate for years but had recently moved to a flat at nearby Scotney Castle as it provided better security. He had known Denis before he married Margaret when they had been two men-about-town, occupying flats in the same up-market block on the King's Road, Chelsea. During the war, Denis married a young woman named Margot but they divorced in 1948. He had been commissioned in the Royal Engineers in 1938 and when the war began joined an anti-aircraft unit in Kent.

Twice mentioned in dispatches, he was appointed MBE (military) for initiative and organisational skills – which included overcoming a liquor shortage at one camp by producing his own gin from neat alcohol and juniper juice. As a dedicated drinker, he always refused ice in his glass because it diluted the alcohol. A neighbour I met at a Dulwich drinks party told me he had been in the same unit as Denis for a time during the war, and that he had a reputation for being a great womaniser. 'When Denis was on the prowl', he told me, 'there wasn't a barmaid safe within a five-mile radius of camp'.

After the war Denis was active in his local constituency Conservative Association and was on the selection board in Dartford when it chose Margaret Roberts to fight the 1950 General Election. After the meeting he gave her a lift in his car - a flashy sports model that he called his 'tart trap'. The relationship developed into courtship. She was in her early twenties, and working as a research chemist. Christopher Powell remembered her as a fresh-faced, attractive woman often carrying books, like a student. Denis admitted that among Margaret's attractions was a good pair of legs. They married in 1951.

The Thatchers arrived punctually at 8pm, with Denis driving. There was another car behind them, occupied by two Special Branch policemen – the bodyguard of the leader of Her Majesty's Opposition. The Powells looked perturbed as they had not expected a retinue and had made no provision to feed them. They explained that they would not be staying and would eat somewhere up the road. We sat on the lawn and Christopher made drinks. Margaret, looking at ease in her long flowered gown, had a weak whiskey and water. She was clearly figure conscious and was proud that she had lost weight. She had even vetted the menu in advance and after the cucumber soup, had her fillet steak without potatoes and gave me her bread roll.

Before dinner, Denis pointed to his car on the terrace below and said the police had advised him to get rid of his telltale personal number plate with the letters D.T. It was difficult enough, they had said, to provide a bodyguard service without the Thatchers advertising their whereabouts. He told me he had found a buyer who was prepared to pay over £1,000 for it – which he would put towards buying a new car.

It was a delightfully relaxed evening spent mostly on social gossip rather than politics. But Margaret did refer to the damage Harold Wilson had done to the image of politicians. She recalled how George Brown told her during the 1963 Labour leadership contest that Wilson had to be stopped from winning, as he was 'not straight'. I revealed that John Sainsbury and other leaders in trade and industry had been invited to a private dinner party to be hosted in the autumn by Kenneth Corfield of Standard Telephones and Cables. They had declined because Wilson was to be guest of honour. Sainsbury had told Corfield that his refusal was not for political reasons but had been prompted by his strong feelings about the damage Wilson had done to the constitution by his 'abuse' of the honours system.

During the evening, I thought that Margaret was rather sharp with Denis at times – even on a matter concerning the Burmah Oil Company of which he had been a director. Surely he should have been given the benefit of the doubt on that subject? He was 61 and it seemed to me that it must come hard for him to play such a subordinate role when he had been very much the dominant man of experience at the time of their marriage. But he had become the junior partner and in due course was to be caricatured as the deep-drinking, hen-pecked husband trying to cope with the demands of 'the boss'.

If it did come hard he didn't show it that evening, and just before dinner ended he made an effort to demonstrate that he had the makings of a socially superior Tory gent. I had revealed in answer to one of his questions that I had spent eight months of my National Service as an Indian Army officer cadet at the Guards Depot, Caterham. Denis then recalled that when he had been stationed with a Guards' unit during the war, the commanding officer had told him that he should consider applying for a transfer to the Guards as he was 'The type of man they wanted'.

Having got to know Denis at that dinner, I made a point of standing near him - usually at the back of the room - when he attended some of Margaret's press conferences during elections. He was enthusiastically supportive and would swear quietly about any media people who appeared to be quizzing her too persistently. I could well understand how in times of crisis he could be her rock. When asked how he put up with the pressure of Downing Street life he would reply laconically, 'Gin and cigarettes'. I discovered that, as a smoker, he was an outspoken supporter of the tobacco industry. In particular, having been an active sportsman, he thought the anti-smoking lobby was being 'ridiculous' in its campaign against tobacco company sponsorship of sports events.

When we met he would sometimes ask about Christopher Powell who was proud to receive a Christmas card from Downing Street, but soon after the Thatchers moved into Number Ten the old friends drifted apart. I was dismayed that, after Christopher's death, Denis failed to attend the memorial service for his erstwhile chum at nearby St. Margaret's, Westminster.

Since the early 1970s Reg Prentice had been fighting a running battle with extreme left wing members of his Newham constituency Labour party. Angered by his outspoken attacks on trade union militants as Shadow Employment Minister, they were determined to get rid of him as their local MP. Wilson had moved him from that post and appointed him Secretary of State for Education on winning the 1974 General Election. I congratulated him on his new job, but I disapproved of his determination to push through widespread and, in my view, over-hasty comprehensive education. When he returned to his old job as Minster for Overseas Development in 1975, the Trotskyites and left wing militants moved to de-select him as Newham's prospective candidate for the next election.

In July he had written to me to say that the prospect for the key Party meeting in his constituency later that month did not look very hopeful. 'It may well be that I shall need to appeal to the NEC'. (The Labour Party's National Executive Committee.) He added, 'If that position is reached it will be helpful if as many messages as possible – from individuals, from constituency Labour Parties, from trade union branches etc. – are sent in to Transport House (Labour Party HQ): if they can be made public so much the better'.

When that crucial local meeting came, he was de-selected as he had feared. On succeeding Wilson as Prime Minister, Callaghan re-appointed Reg to Overseas Development, but he was becoming an embarrassment to the Cabinet by his outspoken public attacks on Labour's left-wing dominated NEC. Then, after abstaining on an important vote in the Commons, he resigned from the Government. His resignation caused a considerable stir. Far from going quietly, he launched a sensational attack on the Government, accusing it of shirking the issues facing the country and appeasing the trade unions. To Callaghan's great relief, however, Reg did not resign from his Newham North East seat for had he forced a by-election and stood as an independent Labour candidate he would have exposed a deep and embarrassing split in the Party.

By the end of the 1977 Labour Party Conference in Brighton, it was known that Reg had decided to cross the floor of the House to join the Tory Party. He did so, he explained, 'To help prevent Britain lurching further down the Marxist road'. In breaking away from the Party on the issue of the growing influence of the far left, he was ahead of the times. In due course the Gang of Four set up the Social Democratic Party, which included Roy Jenkins and Shirley Williams who had spoken up for him. I felt sad that it had come to this and suspected that he and his wife Joan would feel uncomfortable in Tory circles. I did not foresee how his career would flourish.

His adopted Party would provide him with a new seat in Parliament (Daventry) and a government job as Minister of State for Social Security. In that role he was Minister for the Disabled and I was pleased when he announced that his job was to continue the work that Alf Morris had begun. Nevertheless, he was basically out of touch with the mood of the Thatcher administration and, perhaps due to all the stress, his health began to suffer. When we met around Westminster he seemed ill at ease. He retired from the Government in January 1981 and from the Commons in 1987. He was given a life peerage in 1992.

My appointment as parliamentary consultant to the Society of Motor Manufacturers and Traders had come on the eve of a dramatic development in December 1978. As part of anti-inflationary monetary discipline, the Callaghan Government had set a pay rise guideline of five per cent. The Ford Motor Company, however, crippled by a nine-week strike by its militant workforce, decided to ignore this and, in desperation, offered a sky-high increase of seventeen per cent. Ministers had warned that companies who failed to follow their directive should not expect the Government to buy any of their output. Ford decided it was better to lose Government orders for a while than to have no cars to sell.

The Tories spotted an opportunity to embarrass the Government, and forced a Commons debate demanding that the threat of sanctions against companies should be dropped. Callaghan's Cabinet was in a jam. Some thirty left wing Tribune Group MPs were opposed to an incomes policy and were refusing to vote with the Government. Callaghan lost the vote by 285 to 283 and the threat of sanctions had to be withdrawn. The Ford problem had led to the collapse of the Government's incomes policy and Britain was soon to be plunged into the 'Winter of Discontent'.

As if sensing trouble ahead, the SMMT asked me to do some bridge-building in Parliament. My success in running the All-Party Roads Study Groups (APRSG) was well known to the SMMT's director David Gent. He was a dynamic and enthusiastic member of the roads lobby who went on to become director general of the Retail Motor Industry Federation. Gent asked me to set up a similar all-party group for the motor industry and I was pleased to accept, seeing it as an opportunity to strengthen the roads lobby generally. I moved quickly to get two key MPs to agree to be joint Tory and Labour chairmen.

My first choice for Labour chairman was Geoffrey Robinson MP for Coventry North West. He had enjoyed a successful career in the motor industry culminating as chief executive of Jaguar Cars before entering Parliament in 1976. A graduate of Cambridge and Yale Universities, he had intelligence, good looks and a polished style. He declined my offer and I was momentarily stunned by this setback – but luckier with my second choice. My friend Alan Lee Williams, who had got me involved with the Europe-America Conference in 1972, had re-entered Parliament in 1974 as MP for Havering, Hornchurch, and had many constituents who worked for the Ford plant at Dagenham. Alan was happy to take on the job.

Turning to the Tories, I had got to know Hal Miller, the bluff old Etonian, ex-Colonial Service officer who was MP for Bromsgrove and Redditch, through the All-Party Roads Study Group. He seemed ideal – and so it turned out to be. A notice was included on the All-Party Whip announcing that a meeting would be held to discuss the formation of a motor industry group and MPs with constituency links were informed individually.

The All-Party Motor Industry Group was set up with Alan and Hal voted into office as joint chairmen. A press notice was issued announcing that the Society of Motor Manufacturers and Traders would finance the secretariat - all open and above board. Acting as a two-way channel of communication between Parliament and the motor industry, it was to become one of the most active and best attended of the unofficial groups within the Palace of Westminster. To demonstrate that the SMMT was not simply a mouthpiece for the manufacturers, I arranged that Terry Duffy, then President-elect of the Amalgamated Union of Engineering Workers, would be first guest speaker. The following month, July, Sir Terence Beckett, chairman and managing director of the Ford Motor Company, addressed a well-attended meeting. Unlike the All-Party Roads Study Group, no hospitality was offered to the invited MPs and peers, so our parliamentary audience could not be accused of turning up for the food and wine.

I had few City clients, preferring to work for organisations in the fields of manufacturing and construction, but Royal Insurance had been added to my client list soon after I joined Charles Barker and they asked my advice about the possibility of the Callaghan Government taking part of the insurance industry into public ownership. There was a lot of support for this in the Labour Party but from what I knew of cautious Callaghan and his private links with the world of finance I said I did not think it was likely. Royal Insurance then asked me to attend meetings of a committee composed of representatives of what were known as 'The Big Seven' insurance companies set up to monitor the situation. They were jittery and I did my best to steady their nerves – with help from well-informed Labour Party contacts. I discovered after a time that the relieved committee members called me the 'guru'.

The Government's attempt to curb inflation by holding down public sector pay had brought it into conflict with the police. Earlier in 1978, Evie Soames and I were asked to attend a meeting at the Commons with Eldon Griffiths, the Tory MP for Bury St. Edmunds and a well-known journalist. He was also parliamentary adviser to the National Police Federation. The Federation intended to employ a firm of professional lobbyists to help with its campaign for a substantial pay rise for the men on the beat. He asked if we would like to pitch to the Federation, and we were happy to accept.

After a successful presentation, we were hired to help conduct a campaign that was to become of considerable political importance.

Increasing public concern at the steady breakdown of law and order – dubbed 'Laura Norda' by the tabloid press – was central to the Federation's fight for justice. The campaign to win public support was doing well and there was growing evidence that people thought ministers were taking unfair advantage of the fact that the police were forbidden to strike by law. But the Callaghan Government, desperate to hold down wage demands, showed no sign of giving way. Callaghan had at one time been on the Federation's payroll as its parliamentary adviser, which added to the bitterness.

As the weeks passed, the police began to win unprecedented press and television coverage. In a *News of the World* article in February 1977, Eldon Griffiths had spelt out the problem in stark language that the police, for the first time, had begun to consider a national strike. In the face of their call for a fair pay deal, the Government had offered nothing more than a review of their negotiating machinery, a long-term inquiry into the future of the Police Federation and a small pay rise.

Advertisements in the national press spelt out their demands for justice and car stickers with the slogan *'Up with Police pay - down with crime'* carried the message around the country. Filmed by TV crews, the Federation's leaders stomped to 10 Downing Street to present their demands. I was forging a strong bond of trust, goodwill and friendship with the Federation's officers – Chairman Jim Jardine, deputy chairman Basil Griffiths, the highly competent secretary Joe Martucci, and Tony Judge, the lively editor of the Federation's journal *Police*.

The Federation's annual conference at Scarborough in May would present a big opportunity for widespread publicity. The Home Secretary Merlyn Rees, whom I had known since my days on *Reynolds News* when he had organised the Festival of Labour in 1961, had agreed to address the conference. I had great respect for Merlyn who had taken over the Home Office in September 1976 when Roy Jenkins had resigned to become President of the European Commission. He was a popular politician and it seemed to me essential that in dealing with him the police officers attending the conference should behave with dignity. Some Federation members favoured a slow handclap but I feared this might be too difficult to control. I persuaded them to meet Merlyn with stony silence if his speech showed no sign of movement on pay. Merlyn had opposed their £6 a week pay claim and offered instead an unacceptable £4.

All went according to plan in the conference hall and poor Merlyn must have felt chilled by the icy silence as he left the rostrum and walked to the exit. I knew that cameramen would be waiting to get pictures of his departure and emerged from the hall before him, dismayed to find a crowd of boozy young constables, out of uniform, and hemming in his official car. They had arrived by coach too late to get in and had been drinking lager to occupy themselves, on top of what they had consumed en route. They were tanked up and in an aggressive mood. As Merlyn got into the car they surged around, banging on the roof and shouting abuse. The cameramen got it all.

Behind the scenes, however, wheels were turning in favour of a substantial pay rise for the boys. Lord Edmund Davies had been reviewing police pay and conditions for the Government and to everyone's surprise recommended an increase of about forty per cent.

The Times observed:

> 'He has gone back to the generous award of the 1960 Royal Commission and recommended increases intended to bring pay roughly back into a similar relationship with average earnings – well above the relative level that has existed over the past ten years'.

The *Morning Star* commented:

> 'The first thing to be said about the police pay award is that it knocks the Government's pay policy for six'.

The Observer noted:

> 'With law and order the next most popular election issue to inflation, any Government standing even mildly in the way of the Police Federation's demands was on a hiding to nothing'.

The Government announced that the award would be implemented in two stages. Shadow Home Secretary Willie Whitelaw cashed in on the climb-down issue, and promised that, under the Tories, the police would get their increase at once. In the August issue of the Police Federation's monthly magazine, Eldon Griffiths and I were among those advisers thanked for our hard work in helping to bring about such a satisfying result.

Law and order was indeed to be an important issue in the General Election in May the following year. Callaghan's punch-drunk, groggy Government lost a Commons vote of confidence by one vote – 311 to 310 – in late March. The General Election he had foolishly postponed was now forced upon him in the worst possible circumstances.

One of the perks of lobbying for the British Road Federation was that I could occasionally end the day at Ronnie Scott's jazz club. In the 1970s and 80s, after meetings of the All-Party Roads Study Group, Robert Phillipson would lead us to the legendary Frith Street venue to hear such giants as Oscar Peterson, Dizzy Gillespie, Stan Getz, Stephane Grappelli and Bill Evans. Canadian-born Peterson has been acclaimed as the greatest jazz pianist since Art Tatum. Bill Evans, whose delicate pensive style was very different from the driving, forceful playing of Peterson, was one of my favourites. Only a month after I heard him play for the last time, he died aged only 51 in 1980.

Then there was Ronnie Scott himself, a fine tenor sax player who liked to exercise his cockney Jewish wit on punters and staff during the intermissions. He had a repertoire of well-honed one-liners, usually at the expense of his kitchen. 'This is the only club where people are employed to throw people in', he would rasp. 'I'm sure you've noticed the food has improved... we never get complaints, just one or two carried out. But no complaints. And the food must be good – hey, ten thousand flies can't be wrong'.

Sometimes we would see Tory MP Ken Clarke in the audience. He would go on to become not only Chancellor of the Exchequer but a leading broadcaster on jazz.

At 3pm on Friday March 30th 1979, a shattering explosion sent a pall of black smoke spiralling up from New Palace Yard at the Palace of Westminster. An Irish terrorist's bomb, planted hours before, had blown up Airey Neave's car as he was driving it up the ramp from the Commons underground car park. Airey, who had survived so much in World War II, died soon after from his appalling injuries. He had been assassinated by the IRA. As Shadow spokesman on Northern Ireland, he had been typically courageous and outspoken in condemning terrorism. He was target number one for the IRA which had decided to launch a new wave of killings to coincide with the General Election campaign that was about to begin.

A few hours earlier I had waited with Airey at the taxi point in Parliament's New Palace Yard. 'I'm going up West to my tailor', he had said to me. 'Can I give you a lift?'

I declined with thanks as I was heading east to my office. He was taking a taxi because of parking problems around Savile Row. His appointment with his tailor done, he had returned to Parliament to pick up his car. When I heard the news of his assassination I was stunned. I must have been one of the last people he spoke to at the Commons.

His death was a terrible blow to Margaret Thatcher and I remembered with sadness our jokey exchange about sharing the credit for her becoming Tory leader. He had been one of her closest advisers ever since and no doubt would have become a tough Northern Ireland Secretary in her first Cabinet. Just weeks away from achieving top Government office, he had been slaughtered. I felt sick and angry. I had supported the abolition of capital punishment years before, but I found myself close to agreeing with those advocating its return for such ferocious acts of terrorism. Airey, consistently hard line against IRA operations, had himself called for the re-introduction of the death penalty for some terrorist offences. His murder, at the age of sixty-three, was the first political assassination at the Palace of Westminster for over 160 years.

My opportunity to do something about the situation came a few days after Airey's murder. On the Monday morning I received a call from Jim Jardine. He told me of the Police Federation's unprecedented decision to become involved in a general election campaign – on the issue of law and order. Would I help? If Jim had been in the room I would have given him a hug. I could not wait to be involved.

In Britain the police must always stay above politics, never appear aligned with any one party. They could, however, appeal to all election candidates to support a programme for law and order – and that is what the Federation had decided to do. Airey's death had added to their determination. In particular, it had strengthened their belief that capital punishment should be restored, especially for acts of terrorism. Within an hour of starting work for them again, I supervised the first press release of the campaign. It was to play an important role in the election and helped the Tories to win power with an overall majority of forty-three seats in the Commons.

After the election, Jim Jardine told me that the new Home Secretary, Willie Whitelaw, had revealed, as they walked along a Home Office corridor, that he was pleased with what they had done by intervening in the election. Whitelaw added, however, that they had put their necks on the chopping block and commented, 'Goodness knows what would have happened if the Socialists had won!'

He told Jim that so far as the promised pay award was concerned, the Prime Minister had told the Treasury, 'You have got to do it!' Jim was delighted.

The Tories had committed to pay the police the whole of their recommended pay increase at once and not in two stages as announced by the Callaghan Government. Willie Whitelaw was given a hero's reception at a celebration dinner hosted by the Federation. I attended – but didn't see Laura Norda there, although she had certainly earned a seat at the table. Before long she was to raise her head again – and would be the cause of much political embarrassment to her erstwhile champion Whitelaw.

As for me, I was basically a Labour supporter, and found myself in an incongruous position. I had contributed to getting Margaret Thatcher into the position where she was able to oust the only Tory leader I had ever supported (the Alf Sherman saga), and I had now played a part in getting her to 10 Downing Street. I had not voted for her, but I was glad to see the back of Calamity Callaghan. As a result of the pay rise, police recruitment improved – but as their numbers went up so did the crime rate. Burglary soared. Whitelaw, faced with overflowing prisons, pleaded with judges to send fewer to jail.

Then, annoyed by the contribution of car thefts to the rising crime figures, the Government leaned on my client the Society of Motor Manufacturers and Traders, urging car manufacturers to improve vehicle security with better locking devices. I had warned the SMMT about this at a public affairs meeting and in due course the members responded to the Government's desperate appeal.

As I was getting involved with the Police Federation, I discovered that Britain's counter-espionage service was taking an interest in me. For some twenty years I had lunched with diplomats from Communist bloc embassies in London. As the diplomatic and political correspondent for several national newspapers I thought it essential to have at least one contact in an East European embassy.

This had started when the debonair Mikhail Lyubimov, Moscow's most successful spy in London in the early sixties, invited me to dine. We often lunched together and he appeared to enjoy life in London to such an extent I thought he might be persuaded to defect. Years later, I learned that the British Secret Service had nurtured the same naïve hope. When they finally cornered him on one of his spying operations they offered him the choice of working for them or expulsion from Britain. Lyubimov chose the latter and back in Moscow wrote a guide for the KGB on how to be a successful agent in London.

When MI5 caught up with him and he was forced to leave Britain, I cultivated diplomats at the Hungarian and, later, the Czechoslovakian embassies. In dealing with them I always followed certain rules. So that I would never be under an obligation to them, we would alternate paying the bill for lunch. I declined their invitations to visit Moscow, Budapest or Prague or to take part in overseas junkets for journalists. Moreover, I never provided them with information that I had not already published in my newspaper.

When I moved into public affairs consultancy, there seemed little point in keeping up these contacts. I then discovered that certain businesses were keen to build up trade with Eastern bloc countries. It could be useful, therefore, to maintain links with one or two embassies. Moreover, I knew that I could rely on one of the most entertaining members of the Leslie Hale Luncheon Club - clever Ian Mikardo - who was involved in oiling the wheels for trade with the Eastern bloc.

As secretary of the Parliamentary and Scientific Committee, I was privy to scientific and technological developments so my links with Eastern bloc embassies could be inappropriate. During Parliament's 1978 long summer recess, I sought the advice of the committee's President Lord Shackleton who, among his many responsibilities, chaired an official committee on East-West trade.

I always took my main holiday when Parliament was in recess. That year we rented a cottage in Pembrokeshire, and we took my mother with us. One day, she stayed put while we went on an outing and on our return, told us that the police had phoned to say that our bungalow in Dulwich had been burgled. Leaving the family there, I returned to London to find out the extent of the damage. The police showed me how the burglar had entered the living room by drilling out the security bolts from the backdoor – a very clean, skilful job.

As I walked from room to room I was surprised at how little had been taken. Expensive silver and china was still on display, my wife's dressing table with jewellery in the drawers was untouched. My chest of drawers had received attention and a gold pocket watch I inherited from my father was among some items taken. In another bedroom the intruder had wasted time going through a lot of small, empty boxes. It was all very puzzling. What was he looking for? Whatever it was, the police assumed that he had been interrupted by the arrival of Evelyn's father who had come to feed our two cats. The intruder had left by the backdoor and scaling a low wall escaped across our neighbours' large, bosky garden.

I began to draw up a list of stolen items for the police and our insurance company. In our bedroom cupboard, I kept a small battered portable typewriter in a cardboard box. When I went to get it, to type up the list, it was missing. I asked Evelyn where she had put it, she replied she had not touched it. To my amazement, I realised that the burglar had taken it and added it to the list of stolen items. The burglary was becoming more bizarre.

Returning home from a weekend away one Sunday in March 1979, I scarcely got through the door before the phone rang. The man at the other end of the line introduced himself with a faintly diffident, apologetic tone as John Vallance. He asked if I would mind calling on him at the Old War Office Building as he would like to have a talk. His manner suggested he was accustomed to receiving truculent, if not angry, replies to his invitations. He must have been relieved by my relaxed response. I guessed immediately that this was the call I had been expecting for nearly twenty years – the call from MI5, counter-espionage. I asked only two questions: was the call in connection with the Parliamentary and Scientific Committee, of which I was the administrative secretary? And where was the Old War Office Building?

To the first question, he replied 'No', in a voice that betrayed slight surprise and some interest. To the second he instructed me to turn into Whitehall Place from the Horse Guards where I would find it along on the right hand side. The appointment was made for a lunch-time in room 055, a week later. As soon as I put down the phone I dialled the number of a friend whom I knew had been through the MI5 hoop – Charlie Douglas-Home, by then Foreign Editor of *The Times*. When I described what had happened, Charlie immediately confirmed my suspicion. 'Yes, that's Five', he said.

I phoned him because many years before, he had told me how MI5 had called him in as he was leaving the *Daily Express* to become Defence Correspondent of *The Times*. As Diplomatic Correspondent for the *Express*, he had dealt regularly with Eastern bloc embassy officials in London. His MI5 inquisitor had asked him about his meetings with Mikhail Lyubimov.

Charlie told me that MI5 would want to know about the people I had met from East European embassies, and the type of questions they had asked me.

The pieces of the jigsaw were falling into place. Some months earlier, my solicitor and old school friend David Monro, who had experienced some phone tapping in connection with his business, told me that he thought my phone was being tapped. I had not taken his warning seriously at the time, seeing no reason why anyone would want to do this. Now I thought that perhaps he had been right.

At last the mysterious burglary was beginning to make sense. If MI5 had been tapping my phone they would have discovered nothing useful except that we were going away on a certain date. As we did not use the phone to arrange for my father-in-law to come in they would not have known that when sending an agent in to search the place. As for the worthless old typewriter stored in a box in the cupboard, perhaps the burglar thought it might be a decoding machine or, more likely, he needed the typewriter ribbon for his MI5 bosses. I wondered what political story typed years before for the *Daily Sketch* they discovered on it.

I arrived punctually at the Old War Office Building where a receptionist asked me to wait in the drab foyer. After some five minutes I heard a shuffling sound and an enormous ill-dressed woman entered the room and curtly asked me to follow her. She shuffled ahead of me along a bleak corridor without a word. I was reminded of those massive, muscular female interrogators who had added a touch of sadism to the thrillers I had watched for years. My imagination, however, was running away with me. She was not there to twist my arm or any more delicate parts. She was just my guide to room 055. John Vallance rose from behind a desk as I entered. He was a youngish man of medium height with the same diffident manner I had noticed on the phone.

After Vallance had posed a few preliminary questions, I said that perhaps it would be helpful if I told him of my dealings with Eastern bloc spies over the years. For decades, the probing intelligence officers of the Soviet and East European embassies had devoted much time to meeting well-informed British journalists - operating in politics, defence, labour relations and foreign affairs. Soon after entering Parliament for the *News Chronicle* in January 1957, I was introduced by other journalists to a leading Czech Embassy intelligence officer Jan Mravek. He devoted much time to entertaining politicians and political correspondents. An amiable and convivial man, he was often in the Strangers' Bar in the Commons - a drinking hole that one could only enter as the guest of an MP. It was there that I first met him and I was soon receiving invitations to Czech Embassy functions. There was always a good sprinkling of MPs present, mostly left-wing Labourites or right-wing Tories interested in trading contacts with the Eastern bloc. The food and wine at such functions was always plentiful.

My presence at such functions was not so much in the vain hope of getting useful information from my hosts. It was rather to discover which MPs were interested in dealing with them. Although not the type to be privy to government secrets, they generally had inside knowledge of developments within their own parties and had views, based on experience, of the likely trend in government policies. Their information and opinions were useful to embassy agents. They helped to piece together jigsaw puzzle pictures of the political or industrial scene, as they endlessly checked and crosschecked to achieve maximum accuracy.

By associating with the Communist embassies and visiting their countries on trade, cultural or other delegations, the MPs also gave an aura of respectability to these ruthless authoritarian regimes. As a result of Western outrage when Russian tanks crushed the short-lived Hungarian rebellion in the mid 1950s, Soviet agents were less obviously active in London for some years after, and Moscow relied on Czechs and Poles to do its work around the bars of Westminster. Memories are short, however, and by 1960 I was introduced to Mikhail Lyubimov at the Commons.

I told Vallance that by that time I was regarded as one of the best-informed political journalists on parliamentary Labour Party affairs. Working for the Labour and Co-operative movement's *Reynolds News*, following the closure of the *News Chronicle,* I began to meet Lyubimov once every month or two. We lunched at good West End restaurants though never at the same one twice running.

As Charlie had warned, Vallance wanted to know about the people I met from Eastern bloc embassies over the years and the questions they had asked. He was delighted when I told him that although I could not remember all names off-hand, I had kept their introduction cards and would be happy to hand them over. He looked less thrilled when I said that occasionally I had been asked about defence policy – but had always replied that this was not an area I covered as a journalist.

He knew that I had been awarded the Emergency Reserve Decoration and seemed to think it odd that someone who had served as an officer in the front line reserve should have regular contacts with Communist diplomats. As a diplomatic and political correspondent of national newspapers, such links were part of my job and I thought he lacked understanding of the journalist's role.

He asked about the restaurants we used and I mentioned that L'Ecu de France, the smart establishment off Jermyn Street, was one of them. I was not then aware that the banquettes there were bugged by MI5. I agreed to return for another talk, declining his invitation to meet in a restaurant. Sandwiches in the office were fine, and I promised not to forget the business cards. My line that I had told their owners only what had been published in my newspapers was no doubt what other journalists had told him. It was certainly what *Sunday Express* editor John Junor had said when MI5 asked about his lunches with the Russian Embassy First Secretary in 1961 - that the diplomat had received no more information than he would have got from reading the *Sunday Express*.

It transpired that an Eastern bloc official who had defected to the West had handed over a list of people who were considered useful contacts, and my name was on it. It seemed incredible and depressing that MI5 was so under-funded, under staffed and inefficient: for eighteen years they were unaware that I had been lunching openly with Eastern bloc spies and regularly visiting the Russian, Czech and Hungarian embassies. I had always assumed that they had been doing surveillance and I was not sufficiently important to bother with.

I was often right in forecasting political developments but I suspect that another reason spies courted me was that, unlike many journalists and virtually all politicians, I paid my way and always reciprocated gifts.

Some time later, I mentioned the burglary at my home to Geoffrey Goodman, the highly respected and accurate Labour affairs reporter who had been with me on the *News Chronicle*. He had regular access to 10 Downing Street and told me that a number of Harold Wilson's staff had been bugged and burgled by MI5. This extraordinary news threw some light on why MI5 had taken so long to get around to quizzing little me – since the late 1950s its agents had been too busy checking up on each other and eventually on 10 Downing Street.

Britain's secret service had suffered from a debilitating paranoia following various spy scandals. The defection to Moscow of the Foreign Office diplomats Burgess and Maclean, and double agent Kim Philby, who worked for both MI6 and the Kremlin, had shaken confidence and credibility. Philby had served as head of Britain's MI6 office in Washington DC, so our American allies were particularly twitchy about the reliability of Whitehall and put intense pressure on MI5 to unearth any bad eggs. An atmosphere of suspicion and distrust permeated its drab offices.

Officials spent more time looking over their shoulders than looking out for UK citizens like me going in and out of Eastern bloc embassies. No one was safe in certain areas of government. There was a well-circulated but false accusation that Sir Roger Hollis, head of MI5 from 1956-65 was a Soviet agent. Hawkish new recruits to MI5 were encouraged to suspect members of the old guard who had been around during the earlier spy scandals involving Philby and co. And, no doubt with the encouragement of the CIA, some took a close interest in the activities of Prime Minister Harold Wilson and his personal staff at 10 Downing Street. For years before Wilson became premier, his enemies in the Labour Party, ranging from leading Gaitskellites to George Brown, had accused Wilson of being untrustworthy and drew attention, on both sides of the Atlantic, to his activities as a consultant on trade with the Eastern bloc. This is the background to the charges made by ex-MI5 senior officer, Peter Wright, in his book *Spycatcher* who claims there was a move within MI5 to overthrow Prime Minister Wilson in the mid-seventies.

I tried to be helpful and sent Vallance a list of Eastern bloc agents attending the main party conferences. I never heard from him again, nor did an Eastern bloc diplomat ever again approach me. Perhaps they had been warned off by MI5. My involvement in the murky world of spooks was over.

CHAPTER FOUR

Committees, Chunnel and SDP

ord (Eddie) Shackleton, Knight of the Garter, Fellow of the Royal
Society, and enjoyer of the good life, greeted me in the luxurious
office he occupied as deputy chairman of Rio Tinto Zinc (RTZ). As
president of the Parliamentary and Scientific Committee, he invited me to
report my plans for the committee as its newly appointed administrative
secretary. A former Labour MP, he had the reputation of being a skilful
operator endowed with steely determination and the ability to charm.

The committee which I had taken over from Christopher Powell had
been going successfully for thirty-nine years and I was not so arrogant as
to believe it needed a lot of change. Shackleton, however, believed there
was room for improvement and wanted some action before giving up the
presidency. He was certainly a man of action himself, perhaps hoping to
emulate the reputation of his father Sir Edward Shackleton, the famous
explorer of the South Atlantic and Antarctica. A geology graduate of
Oxford, he had travelled in some of the remotest places on earth. He was
particularly concerned about the wellbeing of the Falkland Islands which
he neatly described as 'islands surrounded almost entirely by advice'.
Unfortunately, his good advice was ignored by Foreign Office officials
anxious not to harm relations with Argentina. The result was the Falklands
War of 1982.

He had been MP for Preston from 1946 until he lost his seat in 1955
and was made a life peer in 1958. I got to know him ten years later when
he succeeded Lord Longford as leader of the House of Lords and I attended
his weekly briefings as a Lobby correspondent.

He did not ask me if I was interested in science and technology or
if I had any aptitude for those subjects. He was more interested in
my journalistic background, my wide contacts at Westminster, my
management experience and success at administering the All-Party Roads
Study Group. He might also have remembered that as a political journalist

I was an advocate of the importance of substantial national investment in science and technology. He suggested that I should edit a journal for the P&S Committee to replace the primitive newsletter based on excerpts from *Hansard* that was currently being produced. He asked me also to strengthen the membership, starting with the commercial companies' category. At the time the committee consisted of 75 peers, 123 MPs, 147 scientific and technical institutions from the Royal Society downwards, and 48 companies. Christopher Powell had done well in building it up since helping to launch the committee in 1939 with 14 MPs, 3 peers and two dozen scientific organisations. Shackleton confided in me, however, that too many of the parliamentary members were 'free-loaders' paying no subscription and getting an excellent free lunch at the Savoy Hotel every year without attending the monthly meetings. They were a financial drain on the operation, and contributed little or nothing to the committee's work of providing permanent liaison between Parliament and scientific and technical bodies.

Some of the most active MPs on the committee were friends of mine, including Arthur Palmer from my Middlesbrough days, and Airey Neave, both of whom sent me letters of congratulations on my appointment. Airey, who had Harwell in his constituency and had a deep interest in technology, wrote with typical kindness that he knew I would do a good job. It was to be the last written communication I received from him.

The committee's chairman was Fred Willey, a senior Labour MP who had been a member of Wilson's 'Government of Freds'. He was not as well known to me as Fred Peart, Fred Lee and Fred Mulley, but he gave me a warm welcome. My first major task as secretary was to supervise arrangements for the committee's annual luncheon. This was to be held as always at the Savoy Hotel, with an address by Prime Minister Callaghan on *'Aspects of relations between Government and Science'.* The Prime Minister had been a steady supporter of the committee for years and there was loud applause when he presented Christopher Powell with a Rembrandt etching as a farewell gift on his retirement as secretary. The fortieth anniversary of the committee was approaching and to mark it I got Christopher to help me write a history of the P&S covering those four decades, published by Croom Helm.

The choice of speaker for the fortieth anniversary lunch soon started to exercise Eddie Shackleton's mind. HRH Prince Philip, the Duke of Edinburgh, had been an active member of the committee for many years, being greatly interested in certain aspects of science and technology. Eddie mentioned him as a possibility but I pointed out that the Duke had addressed several lunches in the past, most recently in 1975. We needed an important new personality for this occasion.

I suggested that Prince Charles would fit the bill. Eddie liked the idea. He had been ecstatic when awarded the Order of the Garter and loved nothing better than to rub shoulders with royalty. My suggestion would enable him to get closer to the heir to the throne. The Prince accepted the invitation and well in advance of the lunch, to be held in February 1979, I sent a description of the committee's activities and membership to his private office to assist officials there drafting his speech. The day before the event Shackleton was on the phone to me in a flap.

Prince Charles had received the draft and been appalled to discover that it read like a lecture on simple science. His staff had not bothered to read my description of the committee and it was only when the Prince asked to see the list of expected attendees at the lunch that he realised the prepared speech was hopelessly inappropriate. Like a true Knight of the Garter, Shackleton charged off to rescue him. Charles told him that he had recently had a tour of a number of industrial sites. Could he draw on that experience? Shackleton agreed that he could.

A new speech was hurriedly written and delivered next day to an audience of over four hundred at the Savoy. Entitled *The General Problem of Communications in Industry and the Status and Role of Engineers,* it caused some of the top industrialists present to shift uneasily. The tone was not well judged – and it seemed to me that Charles would be well employed in improving communications in his own small office. The next day *The Daily Telegraph* summed up the occasion with a cartoon based on the famous Landseer painting, *Dignity and Impudence.* The large, majestic hound represented British industry and the small cheeky terrier bore some resemblance to the Prince. I bought the original from the newspaper and sent it to Charles with a note expressing the hope that it would remind him of what I trusted had been an enjoyable occasion. I received no reply.

Apart from arranging the committee's programme of monthly meetings and occasional visits to scientific and technical institutions, I worked on increasing the membership. The number of member companies was expanded, British members of the European Parliament were invited to join and universities and polytechnics were introduced as a new category. The old fashioned newssheet was transformed into a glossy journal called

Science in Parliament and as editor I got a Press pass for political party conferences.

These and other administrative changes, such as the setting up of sub-committees to vet new members and plan the programme, added much to the work of my assistant secretary Sally Tipping, originally recruited by Commander Powell. She took it all in her stride.

On Fred Willey's retirement I arranged for him to be replaced as chairman by an enthusiastic Tory MP Sir David Price (Eton, Trinity, Yale and the Guards). Eddie Shackleton, who was soon to retire as president, informed me that he thought he should be replaced by Tory peer Earl Jellicoe who had not been a very active member of the committee. Eddie and George Jellicoe, however, were close buddies and were said to have swapped lady friends and jobs. Shackleton was keen to give the ex-Tory minister a helping hand following the call girl scandal at the time of the Lambton-Norma Levy affair, and his consequent resignation from office. Some senior committee members, such as Arthur Palmer, were not happy with this proposal. Shackleton, however, got his way and so I got the pleasure of working with the likeable George Jellicoe, who proved to be an excellent appointment.

Meanwhile, Liberal peer Lord Lloyd of Kilgerran, an officer of the P&S deeply interested in the fast growing area of information technology was in talks about the need for an all-party committee on the subject. I was asked to attend a meeting with him, together with Tory MP Ian Lloyd, a leading member of the P&S Committee, and Labour MP Gwilym Roberts. They explained that because the P&S covered the whole field of science and technology it could not devote sufficient time to the important area of IT. A new specialist committee was therefore required and I was asked to set it up. I realised that this development would weaken the P&S to some extent, but I knew that if I failed to do it, someone else would. Moreover, if I were in charge, I could ensure that its meetings did not clash with those of the P&S and I agreed to take on the task.

Within a few months I was approached by Trevor Skeet, another parliamentary member of the P&S who asked me to set up an all-party group on energy issues. He was a pushy, opinionated New Zealander who sat as Tory MP for North Bedfordshire. Bluntly, he made the same point as the more gentlemanly Ian Lloyd about the inability of the P&S to devote appropriate time to this important area. For the same reason that I had launched the Parliamentary Information Technology Committee

(PITCOM), I agreed to Skeet's proposal. But before I could take the initiative another group of MPs moved into the vacuum and set up the Parliamentary Group for Energy Studies. Led by a suave and thrusting Tory MP David Crouch, they asked Christine Stewart Munro, an experienced ex-colleague of Christopher Powell, to provide the secretariat. Skeet pushed ahead with his plan but decided to call his committee the All-Party Minerals Group. I set it up, and it brought my total of all-party committees to five, for three of which I had been the founder secretary. Some three hundred MPs and peers were involved and they were all holding monthly meetings and making occasional study visits in the U.K. and abroad.

At the time, I had some twenty other major clients under my wing and was heavily involved in pitching for new business, so I decided to hand over the secretariat of the Minerals Group and PITCOM to Frank Richardson. As the second in command of my Charles Barker group, Frank had considerable experience in the management of all-party committees. It was fortunate for me that Frank, hardworking and reliable, had followed me to Barkers when the John Addey company broke up.

Margaret Thatcher entered 10 Downing Street in 1979 and as consultant to Imperial Tobacco I took a particular interest in her choice of health ministers. As she was a champion of free enterprise and personal freedom, I hoped that negotiations between the tobacco manufacturers and the Government to renew the voluntary agreement on restrictions on advertising and health warnings would have an easier time. Andrew Reid, who took over as Imperial chairman from Tony Garrett in 1979, had come to know the new Secretary of State for Social Services and Health, Patrick Jenkin, before the General Election and believed he would be reasonable. Gerard Vaughan, who had supported the Nabarro bill, had been appointed Minister of State for Health, but to our horror Sir George Young, one of the most out spoken anti-smokers in Parliament, was appointed junior Health Minister. Sir George, Eton and Oxford, tall and gangly, rode into battle on his bicycle.

For him there could be no compromise with the tobacco industry. He wanted a total ban on advertising and sponsorship. Fortunately, Jenkin, who believed that the industry should move faster to meet reasonable demands of the health lobby, did not support calls for a ban on advertising. He sincerely believed that as a source of information, adverts were a means of persuading smokers to switch to lower tar, less dangerous cigarettes.

With Sir George banging the health drum and a Tory majority in the Commons, our Imperial Tobacco public relations group began to think more seriously about the 'freedom' issue as a means of countering the minister's aims. It was agreed to set up a new organisation to champion the right to smoke. Air Chief Marshal Sir Christopher Foxley-Norris, just retired from the RAF, was appointed to head the new body. An ardent freedom fighter, he had been at Winchester School with Sir John Wilson who chaired the tobacco industry's trade association, the Tobacco Advisory Council (TAC). The new organisation, financed by the industry, was launched in 1979 with the overblown title of The Freedom Organisation for the Right to Enjoy Smoking Tobacco – FOREST for short.

In December 1979 Patrick Jenkin chaired the first session of negotiations with the TAC on renewal of the voluntary agreement. To the industry's dismay, clearly he had been influenced by his junior minister. He proposed an end to all poster advertising and remaining TV and cinema advertising; a cut of fifty per cent in all other advertising; and a tough new health warning on cigarette packets.

Sir George Young was left to conduct the acrimonious negotiations and although the terms were slightly softened, the new agreement was to last for three not five years. To put further pressure on MPs at constituency level, I drew on my experience from the local government and roads campaigns. I suggested the industry should mobilise the support of the corner shops – the newsagents and tobacconists – which would be squeezed out of business if government policies led to a substantial drop in smokers. I pointed out that the families running these little shops were often a focal point of local public opinion and could be important in generating grass roots support for the freedom to smoke. Colin Knowles welcomed the idea with enthusiasm and a proposal went out from our meeting, via Andrew Reid, to the TAC. Once again, the proposal was accepted. A new front organisation called the Tobacco Alliance was set up.

Colin then announced that he had pulled off a coup. He had persuaded Gordon Reece (later Sir Gordon), Mrs Thatcher's highly successful adviser on style and appearance, to become an adviser to Imperial. He would be attending our PR committee meetings.

Reece was a former journalist and TV producer turned PR and image consultant. He had been advising the Tory Party on broadcasting since 1967 and from 1978 to 1980 was director of publicity at Conservative Central Office. In the run-up to the general election he had transformed

Mrs Thatcher from a suburban housewife with poor dress sense and a strident voice into the softer, but firm, well turned-out lady with nicely modulated tones who took over 10 Downing Street. He had worked hard to convince her that the tabloids influenced the mass of the voting public, not the heavies, and he got her on friendly terms with the editors of the *Sun* and the *Daily Mail*. A cigar-smoking, champagne-swigging extrovert, he had great charm and was excellent company. After seeing Mrs Thatcher into 10 Downing Street he left Central Office but remained close to the Prime Minister and was often a guest at Downing Street and Chequers.

Reece, dapper and beaming, arrived at our Imperial PR meeting and quickly lit a cigar. As a dedicated smoker he left us in no doubt that he would use his influence to try to ensure that Mrs Thatcher would support the freedom to smoke campaign and the right of the industry to inform its clients through advertising. He got on well with Denis Thatcher, another smoker, and assured us that he would have his support. But much of the normal business of the weekly meeting was of no interest to him and he was not very well informed on my area of parliamentary developments. After a few more appearances he stopped attending our meetings but when Sir George Young was moved from Health, we had no doubt that Gordon and Denis had helped to persuade Margaret that he was in the wrong job. Reece, who was knighted by Mrs Thatcher, accepted an invitation from the multi-millionaire Armand Hammer to join Occidental Petroleum as vice president for public relations. Returning to Britain from California in 1983 he helped Mrs Thatcher win the next election and again in 1987. He died in 2001 aged 71. Mrs Thatcher said: 'He will always be "One of us" '.

Somebody who was not always to remain 'One of us' in the Thatcher circle was my friend Alf Sherman. An editorial in *The Times* in 1978 described him as, 'the *eminence grise* to the *eminence grise* (Sir Keith Joseph) of the leader of the Opposition', but by 1979 a gulf was growing between Alfred and Mrs Thatcher. Before she became Prime Minister he was one of her most trusted economic policy advisers, and she often shut herself off with him for long sessions – to the annoyance of shadow ministers waiting in the corridor. One described Alf Sherman as sinister but powerful.

On reaching Downing Street, however, Mrs Thatcher decided that she did not want Alfred installed in Number Ten. Soon after, he decided her desire for reform had been diluted by the Tory establishment and then by the Civil Service. His influence was on the wane. Meeting him after the election victory I had expected to find him buoyant but, instead, he seemed despondent. He had always blamed civil servants for much of the country's problems and now that Mrs Thatcher was in Downing Street, he feared she was listening to them rather than him.

In her memoirs, however, she paid tribute to his brilliance and the force and clarity of his mind. In *The Path to Power* she wrote that she could not have become leader of the Opposition, or achieved what she did as Prime Minister, without Keith Joseph, nor could Joseph have achieved what he did without the Centre for Policy Studies and Alfred.

He was always buzzing with challenging ideas, and one that endeared him to my client, the British Road Federation, was that many railway tracks should be converted into motorways. Alfred's support for road rather than rail projects proved helpful in connection with a major transport project looming up. In 1981, I was one of a team of Charles Barker specialists assembled to assist a revolutionary scheme to raise £3,800 million to build a road and rail link across the English Channel.

It was championed by Ian MacGregor, chairman of British Steel – and one of Mrs Thatcher's favourite entrepreneurs. The scheme consisted of a road viaduct and bridge carrying two wide road links coupled to two tunnels designed to carry rail-borne lorries. MacGregor, a tough Scot, wanted to find a new outlet for his steel and together with another nationalised industry, British Shipbuilders, led a consortium that included major construction groups Fairclough, John Howard and Sir Robert McAlpine, Trafalgar House and an American company Raymond International Builders. We were told that our first task was to come up with a name for the project. At home that evening I jotted down ideas until I came up with 'Euroroute' – a name to bridge the language gap with France. When our Charles Barker group met the next day my suggestion was adopted without argument. MacGregor's consortium was delighted – and in the end, in my view, it was the best thing about what I regarded as an unrealistic scheme.

As Edward Heath's Shadow Transport Minister and later a member of his Cabinet, Margaret Thatcher had supported the idea of a channel link. She had strongly attacked the Labour Government when it scrapped the project in 1974 – soon after I sent Alfred Sherman with the All-Party Roads Study Group MPs to inspect the initial work on the French side of the Channel. She liked such big projects – but insisted that they must be financed by private enterprise. MacGregor believed there would be no problem in raising the necessary funds from the British and world money markets.

Christopher Powell was the most experienced parliamentary consultant on the project. Before World War Two he had been employed to run the All-Party Channel Tunnel Committee – one of the oldest such groups in Parliament – and had received fees from the Channel Tunnel Company. He had handed it over to Evie Soames and it was agreed that we could take on the rival Euroroute project only if we operated a system of 'Chinese Walls' within the office. Our clients agreed to this arrangement. Operating on my side of the Chinese wall, I set about trying to persuade MPs and ministers that Euroroute was the best option. MacGregor's consortium, however, found that raising the necessary money for the PR and lobbying campaign was not as easy as had been expected. After some months, we were told they could no longer afford our fees.

Alfred Sherman, an interested supporter of the Channel link project, had done his bit on our behalf during his short-lived period of influence at 10 Downing Street. He played an important role in the shaping of the 1981 Budget but by 1982 his honeymoon with Margaret Thatcher was over. His constant phone calls and agitating had become a source of irritation to the Prime Minister. When I heard that he had been knighted in 1983, I invited him to a celebration lunch at Lockets Restaurant in Marsham Street. Alfred, however, was in no mood to celebrate.

Lord Thomas, chairman of the Centre for Policy Studies, had sacked Alfred after a dispute about the Centre's role and Alf complained that the honour was small compensation. As for his influence in Whitehall, he joked bitterly that trying to sell a policy to a minister was like trying to sell condoms to an impotent man. I feared that he might be facing some financial problems and offered to inform appropriate clients that he was now available to advise them. Meanwhile Mrs Thatcher was becoming increasingly enthusiastic about a channel link, and personally favoured the idea of a privately funded drive-through tunnel while the French favoured a railway.

I suddenly found myself deeply involved again in the battle of the channel link project. At the Tory Party Conference I bumped into my former colleague on the *Daily Sketch* political team Maureen Tomison. She was working for James Sherwood, flamboyant owner of Sea Containers and of the romantic train, the Orient Express. She asked if I would be interested in taking on an account connected with the Channel Tunnel which I assumed would be a wrecking campaign designed to protect Sea Containers' shipping interests.

To my surprise, Maureen revealed that her boss, far from wanting to kill off the Chunnel schemes, had one of his own – for a drive-through road tunnel. His unique project – Channel Expressway – was being kept secret until near the deadline laid down for contenders to announce their schemes – October 31st. Those who supported other plans thought Sherwood's a technical impossibility – a bored tunnel designed for vehicles to drive through all the way from Dover to Calais. They argued that the ventilation problem would be impossible to solve. But Sherwood had discovered new technology capable of dealing with it – and wanted to keep it under wraps until the last possible moment.

The lateness of the announcement posed a formidable lobbying problem for me. Our rivals had been busy for some time trying to win public and parliamentary support for their schemes, including the Channel Tunnel Group's traditional rail-only project. While I was able to mobilise the formidable roads lobby in support, I was not optimistic. Within two months, however, following an intensive campaign, opinion polls revealed that Channel Expressway was the most popular scheme with MPs – especially the Tories, the party of government. It was also shown to be the most popular with the increasingly car-minded general public – and with the quality press. To my delight I then learned that Mrs Thatcher and her Transport Minister favoured the scheme. Surely we must be home and dry!

But it was not to be. The French Government was proud of its superior railway system and was determined to have a rail-only Chunnel. At the time, Mrs Thatcher became enmeshed in the affair of the future of the Westland helicopter company. This led to a major policy clash with Defence Secretary Michael Heseltine, and she did not feel up to taking on Paris as well. She gave way to the French. A bill to provide for the building of a rail tunnel was introduced into Parliament in 1986. James Sherwood, pleased with my efforts on his behalf, gave me a contract for regular parliamentary consultancy work and I also received a letter of thanks from Maureen Tomison in which she wrote, 'I should like to take this opportunity to say that when I approached you to help with Channel Expressway it was because I believed that you were quite simply the best political adviser and I have been confirmed in this opinion by your work for us'.

A key group I had failed to win over was the Commons Transport Select Committee. One member who was clearly going to be a problem was Den

Dover, Tory MP for Chorley who happened to be a consultant to Wimpey, a member of the Channel Tunnel Group consortium. The committee voted by a majority of one to support the Channel Tunnel Group scheme. I strongly believe that committee members with business interests related to the subject matter of an inquiry should be barred from voting.

Since Thatcher's general election victory there had been growing signs of trouble within the Labour Party with left-wingers demanding extreme policies to counter those cooked up by Alf Sherman and others. On the Labour right wing, ex-ministers such as Bill Rodgers and Shirley Williams were discussing the possibility of a new breakaway party with Roy Jenkins. He was waiting to complete his time as president of the European Commission in January 1981, before returning to British politics. Fed up with the bickering in the Party and the incompetence of Callaghan, I had let my membership lapse and started to attend meetings with local Liberals.

My feelings about the Callaghan Government have been well summed up by former Labour MP and Professor of Politics David Marquand – the distinguished son of my old friend Hilary, who had been a minister in the Attlee Government and a former MP for a Middlesbrough seat. An authority on the Labour movement, David has used excoriating words in his fine book *Britain since 1918: the Strange Career of British Democracy*. He described it as the equivalent of a zombie, apparently alive but with no 'moral or intellectual soul'.

I was delighted when Callaghan announced his resignation as Labour leader soon after the depressing party conference in October 1980. I hoped Denis Healey would replace him but while he led on the first ballot of MPs, he was narrowly beaten by Michael Foot on the second ballot – by 139 votes to 129. As much as I liked Michael, I believed he would make a disastrous leader and would lose Labour the next general election. However, as a friend, I wrote to congratulate him, pointing out that he would be the first member of the Leslie Hale Luncheon Club to become a party leader. Within another couple of years the club would be able to claim to include two national newspaper editors – Charlie Douglas-Home of *The Times* and Stewart Steven of the *Mail on Sunday*.

Michael was in favour of nuclear disarmament and opposed to Britain's membership of the European Community. With him as leader, it was certain that pro-Europe MPs on the right of the Party, such as Shirley Williams, Bill Rodgers and David Owen would break away with Roy

Jenkins joining them on his return from his EC Commission post. I was very interested in this development and being unable to take the Liberal Party seriously, decided to join the new Party when it was formed – as surely it would be soon. On Sunday January 25th 1981, Roy, Shirley, David and Bill – to become known as the 'Gang of Four' – launched their declaration that the need for a realignment of British politics must now be faced. The statement, known as 'The Limehouse Declaration', was issued from Owen's riverside home in Limehouse. This was followed in March by the setting up of the Social Democratic Party and I was one of the first thousand to apply for membership.

Some years later, my friend George Thomson, who retired as a European Union Commissioner in January 1977, told me that if he had not been chairman of the Independent Broadcasting Authority by 1981, he would have made it the 'Gang of Five'. Appointed a life peer in 1977 with the title of Lord Thomson of Monifieth, the highly respected and popular George would have been a useful addition to the breakaway group. His family, however, was represented from the start. His son-in-law Roger Liddle, who had worked for Bill Rodgers when he was Minister of Transport, was Bill's political adviser when the declaration was drawn up. Another son-in-law, Richard Newby, (made a Liberal Democrat life peer in 1997) left the Civil Service to work for the fledgling new Party's Council for Social Democracy in the spring of 1981.

When the Parliamentary Committee of the Social Democratic Party (SDP) was set up in March, a number of my friends were among the twelve Labour MPs who resigned the Labour Whip to join. They included Tom Bradley, whom I had known and liked since, when reporting for *Reynolds News*, I covered his 1962 Leicester by-election victory. Tom was a Transport Salaried Staff Association MP, had been chairman of the Labour Party in 1976, and had presided over a TUC conference, giving me his entrance pass when I arrived there and discovered I had mislaid mine. Tom was a railwayman but was in the All-Party Roads Study Group, partly to keep an eye on the roads lobby, and partly because he enjoyed the convivial meetings and tours.

By June 1981 the SDP had fourteen MPs in the Commons – three more than the Liberals. By the end of that month my friend Jim Wellbeloved became the fifteenth, aware that he was putting at risk his Commons seat for Erith and Crayford in the coming General Election. Jim had done a good job as Labour MP consultant to Imperial Tobacco and I argued that the company should keep him on as an SDP adviser. I forecast that more Labour MPs would switch to the new Party in the year ahead, making it a significant force. Imperial accepted my advice.

I hoped that Jim would use his influence in the SDP to slow down Dr David Owen's crusade for the new Party to adopt anti-smoking policies. Imperial would need a Labour replacement for Jim and I recommended former Northern Ireland Secretary of State Roy Mason. He was a pipe-smoking ex-miner with commercial flair, and turned out to be an excellent appointment.

The rule at Charles Barker Watney and Powell was that we could not employ MPs. However, our chairman, George Pulay, had asked me to assist one of his friends in the Lords who needed to earn some money. He was Lord Cullen of Ashbourne, a hereditary peer whose father had been a governor of the Bank of England and much more successful at making money than his son. Charles succeeded to the title in 1932 but did not take his seat in the Lords for ten years and waited a further thirty to make his maiden speech there. He chose to break his silence on a debate on Alf Morris' bill to assist the disabled. His second wife Patricia had been severely disabled when she lost a leg at the fashionable Café de Paris night club when it was hit by a bomb during the war. I met Charles and took a liking to him. As he was not in the Commons, I decided the company should bend its rule about not employing parliamentarians and take him on for a small fee.

Our arrangement ended when he was made a Government Whip, and revived when he gave up the job in 1982. I then persuaded Imperial to take him on as their paid consultant, so our company's rule on not employing parliamentarians was broken for only a short time.

Despite his Liberal Party leanings, Roy Jenkins beat David Owen in the election for leader of the SDP. Jenkins' supporters told me that if Owen had won, the alliance with the Liberals would have been gravely weakened. Meanwhile, it was clear that the ambitious Liberal leader David Steel was seeking to manipulate the association in the interests of his own Party. Having chosen not to join the Liberals, and as an enthusiastic supporter of the SDP's launch, I was uneasy.

With the 1983 Election looming, the SDP organised a much-publicised rolling conference to 'show the flag'. Starting in Cardiff it moved by train to Derby, where I joined it, before travelling on to Great Yarmouth. At Derby, Jim Wellbeloved filled me in on developments. He was not his usual jokey self. No doubt he was worried about his chances of holding on to his traditional Labour seat at Erith and Crayford as an SDP candidate. To add to the gloom, the train ran out of wine early in the next stage of its journey to Great Yarmouth. Surely Roy Jenkins, famed for his love of claret, could have been expected to ensure adequate supplies for his thirsty followers?

Roger Carroll, a former member of the Parliamentary Press Gallery, had been appointed as director of communications for the new party. He had worked for Callaghan and for a short time for Michael Foot when he became Labour leader. I told him I would be happy to volunteer in the press office in the election if needed – and in due course he took up my offer. In May 1983, Mrs Thatcher called the general election and Roger phoned to ask if I could help at the SDP HQ in Cowley Street, Westminster, that weekend as he was short staffed. A summarised version of the SDP-Liberal Alliance manifesto, *Working Together,* was urgently needed. I agreed to write it and, as time was so short and I was assisting in my spare time, I took the material home, working on it late into the night. The four-page summary, printed in red, white and blue, was published on time – and the over-worked Roger was duly grateful.

With the summary completed I was kept busy writing press releases for leading Social Democrat candidates, Bill Rodgers among them. Because of the difficulty of holding his Stockton-on-Tees seat, he had campaigned from his constituency instead of accepting engagements around the country. In this particular speech he promised that the Alliance would take active measures to stimulate the economy and to create one million new jobs over two years. With the Alliance coming a poor third in some of the opinion polls, David Steel was attempting, behind the scenes, to usurp Roy Jenkins as its leader. Steel was well ahead of him in the polls but Jenkins decided to hang on despite his lagging public popularity.

From the start of the campaign, I had attended the Parties' daily press conferences in London in my journalistic capacity as editor of *Science in Parliament.* Starting with Labour's conference to launch its wordy manifesto, later described by Gerald Kaufman as 'the longest suicide note in history', I went on to hear Margaret Thatcher contemptuously put down her gentlemanly Foreign Secretary Francis Pym, who had publicly warned that, 'landslides on the whole do not produce successful governments'. Asked to comment on these truthful words, the angry Prime Minister snapped, 'I think I can handle a landslide all right'. Denis Thatcher, who was standing near me, chortled 'Good for you, old girl'.

A landslide victory it was that she had to handle. Deeply depressed, I watched the Tory blue wave surge forward on election night until Mrs Thatcher was swept back to power with 397 seats. As I had suspected, Labour led by Michael Foot was swept aside, winning only 209 seats, while the Liberals had seventeen and the SDP a mere six. In this electoral disaster the Social Democrats had won only one extra seat – Ross, Cromarty and Skye This was taken by a chirpy young Charles Kennedy who then entered the Commons at the age of twenty-three. He would eventually become leader of the Liberal Democrats and a near neighbour of mine in Kennington.

Twenty-four SDP MPs lost their seats, including my friends Jim Wellbeloved, Tom Bradley and John Grant, who had been industrial correspondent of the *Daily Express* when I covered politics for the paper. They had displayed great courage and integrity – qualities in short supply in the Commons. Jim Wellbeloved became director general of the National Kidney Research Fund in 1984, and, as my wife and I were involved in that important charity in the London area, I continued to keep in touch with him in the years ahead.

Sadly I lost touch with Tom Bradley who, despite the hopes of his friends, never went on to sit in the Lords. He had been chairman of the Commons Transport Select Committee and had done his best to help the railways. In the mid-seventies he had co-operated with the colourful early spin doctor Will Camp in a *No Rail Cuts* campaign. Camp, who earlier in his career came up with the slogan *High Speed Gas* for the Gas Council, went on to run British Rail's public relations office. His expertise made life difficult for me in the running battle to get more money from the Government for road building. And within the Labour movement my problem was exacerbated during policy making debates at party conferences over the allocation of limited public funds between road construction and railway modernisation. The big hearted giant, the Transport and General Workers Union, representing the lorry drivers, was reluctant to fight it out with the smaller railway unions over whether it was more efficient to transport freight by road or rail. So many people had a love affair with trains.

The Thatcher Government's decision to privatise the Royal Ordnance factories brought a cry for help to me in March 1984 from the highly respected Institution of Professional Civil Servants. The bill to enable the thirteen factories that were an integral part of the Ministry of Defence to become an independent commercial organisation had received a Commons second reading in January. It got 354 votes to 206 with a few Tory rebel MPs voting with Labour, Liberal and SDP against the measure. I had noted that my friendly contact, Sir Ian Gilmour, a former Tory Secretary of State for Defence under Heath, had abstained from supporting the Government, describing the bill as 'wrongheaded and unjustified'. Following slow progress in Committee, the bill was expected to complete Commons stages by late May and then move on to the Lords. William McCall, the canny, sociable general secretary of the IPCS, asked me to produce proposals for a lobbying campaign to defeat the measure in the Upper House or, failing that, to amend it in line with the requirements of the IPCS. We agreed that our tactic should be to get enough support in the Lords to produce prolonged committee and third reading stages, thus creating such serious time problems for the Government that ministers would be forced to withdraw the bill.

Tory Governments had traditionally enjoyed a built-in majority in the Lords but with the growth of Crossbench peers it had become less reliable and the Government suffered a run of defeats on technical points. With Christopher Powell and my enterprising executive Corinne Souza, I produced lists of potential allies, organised briefings, lobbied individual peers and advised on tactics. My targets included former high-ranking service officers, former civil servants, peers interested in efficient defence and procurement and those with geographic links to ROFs. Ian Gilmore was active behind the scenes. He helped me to provide information about the efficiency of the closely integrated engineering and chemical production organisation of the ROFs and their expertise in developing up-to-date sophisticated equipment. In October, as the bill came up for debates on report and third reading stages, I helped to mobilise a briefing and an appeal for help from the trade unions affected. At committee stage we had amended the bill to ensure greater control by Parliament and prevent the splitting up of the 13-factory organisation. The Government had warned it would not accept the amendments and would seek to overturn them in the Commons. The unions, who represented the 20,000 strong ROF workforce, expressed fears of enforced transfer out of the civil service, poorer working conditions and a loss of the index-linking system for their pensions.

The Government was accused of repaying a loyal workforce with broken promises and shabby treatment. Backed by reliable lobby fodder in the Commons, the Government largely got its way in the end. William McCall and the IPCS, however, were pleased with what my team had accomplished in the Lords and employed us again to take on unwelcome Government proposals.

It had been a pleasure to deal again with Ian Gilmour. I had first met him when he was PPS to my friend Lord Hailsham (Quintin Hogg) during the 1963 Tory leadership contest. On defeating Heath for the Tory leadership, Margaret Thatcher had made Ian Shadow Home Secretary but then moved him back to his old area of expertise – Defence. He had opposed some of her policies however, and was said by one of her supporters to be 'so wet you could shoot snipe off him'. Nevertheless, on winning power in 1979, she made him Lord Privy Seal. As Foreign Secretary Carrington sat in the Lords, Ian answered for the Foreign Office in the Commons. Then in September 1981, Margaret tired of his questioning her policies and turfed him out of the Government. Freed from ministerial restrictions, appalled by cuts in public spending and soaring unemployment, he became an outspoken critic of what he saw as the undermining of the welfare state. In 1992 he became a life peer and we lost touch.

Within a few years of taking over the Parliamentary and Scientific Committee from Christopher Powell I had become the acknowledged expert on the setting up and administration of all-party groups linked to industries or specialist high technology sectors. As a result, in the summer of 1983 Keith McDowall, a lively former *Daily Mail* industrial correspondent and now director of information for the Confederation of British Industry (CBI) invited me to be the only professional lobbyist to address a CBI conference. It was called *Working with Politicians* and would be held in December, to concentrate on practical advice on lobbying. By the CBI's definition, that meant informing elected representatives of the real concerns of industry – 'a perfectly proper part of the democratic process', according to Sir Terence Beckett, the CBI's director general, in the conference literature. These words were a justification of my own use and subsequent defence of the word 'lobbying' which in 1972 had brought me a rebuke from some in the Public Relations Consultants Association (PRCA).

The aim of the conference was to help businessmen come to terms with the new Parliament elected the previous June. Less than a third of the new MPs had any practical experience of business. Beckett's words echoed my own over the previous decade when he told CBI members, 'It is not possible to complain about Parliament or local authorities failing to act in the best interests of business prosperity if business does not play its part in keeping them well informed'.

The CBI had made great progress in this area of parliamentary affairs. Years before, without a full time parliamentary team of its own, it had asked me to provide coverage of the Wilson Government's industry bill. By 1983, my old colleague Squire Barraclough, whom I had recruited for the *Daily Express* political team, was employed as the CBI's in-house parliamentary adviser.

And in the astute Keith McDowall, the CBI had a man who had been a highly successful member of the Government's Information Service. His last two posts had been director of information for the Northern Ireland Office, 1972-74; and director of information, Department of Employment, 1974-78. Keith chaired the conference and I spoke on the role of the all-party specialist committees. Three MPs and a peer also spoke from the platform.

I had had a rehearsal for my CBI talk. In November 1982 the professional practises committee of the PRCA invited me to address a seminar on the same subject in the Commons. Two MPs with whom I worked – Labour's Alan Williams (the All-Party Minerals Group) and Tory Peter Fry (the All-Party Roads Study Group) also addressed the seminar. Lobbyist Doug Smith who was in business with Peter Fry and with whom I wrote the PRCA booklet on lobbying also took part. He was chairman of the association's Professional Practices Committee.

Peter's activities as an MP consultant to industry attracted favourable media attention in the late 1970s. He had been advising the Lighting Industry Federation, which was anxious to see that a Labour Government Order which made dipped headlights obligatory in towns would not be blocked in Parliament. Having advised the Federation on how to play its cards, Peter then spoke from the Tory benches and voted against the Order. His action was cited as an example of how MPs did not allow consultancy fees to influence their political and parliamentary duties.

There had been important changes of officers on two of my all-party groups. Alan Lee Williams, who had taken on the Labour joint chairmanship of my new motor industry group, had lost his Hornchurch seat in the 1979 General Election. To my great delight I was able to replace him with the wise and experienced George Park, Labour MP for Coventry North-east. The BMC / British Leyland truck and tractor division was in his constituency. As a former senior AUEW shop steward at the giant Chrysler Rootes plant at Ryton in Coventry, his views on industrial relations were heard with great respect in Parliament. He took his seat in 1974 after celebrating his sixtieth birthday. He soon became parliamentary private secretary to the Minister of Transport and then to the Secretary of State for Industry. It was a feather in my cap when he joined the All-Party Roads Study Group and joined us on an overseas tour to the USA.

Alan Fitch, who had enjoyed a long run as the popular Labour joint chairman of the All-Party Roads Study Group, retired from Parliament in 1983. He had started his working life in the coalmines and was to be replaced by another ex-miner, Roy Hughes, MP for Newport. When I first got to know Roy he was an active member of the left wing Tribune group, aggressively class conscious and suspicious of industrialists. As a member of the Transport and General Workers' Union, however, he was deeply interested in road transport issues. He complained of the public's lack of awareness that over ninety per cent of passenger and freight transport was by road. He was to become very friendly with the APRSG Tory joint chairman Peter Fry and, sharing a love of rugby football, they went on to form the All-Party Rugby Union Group.

Another devoted fan of rugger in the Roads Group was my good friend Michael Roberts. Unlike Reg Prentice and Bernard Braine, he had never held a position in any of the companies that employed me. Eventually, I arranged for him to be paid a percentage of the first year's fee from any account that he helped us to win. When he was offered his first Commons post as an Opposition Whip he was not sure whether to accept and asked my advice. I told him he should accept it as in my experience backbenchers who turned down such offers rarely, if ever, got another.

When he entered Margaret Thatcher's Government as a Welsh Office minister we celebrated heavily in the Strangers' Bar with some of his close friends including John Stradling-Thomas, MP for Monmouth. In February 1983 I was appalled to learn that Michael suffered a heart attack while addressing the Commons and died at the Dispatch Box. He had risen to answer a point raised by Roy Hughes from the Opposition benches. Dr Roger Thomas, MP for Carmarthen, attended to him on the floor of the Chamber – but there was nothing he could do to revive him.

By tradition, it is not normally revealed if a non-royal person dies in a royal palace. According to The Library of Parliament, 'It is generally the practise to assume… that the actual point of death occurs outside the precincts of the Palace'. This is connected to problems relating to Coroners' inquests. There was no way, however, that the authorities could hide the fact that Michael had taken his last breath in the Palace of Westminster. This straight-talking popular House of Commons man had done it his way. In her tribute, Mrs Thatcher described him as, 'A most assiduous constituency member, a fine minister, an enthusiast in all he undertook… always partisan, but retaining the respect and affection of all sides of the house'. Michael Foot, as Opposition leader, paid tribute to his gift for kindness and friendship and to his unfailing courtesy.

I had benefited so much from his gift for kindness and friendship that I sometimes felt I could never repay him. Apart from all the good times we shared since my successful Cardiff local government campaign, he had helped me win vital new business. The British Road Federation was of special importance as it led to the Society of Motor Manufacturers and Traders and vehicle manufacturers such as Ford, General Motors, Vauxhall and G.K.N. I particularly liked what John Stradling-Thomas said of him:

'Michael holding court was really a sight to see. His unfailing courtesy and charm were always manifest but woe betide any foolish fellow who went too far. He soon knew that he was up against a doughty opponent. But – and this was the magic – there was never any acrimony. You could argue with Michael but you could never quarrel with him'.

Michael would have been pleased that John replaced him as Minister of State for Wales.

CHAPTER FIVE

On a Killer's Hit List

The year 1983 began with a clear signal that Margaret Thatcher was intent on breaking the power of the National Union of Mineworkers. Ian MacGregor, the ruthless but efficient British Steel boss who had involved me in the launch of his cross-channel Euroroute project, was switched to the chairmanship of the National Coal Board. Some thought that at the age of seventy this tough Scottish trouble-shooter was too old to take on such a daunting task. They underestimated the man who had just streamlined the steel industry and prepared it for privatisation. I saw his appointment as the curtain raiser for a ferocious battle with the miners.

I had a personal interest as there had been miners in my family. During World War One, my mother lived with her Aunt Nell's family in Dover as her own unmarried mother had been too busy working as a top freelance chef to bring her up. After losing her husband on the Western Front, Nell lived with a local man who went to work in the Kent coalfield after the war. In due course, two of her sons, Alfred and George, also got work in the pits. Faced with bad conditions and poor pay they turned to extreme left-wing politicians for a remedy. They read the *Communist Daily Worker* (later the *Morning Star*) and rejoiced when I became political editor of their Sunday reading, the Co-operative movement's Labour-supporting *Reynolds News*.

In time, my great aunt Nell died, and when they, too, died, that little pocket of miners' militancy in Dover went with them. My personal link with the miners had been broken. It would be replaced in time with an important business link.

MacGregor was faced with an industry that was running at a loss of well over £200 million. There were many uneconomic coalmines, and the leaders of the National Union of Mineworkers, Arthur Scargill and Mick McGahey, were preparing for a fight which would have strong political overtones. The crunch came in March 1984.

MacGregor announced that the next batch of twenty loss-making pits would be closed in the coming year, throwing some 20,000 miners out of work. Scargill's response was to call a national strike. In order not to risk losing a vote he abandoned the NUM's democratic procedure of a national ballot.

To support the strike by preventing the movement of coal, Scargill used the weapon of mass picketing of working pits, ports and depots holding stocks. On television I watched the battles between the pickets and the police who were armed with riot shields and batons. I recalled the day I witnessed the young Yorkshire constables attacking the car of Home Secretary Merlyn Rees over their pay claim. I wondered how many of them were now being employed on over-time rates to batter the desperate miners into submission. But by his tactics, Scargill had miscalculated and lost the vital public relations battle, and split the union. The strike began in the spring when coal stocks at the power stations were high and demand for heating was falling. Before it ended some 11,000 striking miners had been arrested by the thousands of police deployed against them.

MacGregor's defeat of the miners in 1985 enabled him to push ahead with his ambitious programme of pit closures and voluntary redundancies. Such measures substantially cut Coal Board losses and increased productivity per man shift from 2.2 tons to 3 tons. There had been a heavy cost in human terms. Thousands of men lost their jobs in one of the most bitter industrial disputes in British history and once proud, hard-working communities were devastated.

Before the strike had formally ended, I got a call from the Barnsley Enterprise Centre, in the heart of the Yorkshire mining area. Their local MP Roy Mason had suggested they should contact me. They needed help to launch a campaign to provide new employment in the coalfield areas affected by the NCB's pit closure plans. Dear Roy! I had never been more pleased with a new business offer. Even my return to Middlesbrough to set up the new county of Cleveland had not given me such satisfaction.

A meeting at my office was quickly arranged. The Barnsley team arrived, headed by a straight talking, business-like Yorkshireman, Hedley Salt. He was deputy leader of Barnsley borough council. Hedley explained the plan would involve affected local authorities throughout Britain and I quickly realised that I had a big task on my hands. He said the name proposed was the Coalfield Communities' Seminar but I suggested that this sounded too academic and neutral. Why not the Coalfield Communities' Campaign

(CCC)? My suggestion was adopted. I promised to send them my proposals together with an appropriate (meaning, modest) fee within a few days. I persuaded my Charles Barker colleagues that would be only right for the work – on a par with what an agency would charge a charity. If we made a success of it, the spin-off in terms of other work for local authorities could be substantial.

Barnsley contained a nest of Scargillites and I stressed to Hedley that Scargill could not be associated with the campaign in any way. Also, every effort must be made to win all-party support for it. I knew that Roy Mason, himself an ex-miner, had been deeply opposed to Scargill's tactics and would approve of my approach. Launch day was fixed for May 15th. The campaign would need a highly respectable cross-party list of patrons drawn from the great and good. It was to include politicians, industrialists and churchmen, many of whom had been dismayed by the violence and divisive nature of the strike. I wanted a former Prime Minister to head the list and be on the platform in London on launch day.

Harold Macmillan, well-known for his deep feelings about the curse of unemployment, would have been ideal, but although he sent a message of support he declined to be a patron. I decided to go for Jim Callaghan and asked Roy Mason if he would have a word with him before I arranged a meeting. I had a suspicion that the calculating, ever-cautious former premier would suspect the CCC of being a front organisation for Scargill's troops. Roy's record was impeccable but, even so, when I met Callaghan in his room at the Commons, he declined my invitation to speak at the launch. Instead, he offered a statement of support and asked me to provide a draft.

By the time Jim had made a couple of alterations it read:

> 'I welcome the formation of the CCC and am very happy to become a patron. There is the urgent need to focus attention on the future of Britain's coal mining areas. The launching of this nation-wide initiative provides the opportunity for a constructive approach to find solutions to the questions – economic, social and environmental – that are now being asked in the coalfields.
>
> 'Britain owes a great debt to its coal mining communities. In banding together to put their case they are not asking for charity; they are simply asking us to recognise the invaluable role that coal will continue to play in the fast-approaching twenty-first century, and that the coal will only be won if it is built on healthy, well-founded local communities.

'All of us have seen the deep sense of loyalty, determination and strength of community of those who live in coal mining districts. If these communities should be sacrificed, the nation will lose much more than its coal – something of our national spirit would disappear, too.

'I wish the campaign every success'.

As Callaghan had declined to appear on the platform, I asked my friend Lord Cledwyn of Penrhos. As Cledwyn Hughes he had served as Secretary of State for Wales and Minister of Agriculture in the Wilson and Callaghan Governments. He was delighted to accept the invitation to be the main Labour Party speaker.

As we would be applying for development grants from the European Community, I asked Barbara Castle, leader of the UK Labour group in the European Parliament, to join our list of patrons. Her name came immediately after Callaghan's when the list was printed and I imagined him hissing at this. He could not stand Barbara. He had helped to block her trade union reform plan *In Place of Strife* and sacked her when he took over from Wilson as PM.

Other patrons included the highly respected Tory businessman Viscount Caldecote, a former National Coal Board chairman and Liberal peer, Lord Ezra, David Sheppard, Bishop of Liverpool, and Derek Worlock, Roman Catholic Archbishop of Liverpool.

Fifty-four local authorities, from counties and city districts to boroughs had signed up by launch day, for which I hired a large room in the Central Hall complex at Westminster. On May 15th at 11.30 a.m. Hedley Salt, chairman of the CCC, opened the press conference. It was attended by a crowd of media representatives and contingents of our supporters from all over the U.K. Remembering the success of our bus tour in the campaign to win a reprieve for Cardiff's steelworks, I repeated the operation.

The double decker carried Hedley and other leading members of the campaign to 10 Downing Street, the Scottish and Welsh offices, and the National Coal Board headquarters. At each stop, they presented a statement of the CCC's aims and asked the PM, Secretaries of State and NCB chairman to receive deputations in due course.

The day ended with a presentation to MPs in the Grand Committee Room at the House of Commons. The consensus was that the launch had been a great success. While I had agreed to handle it and act as political consultant to the campaign, I had told Hedley that he should appoint a separate PR firm to handle on-going media activities. I suggested they should appoint a local Barnsley firm but apparently there was no one suitable. I undertook to find them a good PR man and turned to my old colleague David Powell, who was operating as a freelance consultant and speechwriter to Ian MacLaurin, chairman of Tesco, and writing books. He was too busy to take it on but recommended an experienced consultant named Michael Cornish who turned out to be an excellent choice. Michael and I began a close friendship that has lasted ever since.

I arranged a rolling programme of presentations to appropriate groups of MPs while the research and written work was supervised by a thoughtful young graduate, Bryan Gladstone. Soon, over a hundred local authorities had joined the pressure group, which grew in respect and reputation. Its seminars and presentations were well prepared. A four-day CCC conference on Tyneside in January 1989 was addressed by Neil Kinnock, leader of the Opposition; Bruce Millan, EC Commissioner for Regional Policies; and Sir Robert Haslam, chairman of British Coal, among others. It was raising much needed funds from Whitehall and the European Community Commission to bring new life and hope back into the coalfield communities.

As I was once again a parliamentary consultant to Tesco, I persuaded the company to help the CCC. Ian Maclaurin, encouraged by David Powell, was concerned about the North-South economic and social divide. Years before this, it had worried Prime Minister Harold Macmillan and Quintin Hogg. At a Tesco presentation on retail development to Tory MPs in London, MacLaurin referred to the need to tackle this on-going problem. To his intense annoyance, Sir Marcus Fox, the most senior MP present, denied any such divide existed. 'I represent Shipley, Yorkshire, and I should know', insisted Marcus. 'What are we to do with these people?' groaned MacLaurin after the meeting.

While the Government's battle with the miners captured the headlines, Robert Maxwell had achieved his long-held ambition to become a major newspaper proprietor. The great rogue had bought the *Daily Mirror* in 1984 and as owner of this newspaper, so influential in the Labour movement, he attended the Labour Party's annual conference where his clumsy endeavours to help end the miners' strike drove his aides to distraction. These hapless assistants included Michael Hatfield, a former political journalist and friend, who I feared would collapse from exhaustion.

It was probably thanks to Mike that I attended a *Daily Mirror* party where Maxwell told me triumphantly that this would be a great time for me to work for him. He was handing out jobs galore to ex-ministers, politicians and officials to help him run his empire. With such apparently respectable top people prepared to take his money, others were misled into believing that it was safe to do business with him.

He had offered me jobs several times since 1965 when over lunch at The Savoy he had asked me to write a biography of Hugh Gaitkell for his publishing firm. Knowing Maxwell's reputation for swindling freelance journalists out of their fees, I had declined with the excuse that my then employer the *Daily Express* would not permit me to do so. As his reputation for dishonesty grew I had turned down later offers to join his team.

Resignations from the Government because of the Falkland crisis had one good result for Imperial Tobacco. Argentina's invasion of the islands in April 1982 followed a period of poor British intelligence, bad judgement and fumbling complacency by the Foreign Office. Shamed by their department's failure, Foreign Secretary Lord Carrington and his deputy Humphrey Atkins resigned from the Government.

Soon after Humphrey Atkins returned to the backbenches, Sir John Langford-Holt decided to retire from Parliament, creating a vacancy for a Tory MP consultant for Imperial. Humphrey, appointed a Knight of the Order of Saint Michael and Saint George (KCMG) in 1983, was free to accept the offer of the Imperial post in the same year. Before he had replaced Ian Gilmour at the Foreign office in Mrs Thatcher's 1981 reshuffle, the handsome and charming Humphrey had served as a conciliatory Northern Ireland Secretary – following Labour's Roy Mason in that job. So Imperial Tobacco now had two former Northern Ireland Secretaries on board as consultants.

Their recruitment added to Imperial Tobacco's existing link with the Irish situation. Sir Robin Haydon had retired from the diplomatic service in 1980 with his KCMG honour and looked around for ways to augment his pension. Nine years before, he had been sent to Malawi as British High Commissioner. In that African state, ruled by the despotic Dr. Hastings Banda, he had met representatives of the Imperial Tobacco company who were buying the locally grown tobacco crop. On the strength of this link, he applied for a consultancy with the firm on his retirement, simultaneously negotiating a consultancy with the Charles Barker Group.

George Pulay called me into his office to give me the news and was surprised by my lack of enthusiasm. I had to tell him that in my experience,

Robin Haydon disliked hard work. As a political and diplomatic correspondent, I had encountered him in the 1960s when he was serving in the Foreign Office news department. Although I found him friendly and amusing, in my experience he was too relaxed in dealing with press enquiries. I did not have full confidence in his service.

He was a close friend of another Foreign Office diplomat, Sir Donald Maitland. Maitland was a pro-Europe official much respected by Edward Heath who had appointed him chief press secretary to 10 Downing Street on becoming Prime Minister. Maitland did not appear to enjoy his arduous 10 Downing Street job, which involved late-night phone calls from news hunting journalists. In time, he persuaded Heath to release him into the more relaxed and civilised life of an ambassador – *lying abroad for the good of his country* – and was told to find a successor for the Downing Street post. He thought of his friend Robin Haydon.

As Haydon relaxed on his veranda with a lunchtime gin and tonic in sunny Malawi, he was horrified to be informed one day that he had been recommended for the stressful front-line post at 10 Downing Street. He was flown back to London to be interviewed by Heath and surprised the Prime Minister by politely but firmly declining the job. Heath was flabbergasted but being his obstinate self insisted that Haydon should fill the vacancy. So, as the Government sank deeper into the mire, the Prime Minister was serviced by a reluctant chief press secretary who came out in a sweat at the mere thought of anything akin to effort. It had been a bad appointment – but Haydon's agony was short-lived.

Heath lost the General Election the following year and Wilson returned to 10 Downing Street. Having served as Heath's mouthpiece, Haydon was on Labour's blacklist. He was offered a couple of posts which he declined as unsuitable, finally accepting the appointment of High Commissioner to Malta. When Christopher Ewart-Biggs, Britain's Ambassador to Dublin, was murdered by IRA terrorists at his embassy in 1976, Haydon was moved to fill that bloodstained vacancy.

Having returned from Dublin in one piece in 1980, he was now on our doorstep. When I learned, however, that he had already been appointed consultant to Imperial Tobacco, I realised to my great relief that he could not also work for us. He could not serve us and one of our clients at the same time. I phoned him and explained that there seemed to be a problem. He replied in typically relaxed manner that he could not see why this should be so. Like too many civil servants and politicians, he did not appear to understand the concept of a conflict of interest. I thought it would be more diplomatic if George Pulay explained it to him. Faced with making a reluctant choice, Sir Robin plumped for Imperial Tobacco, a fatter fee, and hopefully, an easier life.

In the same year, while I was enjoying an August holiday, my good friend Michael King died of a heart attack near his Wiltshire home. His careful regime after earlier attacks had not been enough to safeguard him. Imperial Group lost a highly respected public affairs adviser at an opportune time for Sir Robin. He was appointed director of public affairs. I invited him to political lunches and dinners I had organised for Imperial Tobacco, and he was always accompanied by two security men to which he was entitled as a former envoy to Dublin. As Roy Mason and Sir Humphrey Atkins also had two security men each as former Northern Ireland Secretaries, we had to accommodate a total of six gun-toting guards who would eat in a separate room.

Humphrey, whose good looks and suave, courteous style had made him popular with Mrs T, proved to be a good addition to our team. He stayed on as MP for Spelthorne, Surrey, until 1987 when the Prime Minister sent him to the House of Lords with the title Lord Colnbrook.

When Humphrey retired from the Commons, Imperial replaced him with Neil Macfarlane as their Tory MP consultant. As Mrs Thatcher's Sports Minister from 1981-85, Neil had supported sponsorship of events by tobacco companies. An Essex lad, he had played cricket for the county and turned out to be a good team player for us. Although loyal to Mrs Thatcher, he had no time for her son Mark.

As for Sir Donald Maitland, having retired from Whitehall in 1983, he joined my good friend George Thomson, by then Lord Thomson of Monifieth, at the office of the Independent Broadcasting Authority. George was chairman, and I invited him to address the Parliamentary and Scientific Committee. He in turn invited me to a reception at the IBA offices where I met Maitland again. Mrs Thatcher had described him as the best negotiator she had encountered so I had no doubt he would be useful to George.

Compared to Heath, Mrs Thatcher was more successful in her choice of chief press secretary at 10 Downing Street. She was turned down by Tony Shrimsley, assistant editor of the *Sun*, and turned to the highly experienced Henry James, who had recently retired as director general of the Central Office of Information. I had kept in close touch with Henry and introduced him to Peter Earl, who arranged for him to be elected president of the Institute of Public Relations.

On leaving Government service, Henry had become public relations adviser to the main board of Vickers Ltd. Mrs Thatcher knew he was well respected by the media and within hours of entering 10 Downing Street, she called him in and asked him to take over as her temporary press secretary. Vickers agreed to release him for a year.

A year into Margaret Thatcher's Government, an official report that recommended an increase in the maximum weight of heavy lorries led to my involvement in a major campaign on behalf of the roads and vehicle lobby, aimed at ensuring that the controversial recommendation was accepted by Parliament. As the leading parliamentary consultancy in road transport, our clients with a direct interest included the Freight Transport Association, the SMMT, the BRF, the Roads Campaign Council and the Motor Agents' Association. A wider range of clients connected with transporting goods and raw materials by road included Blue Circle Cement, Tarmac, the Cement and Concrete Association, Imperial Group, Allied Lyons, Tesco, Pilkingtons and British Aggregate Construction Materials Industries (BACMI).

I lobbied MPs and relevant Commons committees throughout 1981, and in December all appropriate trade associations held a meeting at the CBI to launch an 'Industry needs heavier lorries' campaign. In 1982 my efforts were directed mainly against a group of some forty Tory backbenchers who, for constituency reasons, were opposing the proposed 40-tonne weight limit. With the Opposition parties, they threatened to defeat the Government, encouraged by a highly organised anti-heavy lorry campaign launched by the environmentalist lobby. At the party conferences in the autumn I organised fringe meetings, and in a key debate at the Tory Conference, our opponents were out-numbered and out-gunned. In November, the Government finally won the day. A 38-tonne limit was introduced along with other regulations for the heavy lorry concerning height, width and axles, to operate from May the following year. The Government won the Commons vote with a majority of 63 – more than its normal majority. The victory was due in no small measure to the work of our Charles Barker team.

Impressed by my work for the heavy lorry campaign, the SMMT and the All-Party Motor Industry Group, the Ford Motor Company invited me to their head office at Brentwood, Essex in January 1983. Tough, hard-working Sam Toy was chairman and managing director, having taken over from Terence Beckett in 1980. Under his strong leadership, Ford UK was to enjoy one of its most successful periods. Less smooth and polished than Beckett, who had gone on to become CBI director-general, he was more forthright in expressing his views about Government policies and the problems and needs of the motor industry. In involving himself in such debates, he wanted to be sure he was armed with accurate, up-to-the-minute intelligence on the political scene. That was to be my job.

Ford wanted me to provide a parliamentary information, contact and consultancy service. At Brentwood I met my old *News Chronicle* colleague John Waddell, who had moved from Fleet Street some years before to a top PR and public affairs role with the company. I got the job at a time when Ford was looking for economies – and expecting trouble from the unions. I produced a busy contact programme for their directors, which consisted of meetings with potentially useful MPs and peers. Parliamentarians with a special interest in technology were flown by helicopter from Battersea heliport to Ford's impressive research and engineering centre at Dunton, Essex.

My position as parliamentary consultant was then strengthened by the arrival of another friend from a previous business relationship. Kenneth Cannell, with whom I had worked closely when he was assistant director of the British Road Federation, had been recruited by Ford as director of public and governmental affairs. To mark the company's 75ᵗʰ anniversary, I helped to round up nearly fifty MPs and peers to attend a celebration lunch.

In 1980, Colin Knowles resigned as head of public affairs for Imperial Tobacco to start a new life in South Africa. Following a reshuffle in the department, a keen, workaholic young man named Peter Sanguinetti also left the company to become head of public affairs for the British Airports Authority (BAA). Soon after taking up this job, he appointed me as the company's political consultant. My range of transport clients was now impressive, ranging from the British motor industry through the shipping and train operator Sea Containers to the operator of Britain's major airports.

I was also becoming increasingly involved in the food and drink sector. Imperial Group, in its efforts to diversify from the threatened tobacco industry, had bought Courage Breweries. It had even hoped that the next Imperial Group chairman might be appointed from the company's drinks sector. In management terms, however, it discovered that in purchasing Courage it had bought a can of worms. It certainly contained no potential chairman. The deputy chairman of Imperial Tobacco, the charming, relaxed Malcolm Anson, who had never been in hands-on control of a company, was therefore leap-frogged into the Group chairman's seat.

Imperial Group also had connections with the food industry. Way back in 1969 it had bought the Grimsby-based Ross Foods. It had been founded by the extraordinary Alex Alexander, who, as a medical student, had fled his Czech homeland in 1939 when Nazi tanks rumbled into Prague. He arrived in Britain and went into the food business after the war. Seeing a future in the freezing of fruit and vegetables, he signed up with the fish-freezing firm of Ross and as chairman and chief executive when Imperial bought the firm, went on to become chairman of Imperial Foods.

With Imperial investing more in food and drink, I thought it necessary to tell the company that Allied Lyons was also my client. They saw no immediate and serious conflict of interest for me and Allied took the same view.

John Beckett, the straight talking, formidable chief executive of British Sugar, added to my responsibilities in the food sector. With the Government owning about a third of the shares, BS had lost its protected status when the UK joined the European Community in 1973. Beckett had been brought in to provide effective commercial leadership in 1975. He turned it into the lowest cost sugar producer in Europe and made bulk deals with supermarkets and food manufacturers.

I had got to know him soon after the Tory Election victory in 1979 when he was striving to convince the Government to sell its share holding and free him from officialdom. However, before he could succeed – as he surely would have done with our contacts and his determination – the firm of S.W. Berisford mounted a take-over bid which in 1982 proved successful. Beckett left and became chairman and chief executive of Woolworths, giving it a vital shot in the arm. Sadly, his influence did not last long enough to save the famous chain of stores. They finally closed on the high street to re-launch exclusively on-line, as Britain nose-dived into recession in December 2008.

With my business dealings in the transport sector, I naturally took a close interest in the occupant of the Transport Minister's seat in the Cabinet. In 1983 Mrs Thatcher gave the job to my ex-colleague and successor at Partnerplan, Nicholas Ridley. Based on my knowledge of him, I advised clients that he was not the most diplomatic of men, had a sharp mind that could cut through bullshit and could be expected to support new expansionist projects provided they were financed by the private sector. He quickly infuriated my client, the Society of Motor Manufacturers and Traders, by turning up to their annual motor show in a French car. The British carmakers saw what I meant when I warned that diplomacy was not Ridley's strong point but he went on to please some of my other clients.

He supported the controversial scheme for the Okehampton bypass, allowing it to cut through a national park. To the delight of the BAA, he supported the authority's plan to expand Stansted Airport, despite local opposition. And sharing Mrs Thatcher's enthusiasm, he speeded up the Channel Tunnel project. If my earlier dealings with Ridley at Partnerplan had been edgy, I had some reason to be pleased with his three years at the Transport Department before he was moved on to Environment.

My links with the booze industry convinced me that it would soon face a serious challenge from do-gooders and health campaigners. I forecast that when eventually the anti-smoking brigade had succeeded in ending advertising and sponsorship by tobacco companies and forced them to plaster cigarette packets with a health warning, they would turn their attention to the producers of alcohol. I had made my views known to Michael King of Imperial Group and suggested that we should ask the chairman of Courage Breweries to give some thought to helping Imperial Tobacco in its defensive fight with ASH and the Government.

The drinks industry, I argued, should regard the tobacco industry as a buffer, protecting it from the attentions of the health lobby, and it was therefore in its interests to ensure that the buffer stayed in place for as long as possible. Courage showed some interest but was reluctant to act on its own. Indeed, if it had the effect would have been negligible. It was agreed, therefore, to invite some other drinks companies to a meeting. I persuaded Allied Lyons to attend and, through a contact in Charles Barker, the large brewing group Bass also agreed to participate, represented by chief executive Derek Palmar, who would later become chairman. I was particularly impressed by Palmar, who had gained wider experience of the industry as chairman of the Brewers' Society, and was knighted in 1986.

I enlarged on my theory of tobacco as the buffer zone and when quizzed as to what the drinks industry could do to help, I drew their attention to the running battle in Parliament with the anti-smoking crusaders. Although the tobacco industry could rely on the support of a goodly number of MPs who had constituency links with cigarette factories; trade union links with employees; or who believed in the freedom of people to smoke, I explained that there was at times a numbers problem when it came to votes.

Support from MPs who had breweries and other alcohol producing plants in their constituencies could be very helpful to the tobacco industry in tight-vote situations. All that was needed was that directors of drinks' companies should take the opportunity to explain the problem to their MPs and discreetly suggest that their votes in the Commons could be of help. I concluded by stressing that my experience with the health lobby on tobacco convinced me that it would turn its guns on the drinks industry as soon as it had won its war against the puffers.

I received a polite hearing and an assurance that my suggestion would be considered. Yet I thought I discerned a hint of scepticism on Palmar's broad, friendly face. I later discovered that the booze bosses did not want to get involved with the tobacco war. My warning to the brewers proved to be well founded. By 2007, the President of the Royal College of Physicians was calling for a total ban on alcohol advertising and sponsorship – and higher taxes on liquor.

In my spare time I had long been active in efforts to help refugees from the appalling tyranny of President Ceausescu's Romania, and to assist the build up of an organisation of free Romanian democrats in Britain. My close friend Ion Ratiu was chairman of the British-Romanian Association, a position he had held since 1965 and by the early 1980s he was calling on me more and more for assistance. I had first got to know him in the late 1950s when his wife Elizabeth, who worked with my wife Evelyn at Harrods, brought us together. A refugee from the Nazis and then the Communists who ruled Romania, he was a far-seeing writer on international affairs and a successful businessman. He had started his own shipping line and made a fortune from property deals in London. I felt I had let him down when I failed to join his public protest in 1978 during Ceausescu's state visit to Britain. This disgraceful affair was initially arranged by Harold Wilson before he resigned as Prime Minister.

Ratiu was arrested while leading a protest by dissidents outside Claridge's Hotel. Her Majesty the Queen did not enjoy having to invest the cruel dictator with a knighthood – Grand Cross of the Order of the Bath. As was Ceausescu's habit, he responded by stealing various small items from Buckingham Palace.

Ion, in his Scarlet Pimpernel role, helped many Romanians escape from Ceausescu's clutches and at his own expense provided homes for them in Britain, France and the USA, as well as helping them to find work. In 1983, a case that attracted much attention involved a young man named Stancu Papusoiu who arrived in Britain concealed in a lorry and was therefore an illegal entrant. Within a few days he gave himself up to the police but, without the right to ask for refugee status or political asylum, he was dumped in a remand centre and eventually deported.

The police and Home Office handled his case unsympathetically but with help from Ion and me, the affair was raised in Parliament. In the Lords there was a call for the resignation of the hard-line Home Office Minister David Waddington. Lord Bethell accused him of making a disastrous error that would have tragic consequences for Papusoiu. In the Commons my friend Sir Bernard Braine went into battle in typically robust style. He was concerned not only by this case but also with the broader picture of the way the Home Office handled refugees from Eastern Europe.

In April 1983, I received a letter from officers of the British-Romanian Association thanking me 'for the way in which you have publicly defended our compatriot Stancu Papusoiu during the last few weeks'.

The letter invited me to join the association's Honorary Committee with the flattering words that my name on their notepaper and my prestige would greatly enhance the standing and ability of the association to discharge its tasks effectively. Among those already on the committee were Lord Amulree, Lord Colyton, Lord Henderson, John Biggs-Davison MP and Sir Sacheverall Sitwell. I suggested they should invite Sir Bernard Braine to join and he was pleased to accept.

My head was now well above the parapet as a trouble maker for the Ceausescu regime. The implications became apparent the following year. At Ion Ratiu's request, I handled the media relations for the first World Congress of Free Romanians, held in Geneva in May. It was supported by groups in California, New York, Stuttgart, Lausanne, Melbourne, Paris, Milan and Venezuela. My first press release was headlined: 'Death threats to Free Romanians'. It went on to announce that leading members of the Free Romanian community in Britain and Western Europe who were involved in the Congress, had received threats to themselves and their families: 'A campaign of threatening letters, some posted in London, has clearly been orchestrated by the Communist regime in Romania which is known to be alarmed by plans for the congress aimed to co-ordinate international action to bring about the liberation of the Romanian people'.

It quoted Ion Ratiu who said he had received a death threat himself. The words used were, 'It is easy to hire an Arab to take you out'. The Ceausescu regime had close relations with some Arab states such as Libya. The threat was reported to Scotland Yard and Special Branch became involved. In Paris, another Congress organiser, his wife and daughters were also threatened and the French police became involved. I arranged for my contact the Earl of Lauderdale to ask questions in the Lords about the involvement of the British police in dealing with the threat to Ion.

In Geneva, the Congress agreed to set up the World Union of Free Romanians with Ion as president. When we returned to London, I suggested that he should launch a monthly newsletter to keep in touch with his worldwide membership. He agreed – and immediately asked me to edit it. I could not refuse, but the work would have to be done in my spare time. Ion agreed to hire a professional lay-out man and with his approval, I took on one of the best in England – my old friend from the *Daily Express*, Peter Johnson.

Peter was at that time doing public relations work for Phillips, a leading London firm of auctioneers, and part-time sub-editing for the *Sunday Times*. He was also personal procurer of toy soldiers for billionaire Malcolm Forbes. He was happy to help.

The first issue of the *Free Romanian* newspaper was published in May 1985. One front-page report revealed that Ceausescu's secret service chief Nicolae Plesita, who had been appointed to stamp out Romania's emerging dissident movement, had been sacked. One of the murders planned by the Ceausescu regime was that of a dissident writer in France. He was to have been killed in a manner similar to that of Georgei Markov, a Bulgarian journalist and broadcaster, assassinated on Waterloo Bridge, London in 1978. The murder weapon was an umbrella adapted to fire a tiny pellet containing the poison Ricin, partly developed by Russia's KGB. Markov was a friend of Ratiu's. They both worked for the BBC's Overseas Service and for the Voice of America.

Ceausescu had ordered Ion Ratiu's murder but another of his secret service chiefs, Ion Pacepa, defected to the West and revealed the plan. He exposed many other plots and poisonings in a sensational book about the regime, extracts of which were published in the *Free Romanian*.

Another story on our first front page concerned a visit by Harold Wilson, by then Lord Wilson of Rievaulx, to Ceausescu's nest of thugs in Bucharest. Having arranged the Romanian leader's prestigious presidential visit to London, he was now cashing in the favour. In 1985, Wilson led a delegation of MPs to Bucharest as a director of the import-export company Rindalbourne Ltd., which specialised in trade with Eastern Europe. The company paid for the trip, and to impress Ceausescu that he still had influence in the Commons, Wilson included Deputy Speaker Harold Walker in the team.

Walker was a decent Labour MP who had served as a junior minister, and we often drank together in the Strangers Bar. He told me that after a sumptuous dinner, the Romanians entertained their British visitors with music and song. Not to be outdone by his hosts, the well-oiled Wilson proposed that he and Walker should sing a song together. To Walker's dismay he chose *On Ilkley Moor Baht 'at*. Neither of the Harolds knew all the words and Walker said it had been a very embarrassing episode.

He knew very little of the horrors of the Ceausescu regime and was appalled when I enlightened him. Wilson, however, had been fully informed by the Foreign office over the years. It did not trouble the ex-Labour leader. He was intent on adding his substantial director's fee from Rindalbourne to his large pension and to the payments for attending the House of Lords. Following the visit, his company got a substantial pay-off in the form of a £100 million trade deal with Romania.

The first issue of the six-page paper was well received. I had a copy sent to Wilson, addressed to the House of Lords. I wondered if his conscience would trouble him as he read about the priest languishing under house arrest in Romania for fighting for religious freedom, watched by armed guards; or of the move to force all women of child-bearing age to have monthly gynaecological tests to bully them in to producing more children.

Over the next nine years the *Free Romanian* carried numerous reports based on independent and US intelligence sources. These proved how wrong Wilson and President Nixon had been to regard Romania as the soft underbelly of the Communist bloc. It was as tyrannical as any states ruled by the Kremlins satraps, and to make life worse for its people, it was far more inefficient.

Early in 1985, Sir Bernard Braine phoned to tell me that he intended to table a Commons early day motion to mark the 40th anniversary of the Yalta Agreement. This had been unilaterally broken by the Soviet Union both in letter and spirit within months of being signed. I agreed to read his draft. When it was tabled, it urged the Government to declare its refusal to accept the division of Europe into spheres of influence that had resulted from Yalta and to reaffirm the right of the peoples of Central and Eastern Europe to genuine self-determination. Within a few months it had attracted some 250 signatures from all parties.

Coupled with this, Bernard wrote to Foreign Secretary Sir Geoffrey Howe about human rights violations in Romania. In reply, Howe said that he had taken up the issue on his recent visit to Romania. He had also raised a number of specific cases including that of Father Gheorghe Calciu, whose appalling treatment I had reported in the *Free Romanian* newspaper.

Calciu, who had become a symbol for religious freedom and for those who yearned to be free of the yoke of Communism, was released from prison in Romania in the summer of 1985 in response to a sustained worldwide campaign. He was imprisoned for more than 20 years and recalled being put in a cell with two criminals ordered to beat him up in the hope that this would kill him.

As editor of the *Free Romanian*, coupled with my other activities in support of Romanian dissidents, Ion Ratiu was in no doubt I was on Ceausescu's black list. I avoided shifty-looking men with umbrellas. In fact, I should have paid more attention to the threat from Irishmen with bombs.

October 1984 found me as usual at the Tory Party Conference, this time in Brighton. I had a room in the Metropole Hotel on the seafront. The PM and most of the leading Government and Party bigwigs were next door at the Grand. After a successful Imperial Tobacco dinner party, I wandered into there at about one thirty in the morning on my way back to my hotel. The foyer and bar areas were packed with people but there was no one I particularly wished to speak to and I left without buying a drink.

Upstairs in her suite Mrs Thatcher was working on her big speech for the next day. I went to my room and clambered into bed. About an hour later I was woken by a loud explosion. An IRA bomb had destroyed the centre of the Grand, severely damaging the Thatchers' bathroom but, luckily for the PM and Denis, their sitting room and bedroom were not damaged. Denis had been asleep and the arrival of Mrs Thatcher's private secretary, Robin Butler, had delayed her brushing her teeth.

In the Metropole, the alarm was ringing and I soon heard people running along the corridor, banging on doors and calling people to evacuate the hotel. At first, I was inclined to stay in bed assuming it was a car bomb on the next road. Having lived through part of the Nazi wartime blitz on

London, I was not particularly alarmed by explosions. But the shouts to evacuate were becoming more strident, so I climbed out of bed and started to get dressed. Finishing my tie with the usual Windsor knot, I left the room and walked down the now empty corridor and staircase to the foyer where only a few people stood about. I was apparently one of the last to leave.

Outside I was directed along the road to a nearby square where other guests had gathered and saw a huddle of media people, including Robin Day, in dressing gowns or coats over night clothes. Having taken the trouble to dress, I felt a heady sense of superiority. Now that I knew the Grand had been the target, I also felt relieved that I had not found anyone I wanted to drink with when I called in an hour or so before.

Ambulances and fire engines clanged along the road and the task of rescuing survivors got underway. Five people had been killed including Tory MP Anthony Berry. Later I watched on television as Norman Tebbit was pulled from the rubble, with his wife Margaret who had been seriously injured. The word quickly spread that it was to be business as usual in the conference hall and the PM would make her speech as planned. Marks and Spencers opened early to hand out clothing for those who had lost theirs and one of our lunch guests wore one of their suits.

I tried to phone my wife to reassure her that I was unhurt but all lines were busy. I gave up until later, hoping Evelyn would assume I was not among the killed or injured. She had of course been very anxious and tore me off a strip when I finally got through, telling me I should have made more effort to contact her.

After the Brighton bomb, party conferences were never the same free and easy events, as security experts took over wielding heavy-handed authority. I never really enjoyed them again.

As I thought about the previous evening, I concluded that security arrangements at the headquarters hotel were appallingly lax. I had been able to walk into the crowded foyer late at night completely unchecked and there was no bag or coat search. An IRA terrorist could have placed a bomb in the busy bar and would probably have caused even more carnage than was wrought by waiting for people to go to bed. By comparison, the security arrangements at the conference hall were so tight as to be irksome.

Back at Westminster, I had run into a problem over the chairmanship of the Parliamentary and Scientific Committee. Tory ex- minister David

Price had completed his allotted time in the post and it was the turn of the Labour Party to provide the chairman. Tory MPs far outnumbered Labour members on the committee which made it more difficult to find an appropriate candidate. The most knowledgeable, intelligent and regular Labour member at our meetings was Tam Dalyell. The problem was that many committee members regarded him as unsuitable because of his 'maverick behaviour' in the Commons. His habit of embarrassing ministers by championing off-beat causes led some of our senior members, such as Lord Shackleton, to fear that this so-called 'loose cannon' might embarrass the committee too if he were chairman.

I had great respect for Tam's integrity, independence and bulldog tenacity when he took up a cause. One of his latest was the controversial sinking of the Argentine warship, the *General Belgrano*, during the Falklands war in 1982. Tam had taken every opportunity to harry Mrs Thatcher on the issue to the point where he was embarrassing some on the Labour benches. They suspected that the jingoistic British public thought the Iron Lady was justified in ordering the sinking of the enemy vessel.

Typically, it was Tam who first posed the famous West Lothian question. He had a knack of putting his finger on a fundamentally important issue. In debates in 1977/78 on the Labour Government's proposal to create a Scottish Parliament, Tam, as MP for West Lothian, drew attention to the consequences at Westminster of such a move. He pointed out that as a member for a Scottish seat he would be able to vote on such subjects as education and health that affected England but would not when they affected his constituency because they would be devolved to the separate Scottish Parliament in Edinburgh. Some thirty years later Downing Street had still failed to resolve this constitutional issue. The Blair and Brown Governments relied on the votes of Scottish Labour MPs to get English legislation affecting England through the Westminster Parliament.

I thought Tam would make an excellent chairman of the P&S Committee but I failed to get the necessary support. He eventually became Father of the House, having served longer than any other member, and when he retired I wrote to wish him well. In reply he sent me a copy of my book on the early history of the committee, and asked me to sign it for him. I put in a dedication, 'To the best chairman the P&S never had'.

With Tam ruled out, I decided to give the committee's old guard more reason to huff and puff. Mrs Renée Short was a flame-haired left-winger described by the media as 'Raving red Renée'. I knew her flamboyant style in fighting for left-wing causes would alarm our Tory - and even moderate Labour – members. She had been, however, a most effective chairman of a Commons Select Committee on health and social service issues and she was knowledgeable in that field. Moreover, some of us thought that it was high time the committee elected its first female chairperson.

I had known her since my *Reynolds News* days when I met her at a party with her engineer husband Dr Andrew Stone. She entered the Commons for Wolverhampton North-East in 1964 and with her theatrical make-up and delivery she quickly caught the media's attention. She had Romanian blood from her father, and held the post of treasurer of the British-Romanian Friendship Association. I tried to convince her that Ceausescu was more of a fascist tyrant than a Communist champion of the people but I had no success.

Trevor Skeet was one of the Tories who opposed her election and suggested he should put his own name forward. I told him it was Labour's turn and that if he challenged Renée, he would split the committee and cause me to resign as secretary. He held back but was determined to get the chairmanship next time. Renée did a good job and alerted the committee to the growing threat of AIDS in the community. She was also a leading campaigner against the tobacco industry. When I told her of my link with Imperial Tobacco she rolled her great eyes and said curtly, 'Well Arthur, you know my views. Perhaps you can find someone else to work for?' I promised to let her know if I did.

For years I had regarded the domestic rating system as unfair and had been pleased when Local Government Minister Richard Crossman leaked to me in 1965 that he was considering a local sales tax. In 1974, as Shadow Environment Secretary, Margaret Thatcher had also been interested in this way of raising money for local government. Eventually, however, she agreed with those who argued that variations from one area to another would have made it impossible for such a scheme to work.

As Prime Minister she ordered ministers to search for a solution as local government was blamed for overspending. The worst offender was alleged to be the Greater London Council. Since May 1981 it had been led by the Labour Party under militant left-winger, Ken Livingstone. In 1983 Thatcher had appointed Tom King as Environment Secretary. He had instructions to produce as top priority a plan to deal with the financing problem. It would have to be ready in time to make it into a manifesto commitment for the coming general election. As for 'Red Ken' Livingstone,

Thatcher had made up her mind to deal with him by abolishing the GLC, originally set up by the Tories in 1964.

Patrick Jenkin, who previously served as Social Services Secretary and Industry Secretary, had hoped to be made Chancellor of the Exchequer. Instead, he was given Environment to deal with rates reform and the abolition of the GLC. In 1984 I won back Tesco as a client, having lost it with the break-up of the Addey company. In 1987 the company asked me for suggestions to help bring about changes it required in the Government's proposals for a Uniform Business Rate, which were to be part of a forthcoming bill to reform the general rating system. Tesco's directors, led by Chairman Ian MacLaurin, were impressed by my company's record on dealing with legislation, and in particular that we had been employed twice in the previous three years by the Institution of Professional Civil Servants to win amendments to bills affecting its members. Our most recent success had been in the previous July on behalf of the Federation of the Retail Licensed Trade Northern Ireland where we had won Parliament's support for the Sunday Opening of pubs in Ulster. The Federation's chairman thanked us for 'the fine work in helping to see the legislation through'.

Action on Tesco's behalf to amend the UBR proposals would bring me up against my successor at Partnerplan again, Nicholas Ridley. He had been appointed Environment Secretary following his spell at Transport, and I had attended a fringe meeting at the Tory Party Conference in Blackpool where he had spoken on the issue. There he claimed that, 'Even businesses that stand to lose a bit initially from the move to a UBR should see that our proposals are still greatly in their interests…'

The Tory leadership's manipulation of the party conference debate on rates reform led to much grumbling behind the scenes and many were unhappy about aspects of the Government's proposals. The platform, however, ensured that few critics were called to speak. The conference voted overwhelmingly for a motion in favour of the proposed introduction of the community charge, 'The fairest and most democratic way of reforming local government finance'.

The Community Charge, better known as the Poll Tax, was to lead to rebellion on the Tory backbenchers with MPs under great pressure from unhappy constituents. Opinion polls revealed considerable opposition to it. Its abolition early in 1992 led to much rejoicing and Mrs Thatcher's chosen successor, the underestimated John Major, replaced it with a more acceptable council tax. Major, a working class lad with an aura of decency who extolled the British traditions of warm beer and cricket, went on to beat the unconvincing Neil Kinnock in the General Election on 9th April that year. I was unconvinced by Kinnock and voted Lib Dem. I recalled that about a decade before, Kinnock had been anti-Europe and pro CND. What did he and Labour honestly stand for?

On Monday Oct 21st 1985, John D. Elliott, the flamboyant managing director of an Australian brewing and trading company, Elders IXL, called a press conference in the City of London. It was held to announce his cheeky plan to take over my client Allied Lyons. He planned to cut out the brewing sector, sell off the remainder and sack the 'tired' senior management. It emerged that the buy-out would rely on mostly borrowed funds.

The chairman of Allied, Britain's second largest brewer, was gentlemanly Sir Derrick Holden-Brown. A chartered accountant before entering the drinks business, he joined Allied from Ind Coope in 1953 and succeeded Sir Keith Showering as chairman in 1982. In 1978, Allied bought J. Lyons, famous for its tea shops and Cornerhouse restaurants. But it was clear that the main target for Elders was the beer division and the steadily growing market for lager. Allied's vice chairman was Sir Alex Alexander who some years before had retired as chairman of Imperial Foods. Sir Derrick could not have wished for a tougher, more doughty fighter to have by his side as the takeover battle began. Earlier in the year when an organised share buying operation became apparent, he employed a specialist merchant bank, S.G. Warburg, to marshal the defences.

The main plank of the defence was to convince shareholders that Allied, a solid successful company, had as much and more to offer than the asset-stripping bidder. A campaign was being quietly prepared to have the bid referred to the Monopolies and Mergers Commission (MMC), which would mean dragging out the fight for many months. I was made a member of the Pratt Committee, chaired by Tony Pratt, Allied's hard working investment controller, set up to channel the corporate defence effort. My direct link to the company, John Mills, head of corporate and economic planning with responsibility for public affairs, was also on the committee.

We were lobbying to be referred to the MMC so I suggested that some friendly MPs, with constituency links to Allied, should table an early day motion in the Commons to call for such a move. But Harry Greenway, Tory MP for Ealing North, beat me to it. His constituency had links with

Lyons-Tetley, and he tabled a Commons question that demanded a referral to the MMC, and a statement from Leon Brittan, the Trade and Industry Secretary.

My observation that 'One prefers to have things controlled rather than shooting off in all direction' was quoted by a *Financial Times* reporter, Christopher Parkes. In strict secrecy, he had been invited by Holden-Brown as 'a fly on the wall', taking notes of the committee's proceedings for a four-part report carried in his newspaper from September 24th 1986. It was an extraordinary arrangement to have made. Parkes wrote an amusing account of the meetings with quotes from members who did not realise they were being reported. It was part of the strategy that Allied was not to be seen attempting to get a referral to the MMC.

I suggested that managers of local companies should write to their constituency MPs and reported back that there was evidence of support. I provided lists of ministers and MPs who could be expected to be helpful. There were about 100 MPs who had constituency links with the company. Then there were others with an interest, such as trade union MPs, Opposition spokesmen, members of specialist and select committees, and over twenty with ministerial responsibilities.

When it came to involving the unions, Holden-Brown was uneasy. But I argued that Labour Party shadow ministers would be bound to consult the unions – as would Labour MPs with constituency links. Therefore it would be advisable for the Allied management to talk directly to the leaders of unions that would be affected. My views were duly reported in the *FT*. Holden-Brown took my advice and a useful lunch was arranged with trade union officials.

Holden-Brown also talked to Government ministers. I had been talking to my friend and fellow Imperial consultant Roy Mason, MP for Barnsley, which had an Allied-Lyons cake factory on the outskirts of the town. He wanted to take some action and I suggested he should table an early day motion attacking the Elders' bid. Drafted by me, it noted with concern the offer from Elders 'whose assets are less than a quarter of those of Allied Lyons'. It also expressed alarm at the possible threat to jobs by a break-up of the successful food and drink group, and called on the Department of Trade and Industry to consider not only competition, but other issues such as the high level of borrowing that would be required by the bidder, and the asset stripping nature of this short term financial operation. It was tabled in November 1985 and quickly drew support from other Labour MPs.

On December 7th 1985, a front page report in the *Financial Times* announced that the Government had referred the £1.8 billion bid from Elders to the Monopolies and Mergers Commission. This would block the Elders' bid for six months – the time the Commission had been given to report. Allied put it to good use. When the Commission gave the go-ahead for Elders to advance, Allied was about to complete its £400 million purchase of a controlling stake in the Canadian drinks company Hiram Walker Spirits. Together with share price increases, this raised to well over £2 billion the probable purchase price of Allied-Lyons. Elders went to find a less expensive way into Britain's booze industry – a route linked to another report on the front page that Saturday.

The report which was the main story above that of Allied Lyons, announced, 'Hanson Trust, the fast-growing industrial holding company headed by Lord Hanson, last night launched a £1.9 billion take-over bid for Imperial Group, the brewing, tobacco and food concern'.

No sooner had the immediate threat been removed from Allied than my major client, Imperial Group, was faced with a battle for survival. Even before this, it had run into serious management problems. Following its disappointing purchase of Courage, it had made an even worse investment in its efforts to diversify - the American hotel chain, Howard Johnson. In 1981, a boardroom coup pushed out the easy-going Malcolm Anson – and replaced him with Geoffrey Kent as chairman. He had displayed high-level managerial skill by turning the Courage mess into a success. Also, he had done a good job in charge of one of the group's tobacco companies so his management experience was ideal. Unfortunately, he lacked any understanding of the field of public affairs – and this was to prove a serious weakness. The all too relaxed Robin Haydon was in charge of that area.

The buccaneering asset-stripper Lord Hanson had made Britain's biggest take-over bid – just four days after Imperial had announced an agreed bid of £1.22 billion for United Biscuits. The Imperial Board immediately rejected the Hanson offer and Geoffrey Kent turned down a request for a meeting with Hanson. Like Allied, Imperial had always been on the bidding end in the past and did not know instinctively how to deal with the situation. Unlike Allied, it was not led by someone with the calm, gentlemanly qualities of Sir Derrick Holden-Brown, who had advised that restraint was a prime quality needed in any company confronting an aggressor. 'Always behave with dignity', he had counselled.

Once again I found myself on a defence committee, but this time the threatened company was less well organised. On the political front Geoffrey Kent had not bothered to cultivate politicians, whom he seemed to view with contempt. Through Robin Haydon, I had offered in the past to arrange functions with ministers and MPs but had been repeatedly turned down on the grounds that Kent was too busy. His view of this aspect of his responsibilities was very different from that of Andrew Reid, chairman of Imperial Tobacco. Reid encouraged the company to have an active parliamentary liaison programme and had asked me to arrange meetings between him and potential high-flyers in the Commons. Like his predecessor Tony Garrett, he had offered me a full-time job with Imperial.

In 1985 / 86 Hanson Trust had reached its zenith. Lord Hanson appeared to have refined a strategy that was virtually invincible. He was about the same age as the sixty-three year old Geoffrey Kent, and was good-looking, charming, well dressed and, in the past, something of a ladies' man. Kent lost no time in launching a war of words against Hanson. Things turned dirty. He pointed out that Hanson had not revealed any concrete plans for the future of Imperial, its business or employees. Indeed, he had been quoted as saying that his experience in brewing and tobacco was 'zero'. There was, Kent insisted, no industrial logic whatsoever in a link between Imperial and Hanson. He urged shareholders to reject the unwanted bid and to vote for the merger of Imperial with United Biscuits.

On the political front, virtually all the activity was with the MP contacts I had built up and nurtured for Imperial Tobacco. At one stage, Robin told me that the rattled and desperate Kent had snapped, 'Haven't we any politician friends?' I replied that we had plenty, thanks to tobacco, and that Kent had shown no past interest in having allies in Parliament. The reality was that Robin had failed miserably with his half-hearted efforts to involve Kent in a rolling programme of meetings with useful parliamentarians.

On January 14th 1986, a friendly contact of mine, Simon Coombs, Tory MP for Swindon, helpfully tabled a Commons early day motion. Noting the Hanson bid with concern, and believing it raised questions of public interest about employment, it urged the Government to refer it to the Monopolies and Mergers Commission. Other friends of mine, such as Labour's David Marshall and Michael Martin (the future Speaker of the Commons), were among the six sponsors.

More of my friends added their names, including Roy Mason and future minister Nick Brown on the Labour side and Charles Morrison and Nicholas Winterton from the Tories. *The Observer* covered the story. Then on February 13th, *The Times* carried the bad news that Trade and Industry Secretary Paul Channon had cleared Hanson's bid and referred Imperial's agreed merger with United Biscuits to the Monopolies and Mergers Commission!

He had accepted the opinion of the Office of Fair Trading whose director general Gordon Borrie was my old friend from Central London Fabian Society days. The OFT view was that there were no competition reasons for referring the Hanson bid but that a combined Imperial / UB would control about forty-five per cent of the British market in snacks and crisps. *The Times* reported that the forty-two MPs who had signed the Commons motion were unhappy with the decision.

Then a row exploded in the Commons as Opposition MPs accused the Government of rewarding Hanson for providing it with a helping hand over the Westland take-over affair, by bidding over the odds for a fifteen per cent stake in the helicopter firm. His intervention had allowed the American Sikorsky camp to beat off the competing bid by a European consortium.

Four Commons motions accusing the Government of unequal and unfair treatment of the competing Hanson and UB bids for Imperial Group were supported by an open letter to the PM from Liberal leader David Steel. The Government, he said, should review its policy on mergers 'which lacked stability and predictability'. Shadow Trade Minister Bryan Gould said 'the incoherence and incompetence of the Government's competition policy passes all belief'.

I had to admit that I thought Gordon Borrie's OFT had no option but to rule as it did. The Westland affair was about whether the firm should join Sikorsky (Mrs Thatcher's preference) or the European consortium of arms manufacturers (the option favoured by Defence Secretary Michael Heseltine). The dispute led to Heseltine's abrupt resignation, alleging a breakdown of Cabinet Government, followed by that of Trade and Industry Secretary Leon Brittan.

Without the protection of a referral to the MMC, Imperial Group lost the battle and Hanson took over. His sharp-eyed team of accountants were soon moving in to prepare for the selling off of assets not required by their boss. He kept Imperial Tobacco because of its useful money flow and the remainder was sold off. This included Courage, which was bought for £1.4 billion by Elders, to give it the place in Britain's brewing industry it had failed to win from Allied-Lyons.

After stirring up so much political trouble for the Hanson camp, I expected to get my marching orders. But his lordship's henchmen decided to give me the opportunity to show what I could do for them and I was retained. Andrew Reid, chairman of Imperial Tobacco since 1979, lost his job at the age of 56.

In March 1988, headlines announced that United Biscuits had bought the Ross Young frozen foods operation from Hanson for £335 million – only two years after Hanson had foiled UB's attempt to acquire it as part of the plan to merge with Imperial Group, the owner at the time.

It marked a further stage in the Hanson carve-up of the old Imperial empire, replenishing Hanson's coffers by almost as much as he had paid out two years before. Since winning the bitter £2.6 billion battle, Hanson had sold Courage Breweries and its pubs to Elders IXL of Australia for £1.4 billion; the hotel and restaurant interests to Trusthouse Forte for £190 million; Golden Wonder to Dalgety for £87 million; and Finlays, the newsagents, for £17 million. He retained Imperial Tobacco and some food interests. The dismemberment was a classic Hanson exercise in not over-paying for an acquisition and then selling the parts for more than the sum of the whole. What an operator!

In the midst of the Imperial take-over battle I suddenly found myself dragged into a motor industry struggle. In February 1986, news broke that the whole of vehicle manufacturer British Leyland was up for sale. The giant American company, General Motors, was the favourite to take over the commercial vehicle sector including famous Land Rover. Trade and Industry Secretary Paul Channon, in an emergency statement to the Commons, confirmed GM's interest and revealed that Ford was interested in the car business, which included the prestige line Jaguar.

Partly because of my reputation as the political consultant to the SMMT and as secretary of the All-Party Motor Industry Group, the Americans decided to employ Charles Barker to assist their bid. Ford did not object. I quickly set up a busy programme of meetings with key MPs for members of the GM team and it became known that the sale to the Americans had been approved by the Cabinet's economic committee – and that Mrs Thatcher was in favour. At one time that would have settled the matter. But Cabinet Minister Norman Fowler, Health and Social Services Secretary, was not on the economic committee and, as MP for Sutton Coldfield, he represented part of the car-making West Midlands.

There was a sudden upsurge of national feeling and flag waving about Land Rover. Behind the scenes a compromise deal was put to GM offering them forty-nine per cent of Leyland's commercial vehicle business. Fowler expressed his concern to Mrs Thatcher and threatened to resign if the deal went through. He knew he had a strong hand as Mrs Thatcher was shaken by the resignation of two Cabinet ministers over Westland. Fed up with the continued haggling, GM broke off the talks and their high-powered team prepared to return to the US. Before departing, they thanked me profusely for my lobbying efforts on their behalf.

In my other main area of transport activity, Britain's airports, I soon understood why Peter Sanguinetti, BAA's public affairs director, had recruited me. I was to serve his chairman, the exacting Norman Payne, whom the *Financial Times* described as the 'grand master of the British aero-political scene'. Payne, knighted in 1985, was an experienced engineer and had started with BAA as its director of engineering. He had a reputation for being tough but from the start I enjoyed a good relationship with him as his political consultant – one built, I hope, on mutual respect. When I joined his team, he had some major, highly political tasks ahead.

When I was taken on in the autumn of 1983 I was told that my main task was to win support from MPs and peers for the development of Stansted Airport. It had to be expanded to cope with a phenomenal growth in traffic but BAA's plans, including the construction of a much-needed new terminal, were controversial. They were opposed by well-organised residents in this green and pleasant area who did not want their lives disrupted and their peace disturbed.

I spent much time ferrying MPs out of London and along the M11 to inspect the site. The success of the lobbying campaign was reflected not only in the final Commons vote on the issue but also in a MORI poll of MPs. This revealed that in 1983, only thirty-one per cent of them believed that Stansted should be developed but by the summer of 1985 support had gone up to fifty-nine per cent.

Heathrow airport, the BAA's flagship, which was becoming the world's busiest international airport, also had to be expanded. And looming on the horizon was the privatisation of the Authority, to be accomplished in 1987. This was helped by the fact that our lobbying campaign had done much to improve BAA's image in Parliament. In 1983 only thirty-one per cent of MPs had a mainly favourable opinion of the airport Authority, but by summer 1985 this had risen to fifty-seven per cent.

As if BAA had not got enough on its plate, it was also involved in an irritating running battle with British Airways led by business world bruiser,

Sir John King. One of Margaret Thatcher's favourite businessmen, King had taken on the chairmanship of the loss-making state-owned airline in 1981. In a ruthless efficiency drive, he had cut staff by some 15,000 in two years, sold off surplus aircraft and turned the failing business into a profitable success by 1983.

As head of the 'world's favourite airline', he then embarked on a series of battles with competitors, ministers and anyone who refused to be trampled on. The last category included Norman Payne, with whom he clashed over the allocation of precious space at airports. To assist him in his political fights, he hired a parliamentary consultant named Ian Greer who was subsequently caught up in the cash for questions scandal.

By 1985, Charles Barker Watney & Powell (CBWP) strengthened its claim as Britain's premier parliamentary consultancy and announced that its impressive client list included eighteen of Britain's top one hundred industrial companies. A MORI poll around that time revealed that MPs regarded the company as the most effective in the business – and the best known at Westminster.

To help win friends in Parliament for BAA – and to counter BA's free flights – Peter Sanguinetti had the bright idea of offering MPs and peers free parking at the airports. In launching this initiative, he consulted me and his MP consultant Jack Aspinwall, the street-wise Tory member for first Kingswood and then Wansdyke. We had both got to know Jack through the tobacco industry as he had constituents who worked at the Imperial factory in Bristol. Unlike some MP consultants, Jack worked at it and made an important contribution. He was a popular member of the Commons and this was underlined after he injured himself in a MPs parachute drop to raise money for a charity.

Confined to a hospital bed, he had many visitors. To put the time to good use, he asked them all to think of anecdotes which he compiled into a book called *Kindly Sit Down – Best After Dinner stories from both Houses of Parliament*. It was published in 1983, with a foreword by Margaret Thatcher. She quoted the American politician Adlai Stevenson who said of one presidential candidate that in the course of his speeches, he succeeded in 'passing the 49th platitude'. I was pleased that the Airey Neave memorial trust benefited from its sales.

My friend Neil Marten's contribution to the book told of his experience when conducting a group of constituents around the Houses of Parliament. When he reached the lobby of the House of Lords he was confronted by the

Lord Chancellor, Lord Hailsham, in all his magnificent regalia. On seeing him Hailsham called out 'Neil!' at which the constituents, misinterpreting the cry, fell upon their knees. The book was so successful that Jack followed it with two others *Hit Me Again* and *Tell Me Another*.

The free parking passes for politicians eventually became unpopular with some BAA shareholders, following its privatisation. A group wanted the airport to declare the passes as political donations, which would then have to be approved by shareholders. BAA argued that as they were given to politicians of all parties, the passes were not political donations. By 2004 they were being supplied to 847 MPs, MEPs and peers. The normal cost of a four year pass was £5,245. At the annual general meeting in July that year, the company won the argument. If the company had not provided such a perk, the bill for these politicians' travel expenses would have been picked up by the taxpayer.

Long before that, Peter Sanguinetti left BAA to become director of corporate communication at British Gas in 1991. Norman Payne retired as BAA chairman in the same year after a quarter of a century of considerable achievement as chief executive and chairman. He had seen the number of passengers passing through the group's airports soar from twelve million to seventy two million and had built six new terminals and a new runway to cope with them. He was replaced by a man I had known in the motor industry – John Egan of Ford and Jaguar, who appreciated the role of public relations and lobbying.

As for John King, his lack of scruples and cut throat methods in running BA eventually ended in disaster after Richard Branson's Virgin Airlines were given permission to operate from Heathrow in 1991. King, already angered by Branson's success in getting some of BA's London-Tokyo routes transferred to Virgin, flew into a fury. He made it known to some of his PR team that he wanted something done about Branson.

King's public relations consultant was a friend from John Addey days, Brian Basham. Having helped me to challenge Addey, he had founded his own highly successful PR firm. Brian later revealed that he advised King to stop reacting and not to allow his vanity to be pricked. This was good advice that King failed to heed. Some of his subordinates went to great lengths to damage Virgin's business in what became known as the 'dirty tricks' campaign. Branson took out a libel action against BA and King, who countersued. A court found in favour of Branson and BA had to pay £500,000 in damages and costs of around £3 million. With that shadow over his reputation, King retired soon after as chairman.

British Airways' public relations director was a tough, blunt Ulsterman, David Burnside, who argued that wooing over fifty MPs with first class up-grades and free flights was no different from a free lunch when visiting a ball-bearings factory.

Brian Basham won libel damages of £20,000 in the High Court in 1996 over a book that described him as 'a peddler of lies' in his role as former public relations adviser to BA. He said the verdict cleared him of allegations that he was a central player in the campaign against Virgin Atlantic. Bursting with energy, he founded several financial PR companies and in the 1980s was known as the 'best bid man around'. He was so successful that he even won business because some companies hired him to prevent him working for a predator. After the John Addey years, he invited me to work for him. I was flattered, but declined. I had other plans…

CHAPTER SIX
Not the Retiring Type

On flying into Beijing with my nine-strong group of parliamentarians and scientists, I soon suspected that the Chinese Government was using us for a trial run for the forthcoming visit of the Queen and Prince Philip in 1986. We were accommodated in a mansion in the same spacious garden compound that contained the small Chinese-style palace built for the royal couple. The walled complex of government guesthouses dotted among lakes and streams was known as 'The Anglers' Rest'.

The delegation from the Parliamentary and Scientific Committee should have been led by the committee's president, the respected Labour peer and industrialist Lord Gregson, who knew China well. Sir Trevor Skeet, however, having achieved his ambition of becoming chairman, belligerently insisted that, as the Commons was the senior democratic chamber of Parliament, he should lead. Faced by this typically pushy behaviour by Skeet, Lord Gregson withdrew from the visit.

Renée Short, as previous chairperson, was also in the delegation, and insisted that as she was the only woman, her husband should join her. The most important member of our team was Sir John Mason, recently retired as director general of the Meteorological Office and permanent UK representative at the World Meteorological Organisation. He was highly regarded by the Chinese who paid great attention to his expert advice on climate. Relaxed, charming and good-humoured, he was an entertaining travelling companion. Another agreeable scientist in the party was Professor Gareth Jones of the Association of Applied Biologists. From the House of Lords came Lord Ironside and Lord Kennet, better known as Wayland Young, the author and journalist with a deep interest in environmental and ecological issues.

We were the guests of an important Chinese committee that linked top scientists with Government. We had forged this connection on the advice of Lord Rhodes, Knight of the Garter and former Labour MP. A First World War fighter pilot ace, he had been a Board of Trade Minister and had led several trade delegations to China. I agreed with his shrewd assessment of China's importance in the future and we won the argument against those in the committee who said we should instead forge a link with Japan.

A fleet of limousines whisked our delegation to important centres of scientific research, industrial sites and major universities. On the cultural front, our itinerary was similar to that being arranged for the Queen. We visited the fabulous Forbidden City in Beijing, the Ming Tombs, the Great Wall and the ancient city of Xian, one time capital of eleven dynasties. From there we drove to see the incredible terracotta army, which had come to light only a dozen years before. Estimated to number some eight thousand warriors, they stand in serried ranks in three great chambers, guarding the tomb of the first emperor of China, Qin Shihuang, ruthless founder of the Qin Dynasty.

As we looked down on the life-size terracotta figures carrying swords, spears and bows or riding horses and chariots, I heard the sharp voice of Sir Skeet, as he was called by the Chinese. He asked a question that revealed he had misunderstood the detailed explanation given by our guide. He thought the figures were mummified humans. Sir Trevor's howlers and gaffes gave our delegation a laugh a day.

There were banquets galore, featuring succulent sea slugs, Peking duck and other local delicacies, washed down with Chinese wine or beer. Sir Richard Evans, the British Ambassador to Beijing, hosted a dinner in the embassy which had been newly decorated for the Queen's visit. He compared well with some other diplomats with whom I had dealt.

One of our last visits was made to China's space rocket centre. It looked primitive compared to the massively funded US space headquarters. A few years later I was pleased to meet Chinese students studying space travel technology at a British university. China was determined to catch up with the United States and Russia in this important field. In September 2008 a Chinese astronaut was to make his first space walk in the emerging superpower's ambitious space programme.

As we drove through Beijing, we often passed through the enormous Tiananmen Square. Five times larger than Moscow's Red Square and capable of holding a million people, Tiananmen was to become known not only for its size, but for the Government's merciless suppression of a great student rally that demanded political and other reforms. After the death of China's dictator Mao Zedong in 1976, the restrictions on economic activity were loosened by his successor Deng Xiaoping and we witnessed the result of this important liberalisation during our visit. But in the fields of culture and politics, progress was much slower and so in the spring of 1989, the students gathered in the great square to voice their criticism of the regime and call for action.

At the end of nine full days, my delegation and the Chinese signed an agreement I had drafted. It covered arrangements for regular return visits, exchanges of information and advice, and assistance with conferences and student training. Our visit had convinced me that we were right in forging the link with China. It had such enormous potential as well as the biggest untapped market in the world. Hopefully, we played some small part in ensuring that Britain would have a role in serving that market.

Back in London, not realising just how quickly the anti-democratic crackdown would come in China, I told friends that this was a good time to go. I warned, however, that central control was still so great that in a short time this opening up process could be reversed. Before leaving Beijing, we agreed that members of the Chinese committee should visit London in about two years' time. In due course, following the Tiananmen Square horror, I had to find a diplomatic excuse for postponing that visit when the Chinese Embassy in London reminded me of the agreement.

The activities of some clumsy 'cowboy' lobbyists at Westminster were getting the profession a bad name. They had been encouraged to move into the business by media reports of high fees earned from successful campaigns. Yet when a director of Charles Barker asked me to sit on a subcommittee on standards of the Public Relations Consultants' Association, I did so reluctantly. From my past experience I did not hold the PRCA in very high esteem. It was put to me, justifiably, however, that this was an opportunity to improve the organisation from inside. The PRCA then asked me to write a booklet on the *Do's and Don't's* of lobbying. I was very busy so agreed to take it on if another experienced lobbyist on the committee would write some of the chapters. He was Douglas Smith, the managing director of Political Communications, and in business with my Tory MP friend, Peter Fry.

In July 1986 our booklet *Lobbying in the British Parliament* was launched at a reception in the Commons. It was sponsored by Tory MP Sir Geoffrey Johnson-Smith, chairman of the Select Committee on Members' Interests.

He was a former minister and breezy ex-television presenter. Years before, he had been employed by the PR consultancy that was turned down by the Corporation of the City of London for having an MP on the staff – John Addey Associates was awarded the account.

In our booklet, we complained that while political consultants played a valuable role in industry, commerce and local government, this was not recognised by either Parliament or the press. Back on my old theme, I wrote:

> 'A consultancy providing a daily information service on parliamentary developments to around a hundred commercial clients and public bodies is fulfilling a communications' role as important as some of the popular daily newspapers. Yet while such newspapers are allowed to be registered at the Houses of Parliament, the consultancy receives no recognition and is provided with no privileges'.

We argued for greater access to parliamentary documents for properly established public affairs consultancies. Politicians of all parties attended our launch, including the Leader of the Commons John Biffen for whom I had considerable respect. A courteous, thoughtful man, he had fallen out of favour with Margaret Thatcher several times. Before he became a popular Leader of the House, he served as Treasury Chief Secretary and Secretary for Trade and as MP for Shropshire North he was a good parliamentarian. I was flattered that he had found time to attend.

The previous year *The Sunday Times* reported that Johnson-Smith's Select Committee on Members' Interests was to look into political lobbying, and the involvement of MPs as paid advisers to pressure groups. It would focus on whether the voluntary code for MPs, disclosing outside income and interests, was working effectively and whether the increasing behind-the-scenes activities of lobbyists needed to be controlled. It then gave several examples of lobbyists who had recently helped pressure groups and companies to put their case in Parliament. It reported: 'The Law Society which fought against Labour MP Austin Mitchell's bill to break the solicitors' monopoly on conveyancing employed a former Fleet Street Lobby correspondent Arthur Butler, who works for an international PR firm, Charles Barker Lyons'.

I had received some publicity for this assignment as, unwisely, I had jokingly told a large meeting of solicitors that it was in their interests that as few MPs as possible should be in the Commons on the Friday the bill was due to be debated. I advised them, therefore, that they should invite their local constituency member to a good lunch that day if they suspected he or she might support the redoubtable Austin. I should have known better than to try to raise a laugh. Some humourless trouble-maker reported to Austin's camp that I had encouraged solicitors to bribe MPs with a free lunch so that they would stay away from Parliament. There was a pompous claim that I was guilty of a breach of privilege. The affair was so ridiculous that it quickly fizzled out.

When the Johnson-Smith committee reported in 1985, I was disappointed that it rejected proposals for a formal register of professional parliamentary lobbyists. It concluded, wrongly in my view, a register would raise 'formidable' problems of definition and enforcement and would probably fail in its purpose 'to identify those persons and companies lobbying for financial reward and those for whom they acted'. Sir Geoffrey Johnson-Smith made clear in his personal comments, however, that he regarded proper, disclosed lobbying as a fully justifiable and acceptable practice.

Some members of the Press Gallery, perhaps envious of our more civilised lives, better pay and shorter hours, had been sniping at lobbyists. Therefore, I derived some satisfaction when the committee recommended that journalists, researchers and others working full time in Parliament should register their commercial interests to prevent abuse of their privileged access to MPs and valuable parliamentary documents.

The Leslie Hale Luncheon Club drank a hearty toast to his success when Charlie Douglas-Home was appointed editor of *The Times* in 1982. He had been one of the earliest members and a regular participant. Since our days on the *Daily Express*, however, he had suffered health problems and within a year of occupying the Editor's chair at *The Times*, he was warned that his medical condition was serious. Like others who had occasional contact with him, I did not realise that his health was so gravely undermined.

I was deeply saddened to learn of his death from cancer in October 1985. He was forty-eight. When I had last seen him a year before, he was confined to a wheel chair and had joked that it was the result of falling off a horse. The Prince of Wales and other members of the Royal Family, together with the Prime Minister, headed a congregation of over a thousand at a memorial service for Charlie at St. Paul's Cathedral in the month after his death. By then, the Leslie Hale Luncheon Club had also died, following the death of Leslie himself in May that year. He had been given a new lease of life by its foundation. It also helped that he had received a life peerage in 1972, after I had suggested to Michael Foot that he deserved one. Despite his disapproval of the Upper House, Michael persuaded Harold Wilson to put his name forward.

Endlessly under siege by the anti-smoking lobby, in 1985 the tobacco industry decided to appoint an expert PR specialist from outside the industry to head a public relations fight back. Clive Turner, dapper and courteous but dogged, joined the staff of the Tobacco Advisory Council (TAC). As a member of the Magic Circle, he used his sorcerer's skill to persuade the manufacturing companies to enter into debate with the uncompromising health crusaders who posed an increasing threat to all who valued the freedom to smoke. Tirelessly and calmly, he argued the case for moderation on radio, television and in interviews for the press. Nonplussed by his balance and good manners, his extremist opponents were often reduced to vituperative and vulgar abuse.

Other anti-smoking campaigners, perhaps not sufficiently intelligent to muster an argument against him, sent him packets of excrement, used condoms and other filth. Understandably, such vile tactics eventually began to wear down even the unflappable Clive. A year after his appointment, he convinced the TAC that they needed to strengthen the industry's parliamentary lobbying by employing their own professional political consultant to reinforce those employed by individual member companies.

Following the departure of Peter Sanguinetti to join the BAA, Trevor King, a neat and exacting young man, took on the job of public affairs manager at Imperial Tobacco. He had been involved with me in the Hanson take-over battle and like me, had been kept on by the victorious buccaneer. In 1986, he asked me if I would be interested in working for the industry's trade association. I said that I would be delighted but assumed I could not work both for a member company – Imperial - and for the TAC as this could be a conflict of interest. Trevor brushed this aside with the cheerful advice that I need not worry about it. He added that I was the best in the business and he would put my name forward. Clive Turner, as chief executive of the TAC, provided the most thorough outline of a potential client's requirements I had ever received and armed with that, I beat two rival companies to win the account.

As the work would mean covering the Westminster and European parliaments, it was the largest account ever to be won for Charles Barker

Watney & Powell. I explained that it was not my practice to argue a client's case with parliamentarians but to set up opportunities for them to do so themselves. I quickly produced a rolling programme of working lunches, meetings and presentations for MPs with constituency, trade union and other links with the manufacturers which went well. I set to work to put pressure on Chancellor of the Exchequer Nigel Lawson to cut, or at least freeze, tax on tobacco products in his next Budget. He gave a friendly reception to a deputation of Tory MPs with constituency interests that I organised. This was led by the helpful Jim Lester (Broxtowe) who served as a junior Employment Minister for two years before Mrs Thatcher decided he was 'too wet'. Lawson puffed a cigar as he listened to their pleas. In support, a Commons early day motion had been signed by some fifty MPs of all parties.

The TAC was delighted with the activity and even more pleased when the Chancellor announced a freeze on tobacco duty in his 1986 Budget. It was the first time for years that there had not been an increase in tax. At a working lunch for Labour MPs soon after, an experienced Northeast parliamentarian Ted Garrett, who knew of my work in other fields, suggested that the industry should ask me to set up an all-party parliamentary committee for the tobacco industry. The companies' liked the proposal so I went in search of two MPs to act as joint Labour and Tory chairmen. My choice for the Tory was Jack Aspinwall. He had a constituency link in the outer Bristol area with Imperial Tobacco and I knew he was sufficiently down to earth and popular to co-operate with a Labour MP. My choice from the Labour benches was Michael Martin who had a tobacco factory in his Glasgow constituency and was one day to be elected Speaker of the House of Commons.

The new committee was to be different from the others for which I had provided a secretariat. Since tobacco was increasingly controversial at Westminster, I decided not to make it a registered committee of Parliament but to run it as an unofficial body that would hold its private gatherings in hostelries outside the Palace of Westminster. It soon began to show results and when the next Budget loomed, I drafted an early day motion to be tabled by Jack and Michael. It recalled with satisfaction the Chancellor's decision to freeze tobacco tax in his previous Budget, and acknowledged the beneficial effect on the Retail Price Index. It also noted that the UK tobacco industry was able to contain the growth of cheap, imported cigarettes. Calling for a repetition, it attracted the signatures of fifty-two

MPs. Among the thirty-four Tories who signed were six knights of the shires and fifteen Labour supporters included future Prime Minister Tony Blair. The Liberals were represented by their future Party leader Paddy Ashdown.

In arranging these tobacco functions for politicians I successfully sought to invite not only ministers, but senior backbenchers such as chairmen of the 1922 Committee of all Tory MPs, and the chairmen of the Parliamentary Labour Party. Their presence at lunches, dinners and receptions in London or at party conferences, gave younger less experienced MPs the confidence to attend functions and support our cause. On the Tory side, I succeeded in winning the regular attendance of two 1922 Committee chairmen in quick succession – Sir Cranley Onslow (1984-92) and Sir Marcus Fox (1992 -97).

The charming Cranley, related to the Earls of Onslow and descended from three Commons Speakers, used his low profile, discreet style to exercise his considerable influence. Middle class Marcus, with his blunt Yorkshire style, was much more outspoken in his support for the tobacco industry and let us all know that we could rely on him to help us. If we had a motion on the Commons *Order Paper* urging the Government to cut tobacco tax, he would make it clear to Tory MPs at our events that he expected them to support it.

Another important Tory supporter was Sir William Clark (later Lord Clark of Kempson) a specialist in finance and taxation. He was never a minister, but he wielded great influence behind the scenes. Serving as chairman of the key Tory backbench Finance Committee from 1979 to 1992, he used his position to caution the Chancellor against damaging increases in tobacco tax. He had forged an early link with the tobacco industry when he won the Nottingham South seat in 1959 and had many constituents who worked in the nearby Imperial cigarette factory. He later represented East Surrey and then Croydon South. A strong supporter of Mrs Thatcher's economic policies, he enjoyed easy access to the Treasury. His jokey nature was reflected in his membership of the All-Party NAAFI Club – 'No aims, ambitions or fucking inhibitions'.

Despite such influential support, tax on tobacco was raised regularly by chancellors looking for easy revenue. This had serious effects on employment in the industry and also on health, as the importation of cheap low-grade foreign cigarettes was facilitated by the growing gap in price between British and Continental brands. Among chairmen of the

Parliamentary Labour Party who regularly attended our functions was the former teacher Jack Dormand, later Lord Dormand of Easington, a much-respected PLP chairman from 1981 – 87. Roy Mason, who had helped me acquire the Coalfield Communities' account, now had a bright idea. A pipe-smoker himself, he suggested that I should set up a Lords and Commons Pipesmokers' Club on behalf of the tobacco industry. The TAC and member companies liked the proposal and, with Roy's assistance, I wrote to all MPs and peers known to be pipe smokers. When a good number said they would join, it was set up with Roy as the convenor. I was soon involved in a programme of visits to pipe-makers, museums and other collections of pipe smokers' artefacts. Twenty years later it had a membership of over one hundred which numbered former Commons Speaker Baroness (Betty) Boothroyd.

The word got around Parliament that the club was a 'good thing' and membership grew steadily. My idea to hold a club lunch on national No Smoking Day in March, with a photo-call, proved a popular annual event with the club's leading characters lighting up amid a haze of smoke. Another fixture I introduced was a lunch on Raleigh Day in October in honour of Sir Walter Raleigh, who had been executed in that month in 1618 by King James 1st. He introduced pipe smoking to England where it became fashionable at the court of Queen Elizabeth. Although not connected with Raleigh's death sentence, King James was one of the first anti-smoking fanatics.

The pipe club became such a success that when it had built up a membership of over forty the tobacco industry decided to open up membership to cigar smokers. The club's numbers swiftly soared towards the hundred, new members being mostly Tory MPs and peers – but Roy Mason continued as convenor.

Arranging tobacco industry events for ministers and backbenchers at party conferences brought me into close contact with a wide range of MPs. Two of these were the Morrison brothers, so unlike that no one would have thought they had the same parents. Their father was the formidable John Morrison, chairman of the Tory 1922 Committee from 1955 to 1964. His activities at the 1963 Tory Conference, where I was a political reporter, alerted me to the top level moves to ensure that Alec Douglas-Home would replace Macmillan as Prime Minister.

Peter Morrison (Eton and Oxford) was an Opposition Whip faithfully serving Mrs Thatcher when I first got to know him. A tough, intolerant right-winger, his temper became shorter the longer he drank. If we had a guest of whom he disapproved – such as a pro-Europe MP - he would stare belligerently at them and mutter in my ear, 'What a bloody wet! Why did you invite him Arthur?'

His ambition was to be Mrs Thatcher's Chief Whip but, in view of his well-known heavy fist, she wisely gave the job to someone less pugnacious. Instead, he served her at the Department of Employment and then at Trade and Industry before becoming Energy Minister in 1987. Valuing his great personal loyalty and ability to keep his ear to the ground, Mrs Thatcher made him her parliamentary private secretary in her last reshuffle as the storm clouds gathered threatening her leadership. He failed her in this key role. He did not keep closely in touch with events and under-estimated the strength of Michael Heseltine's challenge for the party leadership in November 1990.

Peter's brother, Charles (Eton, Cambridge and the Guards) was some twelve years older and went on to outlive him by another twelve. To Peter's dismay, Charles was the wettest wet of all, opposed to Thatcher's leadership and never achieving a ministerial position. Unlike bulky Peter, he was tall, slim and good-looking. At the dinner table he provided charm, civility and relaxed good humour. He was the perfect gentleman. Entering Parliament in 1964 at a by-election in Devizes, Charles supported Heath's bid for the Tory leadership and was made his Shadow Minister for Sport.

My activities for Imperial had made me the most active and effective parliamentary lobbyist for the tobacco industry and I had been careful to keep a low personal profile. Like Christopher Powell, I believed it important to be discreet, to employ people who would not leak stories, and to let my clients take the credit in public for success when this was due. In 1984 I took it as recognition of my success when a new book purporting to take the lid off the tobacco industry's political and other protective activities failed to mention me.

Smoke Ring was written by the successful investigative journalist and broadcaster Peter Taylor who explained that it described the ring of political and economic interests which had protected the tobacco industry for the past twenty years. He wrote that as guardians of public health, governments should fiercely oppose the industry, but in practice the two were often firm allies as cigarettes provided chancellors with one of their biggest and most reliable sources of revenue.

I had been helped in my low profile approach, which had kept me out of Taylor's exhaustive study, by the fact that I was employed by a gentlemanly and traditionally discreet agency – Charles Barker. Unlike some PR companies, we did not boast publicly about our numerous and often spectacular successes or leak stories about our clients.

I was often asked for TV and radio interviews at party conferences, but I always declined as I felt it would be wrong to talk about my clients' problems and campaigns. Public relations practitioners are employed to add lustre to their clients – not to make names for themselves. It is the same in the world of public affairs and parliamentary consultancy. Credit should go to the client unless they have requested anonymity.

Early in the 1980s the left-wing MP for Keighley, Bob Cryer, raised the issue of parliamentary lobbyists with the Speaker. He had first come to my notice as an extremely aggressive student activist at Hull University when he had snatched a microphone from Labour leader Hugh Gaitskell at a meeting. Sponsored by the National Union of Mineworkers, and a staunch supporter of the controversial Arthur Scargill, he entered Parliament in 1974. He soon gained a reputation as a loud-mouthed member of the hard left, noted for heckling and barracking in the Commons chamber. Now he was intent on preventing major industrial organisations, which employed hundreds of thousands of workers, from using lobbyists to communicate legally with MPs. In my view, Cryer did not understand democracy and, as the Gaitskell incident highlights, was prepared to gag free speech when it did not suit his purpose. But in stirring up the issue, he gave lobbyists the opportunity to state our case and get it fairly reported in the media.

Encouraged by Cryer's campaign, the Scottish *Sunday Standard* approached me in December 1982 to ask about administering all-party groups. In a long article, the paper's political editor Tom James wrote that my All-Party Motor Industry Group had visited France as guests of Renault and had been invited to Germany by Volkswagen. Moreover, my All-Party Roads Study Group had been to Switzerland on a trip paid for by the road transport and construction industries. There was nothing secret about these study trips as the MPs leading the groups had given press conferences.

However, James reported that the role of such unofficial parliamentary committees was controversial. He reported:

'There are reckoned to be about 90 All-Party Groups in existence and new ones are always springing up, often initiated by public relations firms as a way of providing easy communications between specific industries and MPs.

'Arthur Butler, managing director of Charles Barker Watney and Powell, is secretary to at least six of these committees, including the prestigious and influential Parliamentary and Scientific Committee'.

He then quoted me as follows:

'What we tend to do is bring the two sides together – people who have a problem and people interested in the problem – and let them thrash it out. I see it as a basic part of the democratic process – it is absolutely open communication. When a committee is set up and industry is going to fund the secretariat it is immediately announced to MPs. No one is in any doubt that the secretariat will be paid for by industry. I estimate that at least half the MPs in the Commons are involved in some way or another with one or more of the all-party committees linked to industry. They must be playing a useful role'.

In the mid 1980s, Sir Ian Lloyd, Tory MP for Havant, and one of the best informed, dedicated and intelligent politicians in the Parliamentary and Scientific Committee (P&S), drew my attention to the important role of the US Office of Technology Assessment (OTA). Since it was set up in 1972, it had provided the US Congress with competent, unbiased information about the physical, biological, economic, social and political effects of advances in technology.

The British Government had been asked to provide Parliament with a similar body. Faced by its failure to respond – as ministers prefer MPs not to be too well informed – Sir Ian suggested that the P&S should attempt to fill the gap. I supported his proposal but it was soon clear that to develop such a body within the P&S was not possible for financial reasons. The committee had no spare funds. A new separated fund-raising body was needed so the committee decided to set up a charity to be known as the Parliamentary Science and Technology Information Foundation (PSTIF). Everyone looked to me to get on with it. Once it was up and running, Sir Ian, the committee's president Lord Gregson, chairman Sir Trevor Skeet and others approached potential donors for funds.

Enough was raised for the PSTIF to operate, which led to the next step – the Parliamentary Office of Science and Technology (POST) set up in April 1989. It had sufficient resources to remain in operation until 1992 /93, with a staff of three to five. Compared to the OTA's budget of $20 million and a 200-strong staff, POST was a frail, underfed child – but a start had been made. Great was the rejoicing when, thanks largely to the determination of Sir Ian Lloyd, POST was granted parliamentary funding by the Commons to take effect from April 1993.

While this was getting underway, Sir Trevor Skeet's three-year stint as chairman was running out. It was Labour's turn and I had to take soundings as to who would be acceptable to the committee. As usual Tam Dalyell was regarded as a maverick by the old guard, and there were no other regularly active and appropriate Labour MPs available. My friend Alf Morris had been too busy to be active on the committee but I thought that he would make a good chairman. He had achieved much in the field of disability - and was also popular and respected. Also, he had been a minister. If Tam Dalyell could not be offered the position, at least it would be going to a politician he respected. I invited Alf to allow his name to go forward and he was elected without challenge.

An important landmark for the committee was on the horizon. It had been set up in 1939 so I had initiated discussions about celebrating its fiftieth anniversary in 1989. HRH the Duke of Edinburgh had long been associated with it. He had addressed its annual lunch on several occasions and attended meetings and receptions. I proposed that he should be invited to be president of the committee for the golden anniversary year and Alfred, who enjoyed his past dealings with Prince Philip, was pleased to agree. The PM, Mrs Thatcher, and a number of her ministers had addressed the annual lunch, but I could not recall a leader of the Opposition having done so. Alfred was enthusiastic about the idea and it was agreed that Neil Kinnock should be invited to address the jubilee year lunch. To please the Tories and involve the Government, I suggested that we invite Mrs Thatcher to give a special jubilee address. This touch of diplomacy worked and she was invited to make her speech in December 1989 in the ornate surroundings of the Royal Gallery in the House of Lords.

Our plans were agreed and Alfred, President Lord Gregson and I went to Buckingham Palace to get Prince Philip's approval of a programme of events to be conducted under his presidency. I did most of the talking and he seemed pleased with our proposals.

Before taking on the presidency, he gave one last address to the committee's annual lunch at the Savoy in March 1989. Some four hundred members and guests attended. Taking as his theme the need for people to be more humble about their ambitions in view of growing environmental problems, the Prince declared, 'Most of the damage done is the result of actions taken with the best possible intentions', citing activities such as the felling of the rain forests and the harnessing of hydro-electric power. In her speech to the committee, Mrs Thatcher, alert to the growing problem, called for urgent scientific research into the phenomenon of global warming. She said Britain would play its part with a planned centre for predicting climate change. The Prime Minister added that the threat to the global environment was more intractable than any other scientific problem and that, while the risks were still being assessed, precautionary measures were needed immediately.

Despite her urgent warning, the world had to wait nearly another twenty years before a panel of UN scientists delivered the most conclusive evidence up to then that mankind was responsible for accelerating global warming and the potentially catastrophic effects. The UN Secretary General said he was 'considering' a summit of world leaders to discuss how the problem should be tackled. After yet more delay, the conference was arranged for December 2009, nine months after some 2,500 leading experts had issued a desperate plea to politicians to act before the planet became an unrecognisable place on which to live.

Introducing Neil Kinnock at the March 1990 annual lunch, Prince Philip, as retiring president, said, 'Quite apart from the opportunity of making personal acquaintance and even friendships, I hope this committee provides an opportunity for scientific activity to be explained to legislators and for policies, if not legislation, to be explained to scientists, always allowing of course that these things are explicable to anyone'.

Kinnock messed up a great opportunity to impress Britain's leading scientists and technologists by making a poor, lightweight speech. Labour members of the committee were dismayed. I was disappointed. Another poor performance at the end of the 1992 General Election campaign at a rally in Sheffield had disastrous effects. It was the final nail in the coffin of Labour's hopes of winning the General Election.

In his presidential foreword to the committee's 1989 annual report, Prince Philip referred with satisfaction to its growing membership. Associate member companies now numbered well over eighty; at Westminster we had 113 MPs and 76 peers; and 23 UK members of the European Parliament were also members. The black spot of the year had been the death of Christopher Powell and the Prince paid tribute to his work in helping to ensure the committee's success.

Despite Mrs Thatcher's contribution to our jubilee celebrations, she was not popular with many in the world of science as her Government had refused to increase its inadequate funding of scientific research. One of her most outspoken critics was Sir George Porter, Nobel Laureate for Chemistry. He had been director of the Royal Institution before he became president of the Royal Society. He fought hard to get Mrs Thatcher to invest in science and in 1987 warned that unless her Government stopped downgrading Britain's scientific research the country would join 'the Third World of science'. A convivial Yorkshireman who entertained me to dinner at the Royal Institution, he was a very effective communicator and I thought he would have made an excellent president of our committee.

I had become a member of the Worshipful Company of Tobacco Pipe Makers and Tobacco Blenders, a City livery company. As a result I began to learn more about the role and history of these City institutions. And since I was once again parliamentary consultant to the Corporation of the City of London, I tried to do some bridge building. The Corporation needed more friends among the general public and I thought that it should harness the support of the thousands of members of the livery companies. I proposed that the Corporation should make direct contact with liverymen, such as myself, by publishing a regular newsletter to be distributed free of charge. Members of the Corporation's key Policy and Resources Committee showed polite interest but the idea was not taken up for some years, until after I had retired as consultant to the notoriously slow-moving institution.

The Corporation was more interested in getting me to organise visits by groups of MPs to the building site for the new Barbican Arts Centre so I invited some with known interests in the arts. As I conducted them around the construction site I became increasingly concerned. The centre lacked a clear, imposing front entrance and its various floors and corridors were like a maze. It was finally completed in 1981 and when I attended productions, I would invariably lose my way – and my temper. It would be twenty-five years before the Corporation would bow to criticism about the design. A new entrance and reception area with illuminated signposting throughout the centre were eventually installed.

In the summer of 1987, I had a business planning lunch with Angela Heylin, a high flying consumer affairs PR operator who had been given oversight of our successful parliamentary division, unnecessarily in my view. I pointed out that under the company rules I was due to retire in eighteen months at the age of sixty. She was clearly surprised. Perhaps I looked young for my age. So far as business was concerned, my forward planning days were over.

Originally dominated by the advertising business, Charles Barker had assumed that by the age of sixty, a director would be washed out and fit only for the golf course. By contrast, a sixty-year old parliamentary consultant would be at the height of his ability and earning capacity. This had not registered with the company big wigs.

To get me out of the daily management of CBWP, I was promoted to vice chairman for my remaining year or so of fulltime employment. There was also the prospect of consultancy work after that, although the details would be spelt out nearer to my sixtieth birthday. This arrangement did not appeal to me. I had no intention of ending full-time work so soon. I discussed my situation with a few of my long-standing clients. The Charles Barker management did not appear to have understood the strong personal link that could exist between a consultant and his clients.

My soundings revealed that about eight of my clients would follow me to another company, among them Imperial Tobacco, the Tobacco Manufacturers' Association (formerly the Tobacco Advisory Council), Sea Containers and Tesco. I shared two clients, (BAA and the SMMT), with another PR company - a subsidiary of the Valin Pollen group, McAvoy Wreford Bayley. Not wishing to set up my own company, I decided to join a PR firm without a parliamentary division and establish one for them. MWB fitted the bill and were pleased to have me. BAA, the SMMT and All-Party Motor Industry Group liked the arrangement and joined my group of breakaway clients. As Charles Barker Lyons had made clear they did not want to keep the time consuming but low fee Parliamentary and Scientific Committee I also arranged for that to move with me.

I finalised arrangements with MWB in August 1988 and informed Charles Barker that I would not be available to them on my retirement on my birthday, January 20th. Then one by one my chosen clients gave notice of the termination of their contracts – to the fury and consternation of the Barker's board. I explained what was happening and gave an assurance that only a limited number would be moving with me. I had no wish to threaten the livelihoods of the team of hard working, first class associate directors, executives and secretaries who had been working with me. Sadly I had to let some of them know that as much as I would have liked to take them with me, it would have opened me up to legal action by Barkers. I was particularly sad to leave my friend and colleague Frank Richardson who had been a great support since joining me from John Addey Associates.

It was my good fortune, however, that two valuable people who had worked in my team were able to join me at my new company – Corinne Souza, the highly intelligent and well organised executive who had left Barkers some years before, and Teresa Moriarty, a very reliable secretary. My move made the front-page of the industry's trade magazine *PR Week*. It seemed to me that I was moving just in time as there was a buzz that the acquisitive Martin Sorrell might decide to take over the company. In such a situation, my position as a sixty-year old consultant would have been precarious. Sorrell, however, who had bought the advertising agency JWT in 1987, decided instead to expand his empire by purchasing the Ogilvy and Mather agency in 1989.

When I joined the Charles Barker group, it had the reputation of being a blue-blooded, well-ordered company but by the early 1980s it had run into trouble. In June 1983 it surprised the City of London with a boardroom putsch in which the aristocratic Julian Wellesley, chairman since 1978, was voted out of office. In 1983 Barker's ranked sixth in the UK's advertising league table and, as press comment put it, the company's performance in the past few years lacked the sparkle of some of its younger rivals.

Wellesley had been concerned by reports that Christopher Bosanquet, as managing director of Charles Barker Lyons, had not been acting in the best interests of the company. Within my division I found evidence of this. For personal reasons he had interfered in our promotion arrangements – with a damaging effect on our profitability. When the chairman George Pulay asked why our profit had slumped, I explained the problem. He looked in turn surprised and perturbed and said he would take up the matter with Bosanquet. He also raised it with Wellesley who was strengthened in his view that he must take drastic action. Being a gentleman, however, he warned Bosanquet in advance of his intention.

Bosanquet used the time to draw the attention of board members to the group failings, which he claimed were the fault of Wellesley's management style. In the event, instead of Bosanquet being in the dock, Wellesley was removed from office and Antony Snow, a former vice chairman of the company returned to take his place. He was a clever, polished, successful businessman with film star good looks who had been working for Corning Glass in America for six years. According to one of the directors involved in the coup, the board had decided to bring in a better salesman. As often happens, the man who initiated the putsch was not to survive long. Snow was a close friend of Wellesley and following his return to the company, Bosanquet was given his marching orders. The company went on to buy the headhunting firm Norman Broadbent, and changed its name to BNB Resources.

News of my impending departure from Charles Barker Watney & Powell was the cause of some gossip at the Tory Party Conference in Brighton in October. Sir Gerard Vaughan approached me, all smiles, and invited me to join a public affairs consultancy in which he had an interest. He appeared surprised and peeved when I declined his invitation because I had agreed to join another agency. Apparently he knew that a number of clients, including Imperial Tobacco, were moving with me and, as he had campaigned against the marketing practices of the cigarette manufacturers, I thought it odd that he was prepared to have the leading company as a client for the PR consultancy with which he was linked.

Of the clients I was leaving behind, the successful Coalfield Communities' Campaign, which I helped to launch, was by then well established and less in need of our services. Frank Richardson had taken over my work for the British Road Federation which had been hit by a drop in financial support and forced to make economies. The Corporation of the City of London had just sacked Charles Barker Lyons and the chairman of the Policy and Resources Committee, Peter Rigby, said he hoped I would regain the account with my new company. Peter, a no-nonsense, hard-working Common Councilman, had given me valuable support and encouragement as well as some tough challenges.

Other more recent clients I was leaving included the huge octopus-like Japanese investment corporation Marubeni. They sent my monthly reports on the UK political scene back to a government office in Tokyo. I would also be leaving behind Motorola, for whom I had helped introduce the mobile phone into Britain. Twenty years later I had still not bought one of the ubiquitous gadgets for myself.

My last good deed for Charles Barker Watney and Powell was to set the wheels turning for the establishment of yet another all-party group for it to administer. Over lunch at The Turf Club, the amiable Earl of Bessborough, with a strong interest in science, urged me to set up a parliamentary committee for space technology. Encouraged by his enthusiasm and support, I brought together MPs and representatives of interested technology companies to discuss the project. As a result the All-Party Space Committee was established soon after my departure from Barkers. Frank Richardson was secretary – and it went on to become one of the most successful of the parliamentary groups linked to high-tech industry.

CHAPTER SEVEN

Jinx Again

I was warmly welcomed at the expensive Grosvenor Gardens offices of McAvoy Wreford Bayley. At one time the building had housed the Belgian Embassy, and the first floor meeting room, lit by glittering chandeliers, was protected by a preservation order. The company was owned by Valin Pollen International, an advertising and PR agency enjoying soaring success. Set up in 1979 by Reg Valin and a small group of former Charles Barker City executives, it had gone on to enjoy the best earnings record in the profession and had become the darling of the City by the mid 1980s.

To the eight clients I had taken with me, MWB added a couple more, including Yorkshire Water. It was not a bad start.

A favourite client I had left behind at Barkers was Ford of Britain, for whom I supplied an information service but no lobbying. Knowing that I would continue to help them through the All-Party Motor Industry Group, they had not bothered to move with me. Within a few months, however, Ford's head of public affairs Kenneth Cannell called to invite me to lunch to discuss a proposition. Over grilled sole and a good dry white wine, he told me that Ford intended to make a bid to take over Jaguar Cars.

Ford had started to look seriously at Jaguar in 1988. Once part of British Leyland, Jaguar had been privatised under the chairmanship of Sir John Egan, but by the end of the 1980s he had foreseen serious trouble ahead. He was ready to abandon ship if someone could be found who was willing to salvage the company. He had put out feelers and was soon talking to Ford and General Motors. An offer of £600 million from GM for a minority stake did not appeal to Egan.

According to Ken, Ford's bid could prove to be controversial. The company was in need of effective lobbying in Parliament to prevent a flag-waving backlash like the one that had stalled GM's bid for Land Rover some years before. Would I take on the job? I did not need to be asked twice. I added, however, that for propriety's sake I first needed to get clearance from the SMMT – as I had done before helping GM some years earlier. This was forthcoming and the Ford account was switched from Barkers to MWB.

It was my task to ensure discreetly that contact was made at the right time and right level with parliamentarians. I arranged for Ford's chairman to put his case to Labour leader Neil Kinnock over the phone. It was pleasing that some MPs congratulated the company on the careful and efficient manner in which they were kept informed of fast moving developments. Ford made Jaguar an offer they could not refuse - £1.6 billion for an asset said to be valued at only £250 million. As part of the deal, the Government agreed to end its 'golden share' arrangement with Jaguar. On the point of launching a new attempt at an agreed bid, General Motors were left standing at the starting post.

Ford took over, but when their management team arrived at the Jaguar plants, they were appalled to discover run down factories that resembled Third World workshops. An enormous investment was required. Jaguar became Ford's black hole money pit. In the next fifteen years it was to cost its buyer some £2.5 billion. Meanwhile, John Egan, who had presided over Jaguar's decline, skipped off to become chairman of another of my clients – BAA.

I was less lucky in winning back the Corporation of London as a parliamentary client. I made sure MWB had the opportunity to pitch for the big PR account but the company was too relaxed and deservedly failed to win it. I was informed that the City Corporation did not want to split the service between two agencies and so, regretfully, the parliamentary work I had done for so many years would be going to the successful contender. I was not too disappointed. Although I had enjoyed working with the excellent Peter Rigby, I had found the slow-moving corporation to be a source of frustration.

Meanwhile, *The Free Romanian* was still publishing and Ion Ratiu continued to lobby in London and Washington for sanctions against Romania. Both were causes of growing irritation to Ceausescu. While lobbying US congressmen in Washington in the summer of 1989, Ion received a call from the Special Branch in London. They said they had been informed by the Belgian and German police that two Romanian female agents had been dispatched to London to kill him. Handsome, rich and debonair, Ion had a reputation as a ladies' man. The plot, apparently thought up by Elena Ceausescu, was not only to murder him but to damage his reputation by making it appear he had died in an orgy.

On his return to London, Ion called me into his luxurious office in a block he owned on Regent Street, overlooking Piccadilly Circus. He was used to death threats and appeared as relaxed as ever. But he assured me he would be on the watch for the ladies who lunged and Elena's death squad never got near him. Typically, he was more worried that Ceausescu might strike against some of his London associates, such as me, who would not receive the benefit of a warning call from Special Branch.

To the editorial team of *The Free Romanian*, Ceausescu's assassination attempt was seen as an act of desperation by a tyrant whose personal grip on power was crumbling. In its December 1989 issue, I reported that the balance of power of the Warsaw Pact leadership had shifted dramatically against the Communist old guard. Listing reformist developments in East Germany, Czechoslovakia and Bulgaria, I wrote, 'The walls come down everywhere in Eastern Europe. Only Ceausescu holds out. Only he refuses to change…'

The paper warned that unless Ceausescu and his family departed, the outcome would be bloodshed.

Bloodshed it was to be. On December 22nd Ceausescu's drunken, playboy son Nicu ordered Securitate police forces to fire on unarmed demonstrators in Sibiu, an area under his control. Eighty nine were killed and two hundred and nineteen wounded. On Christmas Day, Nicolae Ceausescu and his wife Elena were executed in an uprising in Bucharest secretly backed by Moscow. As I celebrated Christmas with family and friends in Kennington, an exuberant Ion phoned me. Already, he was talking about returning to his homeland where he had not set foot for fifty years and he flew into Bucharest the following month. On his second trip soon after I had a seat on the plane, together with Peter Johnson, joint editor of the Free Romanian. It was carrying much-needed aid supplies. Larry Adler, the world famous American-born exponent of the mouth organ and campaigner for human rights, was also on board. As his aid contribution, he took boxes of condoms.

May had been the month chosen for elections for a new Romanian Government, and it was also the fifth anniversary of *The Free Romanian* which was already being published in Bucharest as well as London. At the age of 73, Ion had been selected as presidential candidate for the National Peasant Party that he had substantially funded. His campaign called for a switch to a market economy, support for the independent farmers and firm links to the Western democracies. He was faced by remnants of the vicious Ceausescu regime led by Ion Iliescu and his Communist National Salvation Front. During the campaign Ion and his ever-supportive wife Elisabeth were physically attacked, one of his senior aides was badly beaten and two supporters were murdered.

In London, I was putting pressure on the Thatcher Government to try to ensure that the elections would be free and fair. In reply to questions in Parliament, Foreign Office Minister of State William Waldegrave revealed that local government officials were being sent to observe the campaign. Over 100 tonnes of paper would also be sent so that Opposition parties could print their policy pamphlets. When the ballots were counted, Ion came in a poor third, gaining only four per cent of the votes.

Within a month of winning, the new President Iliescu, irritated by democratic opposition to his policies, stood by as club-wielding miners roamed the streets of Bucharest beating up, and intimidating, opponents of the National Salvation Front. Ion's printing works was broken up, his house invaded and others were taken away in a lorry but survived. Although Ion failed in his bid to form a government, he had been elected MP for Turda and would in time become Speaker of the Romanian Parliament.

The Ratius survived the death threats of Romania's Communist thugs but, nearer home, two more of my political friends were to die as a result of IRA terrorist action.

When we moved into our new home in Kennington in 1981, the house at the other end of the recently built neo-Georgian terrace was already occupied by the Conservative MP for Eastbourne, Ian Gow and his charming wife Jane. He had been in Parliament since 1974, but I knew him only by repute. In particular, Airey Neave had told me that Gow was a man to watch and cultivate. His knowledge of Gow stemmed from Ian's deep interest in the problems of Northern Ireland and his belief that Ulster's future had to be in union with Britain.

Despite Airey's advice, I did not wish to embarrass Ian by having a professional lobbyist take advantage of the fact that we lived a few doors apart. As Margaret Thatcher's deeply loyal parliamentary private secretary, he was a lobbyist's dream contact. Nicknamed 'Supergrass' in the Commons, he appeared to know everything that was going on. Before his assassination in 1979, Airey had made known that he wanted Gow to be his Minister of State for Northern Ireland when the Tories won the coming election. Instead, following his stint as her PPS, Mrs Thatcher made him Minister of State for Housing and Construction in June 1983 and then Treasury Minister of State in 1985.

He resigned from that post in protest at the Anglo-Irish Agreement that concluded in November. We entertained each other at drinks parties. On one occasion when he had invited Margaret Thatcher, the security police did a check-up in advance and were taken aback to discover that Ian's next-door neighbour was a fit looking young Irishman named Michael O'Rourke. Ian was fond of wine and loved gardening. Sometimes on my way home I would stop to share a bottle with him as, glass in one hand and hose in the other, he tended his fine pale roses.

In 1989 his name had been found on an IRA hit list not far away in South London and he was advised to take care. In view of his outspoken views on Northern Ireland and strong condemnation of IRA activities, it was not surprising that his life should be threatened. But he paid little heed to the warnings. I noted with dismay that he did not bother with basic security checks on his car parked in our road, before he drove off each day. Airey had been killed by a car bomb. On Monday July 30th 1990, it was indeed an IRA car bomb that killed Ian outside his constituency home, 'The Dog House', in Hankham, near Eastbourne. He was 53.

The year after Ian Gow's assassination, my friend Lord Kaberry, an important and influential ally of the tobacco industry, died after he was injured in an IRA bomb attack on the Tory Carlton Club in London. The bombing took place a month before the assassination of Ian Gow. Lord Kaberry had not been severely wounded, but he was badly affected by shock and smoke inhalation and was unwell until his death nine months later in hospital in his native Leeds.

Donald Kaberry, a burley, straight-talking Yorkshire solicitor, had been elected MP for North West Leeds in 1950, making assistant chief whip a year later. He became vice chairman of the Party in 1955 and Harold Macmillan made him a baronet in 1960. Using his Whip's experience and considerable influence, he had helped me kill off the Nabarro bill. He later became a stalwart of my Tory backbench tobacco industry group and then of the Lords & Commons Pipe and Cigar Smokers' Club, having moved to the Upper House as Lord Kaberry of Adel, a suburb in Leeds.

It was typical of the humour of this tough World War II artillery colonel that having been carried from the Carlton Club on a stretcher following the bomb blast, he told his friend Lord Whitelaw, 'I don't think I'll be able to vote in the Lords this afternoon'.

Donald's grit would have been appreciated by another tough character with whom I came into contact in 1989 – the formidable Israeli leader Ariel Sharon. A bright fashion PR consultant Jenny Farndale had got to know my wife through the rag trade. A former employer had asked her to recommend someone with political experience to advise on how the controversial Mr Sharon could win friends and influence people on a forthcoming visit to London. Intrigued by such a challenging prospect, I thanked Jenny and went to meet her ex-boss, fashion millionaire Cyril Kern at his elegant Belgravia home. His friendship with Sharon had begun when he had volunteered for a spell with the Israeli army at the age of seventeen. Sharon had been his commanding officer and they had become life-long friends, Kern holding the Israeli warrior in great esteem and affection.

On his return to London, the good-looking young man had joined his uncle's fashion firm, Reldan, and eventually became chairman of the successful company. As we discussed the Sharon project over a drink, I discovered that he had fought under him in the Six Days War in 1967. In that short conflict Sharon had distinguished himself, before, in the Yom Kippur War of 1973, outshining all other commanders in courage and tactical ability. But he also had a reputation for ruthlessness. As Defence Minister in 1982 he had persuaded Israel's Prime Minister Menachem Begin to invade southern Lebanon to tackle Palestinian terrorists.

During the campaign the Phalangist, Lebanese Maronite Christian militiamen, carried out a massacre at Sabra and Shatila refugee camps with the loss of countless innocent Palestinian lives. Following an investigation, Israel's Kahan Commission concluded that Sharon was indirectly responsible because he had disregarded the prospect of violent revenge by the Phalangists. Sharon resigned, but remained in the Government as Minister without Portfolio.

As a politician, he had been cold-shouldered by the Labour Party as being too controversial. He then went on to play a leading role in setting up the right-wing Likud movement with which he campaigned strenuously for an expansion of Israel's borders to improve the country's security. Kern said he would arrange for me to meet Sharon in his suite at the London Hilton the day after his arrival.

I was there on time. Squat and pot-bellied, the sixty one year old legend still looked tough if not particularly fit. I noticed he had a clumsy walk as he came towards me, hand outstretched, a quizzical smile on his broad, weather-beaten face. It was a face that reflected his pugnacious nature. He had inherited his aggressiveness from his German-Polish father who brought him up on a Jewish farming settlement in the days when the British ruled Palestine and had grown up with a deep love of the land. As we talked, I made notes to help me devise a PR programme that would win him the respect of the top people he needed to influence. My client was bloodstained from desert battles. It was essential that he make the case that these had been battles for survival, not from ambition for aggrandisement.

He dealt with this problem well in an address to a packed black-tie dinner at a Park Lane hotel. With the aid of a large map he described dramatically the desperate geographical situation of his country, hemmed in by states dedicated to its destruction. Israel's narrow, elongated shape was a defence minister's nightmare.

On a different plain, I sought to play up a side of Sharon that would appeal to the knights of the shires and retired military men – his role as a farmer who loved the land and his horses. There was much in his background and sentimental nature to appeal to the readers of *Country Life*.

I never met him again and had no further dealings with him – presumably because in the light of developments, he no longer had need for my type of consultancy work in Britain. Years later I watched with admiration as the old soldier, who played a leading role in expanding Israel's borders to create a vital buffer zone, forced the withdrawal of Israeli settlements from Gaza and the West Bank through the Israeli Parliament, a policy since rescinded. He was to become Prime Minister in 2001 and accepting the need to dismantle the settlements in the face of bitter opposition from his own Likud Party, he abandoned Likud and set up the centre-right Kadima movement.

It was a masterly manoeuvre, paralleled by his war-winning strategies on the battlefields. It appeared to assure him a victory in the coming election and also a new form of security for Israel's frontiers. The opinion polls indicated that he was 'top of the pops' with the priorities of his new National Responsibility Party being security and war against poverty at home. Then the battered old bulldozer faltered and stalled as he dominated the centre ground. Sharon, worn out by decades of struggle, was taken seriously ill.

As I busied myself building up the parliamentary division for MWB, there was a distinct smell of burning from the offices of Valin Pollen International further up the road. The company had been so successful that it had used surplus funds to buy an American firm. Unfortunately the new acquisition had been run by the conman Don Carter, who defrauded the US Treasury of huge sums in unpaid taxes.

Mr Carter ended up in jail and Valin Pollen inherited the tax bill that the company owed to the US Government. Carter could have inspired the character of Gordon Gekko, the ruthless financial spiv in Oliver Stone's film *Wall Street*. Indeed, his office, in which he locked himself as the police moved in to arrest him, was featured in the film.

In August 1990 *The Times* business section reported that a £7.1 million rescue bid from a Mr Peter Earl's Tranwood mini-merchant bank 'comes as the only acceptable alternative to a complete collapse for the former Valin Pollen agency, humbled by its involvement with the now jailed Don Carter'. It added, 'The Tranwood bid has hardly been welcomed by VPI, not least because Mr Earl's intriguing track record, including failed bids for Storehouse and Extel, does little to add to VPI's credibility as a public relations group'.

The market took its own view and VPI shares slumped to 9.5 pence. This Peter Earl was not my old friend of STC and later of Sea Containers, where he took over as public affairs manager from Maureen Tomison.

Reports were circulating that Grey Communications International (GCI) was in talks with VPI about buying its subsidiary MWB. Alastair Eperon, MWB's hard-working chief executive, was quoted as saying that he saw benefits in joining the GCI group, whose London agency was GCI Sterling. In September 1990, GCI acquired MWB from the receivers of the VPI group, and in January 1992, GCI Sterling and McAvoy Bayley (as it had become), merged. These developments put me in touch with the convivial and expansive chairman of GCI Sterling, John Brill. He was impressed with my client list and encouraged me to expand my side of the business by seeking a merger with a small but highly respected firm – CSM Parliamentary Consultants.

This was managed by Christine Stewart Munro. She had been trained by Christopher Powell and had been his deputy when Watney & Powell was bought by Charles Barker. Having broken away, she had set up her own company but remained a close friend of Christopher's. She came to lunch and brought Michael Ancram, her chairman and a Tory politician who later became chairman of the Conservative Party. Pleasant and gentlemanly, he was the son of the 12th Marquess of Lothian. The lunch went well but Christine rightly decided to stay independent and when I retired from Sterling PR, I joined her board of directors.

As political consultant to the Tobacco Manufacturers' Association (TMA) I could organise my parliamentary lobbying on a wider scale than when I had worked solely for Imperial Tobacco. I could now bring together MPs and peers linked to all the member companies of the association. In the Commons there were some fifty Tories, thirty Labour members and a few Ulster Unionists and Liberals. The MPs ranged from right wing Conservatives such as John Carlisle, to extreme left wing Socialists such as Eric Heffer, who had once described the Tories as '…a load of kippers – two faced with no guts'. In the House of Lords, over twenty supporters included my old friends Lord Mason, Lord Colnbrook (formerly Sir Humphrey Atkins) and Lord Cullen. They could be relied upon to get the better of most exchanges in the Upper House on tobacco issues.

The annual pre-Budget deputations to the Chancellor were now a regular, highly organised affair for friendly Tory and Labour MPs. After a detailed briefing by an industry tax expert they were then photographed on the steps of the Treasury on their way to meet the Chancellor. The pictures were sent to their local papers to show they were doing their bit for their constituency tobacco factory and its employees.

The lunch and dinner parties I organised for my tobacco clients at party conferences had become very popular with politicians and their spouses. Among the ex-Labour government ministers who attended, one of my favourites was Denis Howell. He was the first Football Association referee to enter Parliament, and went on to become the first Minister for Sport in 1964. He enjoyed a good cigar and was an important supporter of tobacco industry sponsorship of sporting events.

I was particularly pleased when Barbara Castle accepted an invitation to a tobacco lunch at the party conference in 1989, the year she had retired from the European Parliament and accepted a life peerage as Baroness Castle of Blackburn. She had enjoyed smoking for years, and I hoped she would speak up on behalf of fellow puffers in the Lords. To the best of my knowledge she never did - but she was good company at our functions.

She was always impeccably turned out, and was still using her famous feminine wiles in her late seventies. Celebrating her 80th birthday at the 1990 party conference, this consummate politician again joined us for a lunch. She had spent a lifetime fighting for respect in the very male world of Parliament. She once observed, 'Men are so terribly sex conscious that if a man disagrees with you he probably resents you sexually'. She continued to fight her battles at party conferences throughout the 1990s, frail but as fiery as ever, and won a standing ovation just before her 89th birthday.

A less welcome Labour member of the House of Lords was Lord Cocks of Hartcliffe, a former MP for Bristol South. He had become involved with Imperial Tobacco, which had a factory in the area. He wanted to be a paid parliamentary adviser to the embattled company and could not understand that as the local MP this could lead to a conflict of interest – his employer versus his constituents if Imperial decided to make cuts at the local plant. He was furious when, due to me, James Wellbeloved was appointed as the company's Labour MP consultant. To soften the blow, Imperial provided financial assistance in the form of equipment for his constituency office. Indeed, he missed no opportunity to squeeze perks out of the company in return for giving it not always good advice.

Whenever he attended tobacco functions, he was rude, bad tempered and aggressively opinionated about the industry's tactics. His language became so unacceptable in front of ladies that it was decided to remove him from the entertainment list. So, like the bad fairy, he was not invited to a Labour conference function in 1989. Scanning the list of events in the hotel foyer he saw that the TMA was hosting a dinner party and as we sat at the table, the drunken Lord Cocks lurched into the private room. Sir Robin Haydon, who had been made redundant by Imperial Tobacco, was being employed by the TMA to host such functions. Typically, he did not know how to handle this intrusion. Cocks demanded to know why he had not been invited. I moved to deal with him when, suddenly, a trade union guest near me rose to tell him that the TMA had chosen to make this a trade union rather than a parliamentary event - and by invitation only.

This quick-witted intervention wrong-footed Cocks and as he paused, I moved in and conducted him from the room. Cocks had been a foul-mouthed, heavy-handed Chief Whip during Callaghan's premiership and I could not understand how he came to be appointed vice chairman of the BBC in 1993. With him on board it was not surprising that broadcasting standards began to slip. The trade union official who had put him in his place at our dinner was Mike Mulhern, in charge of the tobacco sector for the MSF union (Manufacturing, Science and Finance). He went on to play an increasingly important role in fighting to preserve jobs in the industry. Ken Gill, the newly elected Communist general secretary of the union, was also a guest at the function. He had considerable skill as a portrait caricaturist and drew a good likeness of me on a menu card. I was so pleased I had it framed.

Robin Haydon, who had failed to deal with the invasion of our dinner party, was a charming and entertaining host and popular with our guests. But it was left to me to arrange everything for him in advance from drawing up the menu and preparing the table plan to producing potted biographies of those attending. What made me twitch was that, although he had nothing else to do, he invariably turned up at the last minute. At times he would even get there after the first guests had arrived, which left no time for a final briefing. His first request was for a large gin and tonic. Like other Foreign Office types I have dealt with, his main aim was to avoid any form of work-related stress. But unlike some other ex-ambassadors, he was no snob and had a warm and kind nature.

A few weeks after the 1989 party conferences, the country was stunned by the resignation of the clever Nigel Lawson as Chancellor of the Exchequer. He went in protest at Mrs Thatcher's refusal to get rid of meddling, opinionated Alan Walters as her personal economic adviser. In a swift reshuffle, he was replaced by John Major whose short-lived Foreign Office job was passed to Douglas Hurd. Tory elder statesmen were alarmed by Lawson's departure and saw it as a sign that the Prime Minister was living in an ivory tower. Her days were numbered.

Major was elected Tory leader the following year and Norman Lamont was appointed Chancellor of the Exchequer as reward for nominating him for the leadership. The move was to be regretted by my client, the motor industry. Lamont's first Budget in 1991 was a severe blow to the motor manufacturers, already reeling from the effect of a recession. He struck at the company car market which accounted for more than half the industry's domestic sales.

I found Derek Barron, head of Ford of Britain, deeply depressed by the Government's apparent lack of understanding of the industry's problems and needs. Geoffrey Whalen, the civilised cricket-loving head of Peugeot UK, who had just served as president of SMMT, was equally fed up, as was George Simpson, chairman of Rover. The All-Party Motor Industry Group, developed for lobbying within Parliament, was no longer as effective as it had been. Sir Hal Miller, Tory MP for Bromsgrove, who had been a successful and forceful joint chairman of the group since I had set it up in 1978, had recently retired from the Commons to become chief executive of the SMMT. I had resigned as secretary in 1990 after Vauxhall Motors, owned by General Motors, had complained that it was unacceptable that, as the political consultant who had helped Ford to buy Jaguar, I should continue to run the APMIG. Before taking on the assignment, I had taken the precaution of clearing this with the public affairs department of the SMMT. Unfortunately, they had not cleared it with the member companies. Rather than see the APMIG pass into the hands of a rival PR firm, I persuaded the SMMT to run it, with help from me in the background. Within a few years – and after I retired – I learned that this once thriving and successful group had gone out of existence. Some incompetent employee at the SMMT had failed to re-register it with the House of Commons authorities. It was eventually revived under a different name.

Sir Hal Miller's presence at the SMMT turned out to be important in mobilising the member companies to lobby for a better deal from the Government. I used my influence with Ford, and Geoffrey Whalen of Peugeot, with whom I had kept in touch, also weighed in with a public call for the abolition of the ten per cent special car tax. Behind the scenes, Colin Hope, SMMT president and chairman of Turner & Newall, led the car firm chiefs in and out of key ministers' offices putting the case for urgent action to avoid thousands of redundancies and the terminal decline of the industry.

This highly organised lobbying paid off. In his pre-election Budget in March 1992, Lamont dished out over £1 billion to the motor industry. The special ten per cent car purchase tax was halved at a cost of £765 million a year to the Treasury – reducing the price of a £10,000 family car by £400. The £8000 ceiling on capital allowances for company cars was raised by fifty per cent to £12,000 at a cost to the Government of £220 million; and the ban on taxi, car hire and driving school firms from reclaiming VAT on their vehicles was removed, at a cost of £50 million in the next financial year. The motor industry had won a great victory. I had urged the industry to step up the pressure on the Trade and Industry Secretary, Nicholas Ridley, who had held that office since 1989. In view of his free market philosophy, he believed that such a department of state should not exist and he was not a natural interventionist.

Roger King, the lively Tory MP for Birmingham, Northfield, who had been vice chairman of the APMIG, caused a stir in 1992 by following Hal

Miller's example and joining the SMMT – as director of public affairs. That two Tories who had been officers of the All-Party Motor Industry Group had been given jobs by the SMMT within a couple of years was a cause of much annoyance to Roy Hughes, Labour joint chairman of the group, and his Labour colleagues. The trust I had sought to build between the motor manufacturers and the Labour benches in the Commons had been severely weakened. As chairman of both the All-Party Motor Industry Group and the Roads Study Group, Hughes had become the most important backbencher in the field of road transport in the Commons. He had taken over the APMIG on the retirement of the much-respected George Park.

On November 5th 1991, the bloated body of Robert 'Captain Bob' Maxwell was recovered from the sea off the Canary Islands. He was 68. There were suggestions that he had fallen overboard from his luxurious yacht *The Lady Ghislane*, or suffered a heart attack. I suspected that the great confidence trickster had pulled off his last deception by faking accidental death while committing suicide to avoid pending ruin and disgrace.

Having borrowed from undiscriminating banks to repay other banks, he knew that his precarious paper empire was about to collapse. He also knew that his family was facing financial disaster and would need the £20 million his insurers were committed to pay, provided he did not commit suicide.

I received my last job offer from him at a magnificent display of Ford cars and technology, staged by my client in the East End of London some years before. He had been invited as a guest – and, hopefully, as a potential buyer of a fleet of Ford cars for his business. Seeing me with my wife Evelyn, he gave a huge grin and asked what I was doing there with my 'lovely lady'. He seemed impressed when I said that Ford was one of my clients. 'When are you coming to work for me?' he asked. 'You really must think about it'.

Not wishing to offend one of Ford's potential clients, I said I would indeed give his offer some thought. 'Good', he replied, and lumbered off to the refreshments to assuage his enormous appetite. 'The old crook never gives up', I remarked to Evelyn. Apart from his request in 1965 that I should write a biography of Gaitskell for his publishing firm, this was his third or fourth job offer to me in some twenty years. In my opinion, anyone who went to work for him at a high level after the 1970s had seriously flawed judgement. This view did not extend, however, to those, such as the unlucky Mirror Group employees, who were taken over by him. It was common knowledge that a Board of Trade enquiry in the 1970s had declared Maxwell as a person who could not be relied on to exercise proper stewardship of a publicly quoted company. Despite this, many top people joined his payroll.

Optimism was in the air at the Labour Party's 1991 annual conference as Neil Kinnock's team contemplated winning the forthcoming general election. In some eight years as Opposition leader Kinnock - aptly nicknamed 'the Welsh windbag' - failed to ever dominate the House of Commons. He never won the respect of the Chamber and I agreed with my friend Peter Shore that he never really looked like a potential Prime Minister. Nevertheless, having espoused left wing causes in the past and having used the Left to win power in the Party, he had recently been successful in destroying the influence of the most extreme elements. With the help of ambitious Peter Mandelson, who had been director of campaigns and communications for the Party from 1985 to 1990, he had also succeeded in giving Labour a more modern, middle class look with gimmicks like the long stemmed red rose emblem.

Twenty Labour MPs and peers had attended my lunch and dinner parties for the tobacco industry at the 1991 Conference. Among them were Shadow Treasury Ministers Nick Brown and John Marek, and Northern Ireland spokesman Roger Stott – all very supportive and helpful. Trade union officials included two extremely competent women, MSF national secretary Mrs Terry Marsland and Mrs Brenda Warrington, chair of MSF's National Tobacco Committee. The latter was to play an important role for the industry in due course.

At the 1991 Tory Conference, Education Secretary Kenneth Clarke was among members of the Government and senior MPs to attend tobacco functions. Representing a Nottingham area tobacco industry constituency, he was accompanied by his wife Gillian, who smoked a cheroot. A year later, as Home Secretary, he appointed Sir Patrick Sheehy, chairman of the giant tobacco firm BAT, to carry out a review of police pay. This was to bring the Government into conflict with my old client the Police Federation. When the Tories lost office, BAT subsequently appointed Clarke as the company's deputy chairman.

Due to an ill-judged campaign run by Kinnock, the Tories retained office in 1992. Labour's election disaster was heralded a week before polling day by an awful rally in Sheffield that was advertised as 'the greatest of the decade' and orchestrated by Mandelson.

Kinnock had the good sense to resign quickly following the catastrophe. He had been leader of the Opposition for nine years – the longest in Britain's parliamentary history. I was glad to see him go as I had little faith in his judgement. By contrast, I held his successor John Smith in high regard. He had won wide respect as Shadow Chancellor and enjoyed an overwhelming victory in the leadership election.

He entered Parliament in 1970 so I had not known him when I was a journalist. But through my clients' interests I had contact with him when he served as Opposition spokesman on Trade, Prices and Consumer Protection in the early 1980s. In that role, he had been guest of honour at a directors' lunch at Charles Barker where he had been good value. Our contact continued when he took over as Shadow Chancellor in 1987, and launched his famous *prawn cocktail offensive*. This busy round of lunches and dinners was a bid to build bridges with the City of London and persuade its denizens that they could live comfortably with a future Labour Government.

He was not a colourful orator but as a successful Scots barrister he had an incisive legal style. To the public he appeared trustworthy and competent and under his leadership Labour led the Tories in the Gallup opinion polls. He seemed destined to become the next Prime Minister. Yet all was not well. He had suffered a heart attack as Shadow Chancellor and after that had sought to keep fit and lose weight by strenuous hill walking and dieting. His friends were reassured by his brave attempt to shrug off the problem but I took a more serious view.

Lunching with Nick Brown in Westminster, I aired my concern. Having witnessed similar cases, I argued that the attack should be seen as a warning to Smith not to put himself under too much pressure – the type of pressure he would encounter in a general election. Suppose he had a more serious attack during such a campaign? Nick looked suitably horrified but I suspect he did not take my depressing assessment too seriously. Fortunately for Labour, my scenario never came to pass. The stress of operating as leader of the Opposition, even before a general election, proved too much for John Smith's constitution. He died from a heart attack in May 1994 at the age of fifty-five.

I had rejoined the Labour Party after witnessing Smith's clear control of the annual conference and the election of his promising young lieutenants – Shadow Chancellor Gordon Brown and Shadow Home Secretary Tony Blair - on to the previously left wing dominated National Executive Committee.

Blair was unknown to me except by reputation. He had constituents in
Sedgefield who worked in a local tobacco factory and had supported one of
the Commons motions I had drafted calling for a cut in tobacco taxation.
However, he had never accepted an invitation to a tobacco industry function.

I had got to know Brown when we both opposed a Tory Government
privatisation bill affecting the interests of one of my clients – the Institute
of Professional Civil Servants (IPCS). I had prepared a few press releases
for him and had been impressed by his energy, intelligence and feel for the
media. He was open to suggestions, confidently relaxed and grateful for
my assistance. I certainly saw no sign of the control freak that he would be
accused of becoming later in his career.

More politically mature than Blair, he entered Parliament at the same
time as the other future Labour leader and they shared a small cramped
office. At a dinner in London hosted by the British-Romanian Association,
I met his former girlfriend from their days at Edinburgh University – the
attractive Princess Margarita of Romania. Ion Ratiu gave me the honour
of sitting next to her and I found her lively and intelligent.

Blair, the young, good-looking happily married barrister with a flair for
producing catchy media-friendly phrases, was elected Labour leader with the
help of Peter Mandelson, MP for Hartlepool. John Smith was unimpressed
by 'Mandy's' role in the 1992 General Election and had decided not to use
him as an adviser. Mandelson initially harnessed himself to Brown. Then
he decided that Blair had more flair and was a better bet, and switched
allegiance – to Brown's great annoyance. The scene was set for much bitter
trouble at the top. In 1994 Blair recruited Alastair Campbell, political editor
of the *Daily Mirror*, to deal with the media. A blunt, pugnacious son of a
Scottish vet, he was known for boozing and bagpipe playing.

His closeness to Blair allowed him to influence policymaking and from
the start he was distrusted by some on Labour's left wing. I saw him in
action at Labour's 1995 annual conference when Blair, under the slogan
New Labour, New Britain spelt out his dual ambition to change the Party
and the country. Blair had a gift for speaking with conviction. Former
Liberal leader Paddy Ashdown recalled frustration in dealing with Blair on
a possible Labour-Lib Dem coalition. Ashdown said of him, 'He always
meant it when he said it'.

While the motor industry had much to celebrate following the 1992
Budget, the tobacco industry was having less success with its lobbying.
In the run-up to that Budget, the manufacturers wrote to Chancellor

Lamont. They reminded him that the large duty increase on cigarettes in the 1991 Budget was twice that required to match inflation, and had added about 0.4 % to the annual rate of inflation. It was pointed out that UK cigarettes were the second most heavily taxed in the European Community and were virtually double the price of those in France – creating greater opportunities for smugglers. The Government's *Health of the Nation* report in 1991, however, strengthened the hand of those demanding that smoking was 'the largest single preventable cause of mortality'. It set out to reduce smoking by some thirty per cent by the year 2000.

Following a slow but steady decline in the number of smokers, Imperial Tobacco said in 1991 that there were just under seventeen million compared to just over that figure in 1986 – a decline of less than two percent in five years. It admitted that cost had the greatest effect on numbers. In 1991, Lamont had slapped on an extra 22 pence in tax on a pack of twenty cigarettes. In 1992 he added another 13 pence. By 1993 the total number of smokers in Britain dropped to 14.5 million. In 1992 the Government's Smee report pointed to a direct relationship between advertising and consumption. Demands by the anti-smoking lobby for a ban on advertising became more strident.

For years Tory Governments had opposed a blanket ban on tobacco advertising but in the autumn of 1993, I learned that Health Secretary Virginia Bottomley had run into problems in the Cabinet when three members argued in favour of such a move. The triumvirate was made up of Michael Heseltine, President of the Board of Trade, John Gummer, Environment Secretary and William Waldegrave, Chancellor of the Duchy of Lancaster and a former Health Secretary.

The Cabinet split could not have come at a worse time. Yorkshire Labour MP Kevin Barron had done well in the annual ballot for private members' bills and had introduced a measure to outlaw all tobacco advertising beyond the point of sale.

There had been other attempts in previous years but these had not had the allocation of Commons' time that Barron's bill could claim and had been swiftly killed off. In 1993, however, twenty-one Tories had been among the 206 MPs to support a token bill to make tobacco advertising illegal. The Government knew, therefore, that in a vote on Barron's bill, its 17-seat majority might well be overturned.

Mrs Bottomley took the view that the available evidence did not justify a ban. She was not convinced that it would be more effective than the

Government's long-standing successful voluntary agreement with the industry to limit advertising which by then had disappeared from radio, TV, the cinema, teenage magazines and some shop fronts. In fact, Britain had a better record of falling tobacco consumption than those European countries that had already banned advertising. Despite her stand, Barron's bill received a second reading in the Commons in February 1994 and, following its committee stage, arrived back in the Commons chamber for its report and final stages on Friday May 13th. For Barron, Friday the 13th was to prove to be a very unlucky day. Not that luck had much to do with the outcome.

With my assistance, the tobacco industry had mounted a highly organised lobbying campaign to kill off Barron's measure. Tory MPs friendly to the industry had tabled 108 amendments and four new clauses to the bill, to make sure it ran out of time. The Tobacco Manufacturers' Association had been responsible for co-ordinating the operation with which I had been closely involved. Most of the Tory MPs who tabled the amendments had attended functions of my unofficial all-party group for the tobacco industry that held regular working lunches at restaurants in the Westminster area. They included the very active right wing MP for Luton North John Carlisle and Sir Trevor Skeet. While Skeet had been a problem for me on the P&S Committee, he was extremely helpful when it came to tobacco.

Behind the scenes, the TMA's chain smoking consultant John Russell, an expert draftsman, had produced amendments for MPs to table and supporting speaking notes.

Barron complained that he had been 'mugged' by the Tory backbenchers. He had, in fact, been tactically and legitimately outmanoeuvred. Labour members of the all-party group had stayed away from the Commons that Friday, tending to constituency business.

But only hours before the Commons clash on the bill, the industry had been obliged to agree to stricter voluntary controls on cigarette advertising in its talks with the Government. Unveiled by junior Health Minister Tom Sackville, the package was timed to appease Tory MPs who might have helped Barron in a crucial vote. The controls aimed to cut promotional spending on cigarettes by forty per cent and were to last for at least five years. They also proposed the removal of advertising on shop fronts by 1996, the end of advertising on buses, taxis and other mobile sites, and no more posters at small sites such as bus stops and within 200 metres of a school.

Among other controls, humour in cigarette advertising was forbidden –
a move that gave scope for wry comments by columnists and leader writers.
The ban followed complaints to the Advertising Standards Authority about
advertising for Imperial Tobacco's *Embassy* brand that featured a jowly
comic strip character called *Regal Reg*. In his *News of the World* column,
cigar smoking Woodrow Wyatt, described Virginia Bottomley as the
nanny Goddess. She had already been nicknamed *Golden Virginia* (a brand
of tobacco) by the anti-smoking crusaders for refusing to ban adverts.

The *Sunday Telegraph* projected that, 'Tobacco advertisements will become
more subtly witty – and therefore, more alluring than ever. The new code of
practice would make one laugh, if it did not make one weep'.

Although the tobacco industry had won an important parliamentary
battle, the writing was on the wall. On May 14th the press carried a report
that according to the latest Gallup Poll nearly half of voters thought
Labour would win the next general election. Following the death of John
Smith, Tony Blair and Gordon Brown were sounding out their colleagues
to determine who should be the Party's next modernising leader. The forty-
one year Shadow Home Secretary, Tony Blair, had already established a
clear lead over the forty-three year old Gordon Brown, the Shadow
Chancellor. Both knew that the winner would stand a good chance of
being in 10 Downing Street within three years time. After so long out
of power, the Party had succumbed to the lobbying of extreme pressure
groups such as ASH (Action on Smoking and Health). The portents were
not good for tobacco.

Faced with this growing threat from the revived Labour Party, I urged
the TMA to woo the trade unions whose members in tobacco factories
would be affected by a big reduction in smokers.

When I joined McAvoy Wreford Bayley in 1989 I had warned that I did
not intend to work for more than four or five years. Although I had gained
some clients since moving in to Grosvenor Gardens, such as Grand Met.,
I had also lost some. The new Hanson men running Imperial Tobacco
were continually looking for economies. They decided to run down the
public affairs team and with some justification pointed out that since I also
advised them through the TMA they did not need a separate contract with
me. And due to my consultancy work for Ford, I had also lost the All-Party
Motor Industry Group.

With the takeover of oil company Ultramar, I had lost another client.
My work at BAA was less enjoyable since Peter Sanguinetti had left to

become head of public affairs for British Gas. And my old friend at Sea Containers, the highly professional Peter Earl, had left to enjoy a well-earned retirement. As I entered 1992, I began to think seriously that it was time for me, if not to retire completely, at least to give up the bulk of my work. I informed the directors of my new employer, Sterling PR, and, to my delight, when the forthcoming vacancy was advertised, a bright up-and-coming consultant named Gillian Morris was appointed. She was the daughter of my old friend Alf Morris and I knew she would do a good job for such favourite old clients as Ford.

I intended to retain a couple of clients who did not need a time-consuming daily information service. The TMA wanted me to continue my lobbying work and I aimed to work for the P&S Committee for just a few more years, while looking for a suitable successor. I was fortunate in having as my assistant secretary the highly efficient and very likeable Mrs Annabel Lloyd but I suspected the committee officers would look for someone with wider experience to replace me. My assumption was correct. Years later, however, I was delighted to learn that, belatedly, Annabel had at last been promoted to administrative secretary.

G.C.I. Sterling hosted a lively retirement party for me at a restaurant near the Houses of Parliament. Among the guests were old journalist pals such as Ian Aitken, by then political editor of *The Guardian*, and old parliamentary friends including Alf Morris. To my surprise Iain Mills, the boyish-faced Tory MP for Meriden, who was joint chairman of the APMIG, took the opportunity to say some very kind words on behalf of the group and other parliamentary committees I had administered. Iain did not know how near the APMIG was to death – and nobody there that evening could have foreseen the nearness or the appalling circumstances of his own.

Soon after my retirement from GCI Sterling, Christine Stewart Munro invited me to become a director of her highly respected company CSM Parliamentary Consultants Ltd. – the firm with which I had previously sought a merger. Trained by Christopher Powell, Christine and I shared a similar style of operating and applied the same standards. In 1980 she pipped me to the post by forming the Parliamentary Group for Energy Studies, which she successfully built up until its membership included some 200 MPs, peers and MEPS, together with 130 companies, institutions, trade associations and regulatory bodies. She also administered the All-Party Groups for the Chemical Industry and the Retail Trade and was to go on to found the All-Party Group for Building Societies and Financial Mutuals in 1996.

She advised companies, charities and professional bodies on legislation and relations with government and political parties. Her chairman by then was the charming and gentlemanly Sir Brooks Richards, a man of cool courage who served in the Special Operations Executive in World War II. He was later appointed ambassador to Saigon during the Vietnam War. I was in awe of his wartime exploits and I felt honoured to be on a board of which he was chair. When he died in 2002 aged eighty-four, I wished that I had enjoyed the pleasure and privilege of knowing him for longer.

After a decade of exposing the tyrannical practices, inefficiencies and scandals of Romania's governing Communists, the English edition of the monthly *Free Romanian* newspaper had run its course by the end of 1994. The October edition warned readers around the world that due to prohibitive costs it would cease to be produced in Britain, and as from January 1995 production would be switched to Romania. Proprietor Ion Ratiu had a printing press there producing a national daily newspaper and there was also a need to carry less international and more Romanian domestic news. The English language edition would no longer be printed and those who could read Romanian could subscribe to *Romanul Liber* mailed from Bucharest. Ion publicly thanked Peter Johnson and me as joint editors for doing, 'a superb job in writing and presenting interesting and provocative stories'.

So yet another paper was about to die under me – this time one that I had helped launch. I made sure it went down fighting. In the final, December, issue readers were reminded that President Ion Iliescu – who had served in the administration of corrupt dictator Nicolae Ceausescu – had packed his own government with former Communist ministers and officials.

Despite the fact that his home in Bucharest had again been damaged in an arson attack by neo-Communist thugs earlier in 1994, Ion refused to cut back on his media battle against Iliescu. Violence aimed at deterring my courageous friend made him more determined to carry on his fight for true democracy in his long suffering country. In recognition of his efforts and financial support, he was elected deputy chairman of the new moderate to right-wing party formed by the merger of his National Peasant Party and the Christian Democrats. In the run-up to the 1996 General Election, however, he was disappointed when Emil Constantinescu, a geology professor, was chosen as the Party's presidential candidate.

Ion argued that he would get a better result in the ballot and when Constantinescu won the presidency he found it difficult to accept the situation. He firmly believed he would have made the best leader for Romania – and I have no reason to doubt that he was right. To the end, he retained his English-style manners, Churchillian bow tie and his wealthy businessman operations, which provoked distrust in too many of his countrymen.

Ion died in January aged 82, ten years after he had returned to his country with hopes of playing a leading role in transforming it into a Westernised democracy. He died deeply disappointed that Romania had not developed into the modern state of which he had dreamed. With his death, I lost a dear, generous and brave friend – an extraordinary man of immense energy and considerable business flair who brought colour and excitement into my life. Romania lost a far-seeing and dedicated patriot. Over 10,000 people attended his funeral in his hometown of Turda in January 2000.

His widow Elisabeth, who had staunchly supported his endeavours over the decades, continued to visit Romania on vital charitable work. She received a national award in recognition of her dedicated service to her adopted country. Ion could not have achieved so much without her help. Evelyn and I have warm memories of the holidays the four of us spent together – in Amsterdam, Dublin and Stresa. We were also guests in their hospitable homes in Zermatt, Washington DC, Savannah and finally, after so many years in exile, i Buchret

CHAPTER EIGHT

A Helping Hand for Blair

The body of Iain Mills MP was found in his run-down London flat in January 1997. He had been dead for two days. He was fifty-six. Empty gin bottles littered his grimy living room. An inquest verdict recorded death by misadventure caused by acute alcoholic intoxication. I was shocked to hear the news. I had known him as a charming, relaxed, well-balanced person. What had gone wrong for Iain who had shown great promise as a young politician? A good speaker and organiser, he had won the Midlands seat of Meriden from Labour in 1979 with a 4,127 majority. With his friendly out-going manner, he had been popular in the constituency and by 1992 had increased his majority to 14,699. Within two years of entering the Commons, he had become parliamentary private secretary to the formidable Norman Tebbit, Secretary of State for Employment. When Tebbit moved to Trade and Industry, Iain stayed on as loyal and unpaid aide, strongly supporting his boss's efforts to curb the trade unions. He had been deeply depressed by the weakened state of the often strike-bound motor industry in his Midlands area.

Despite his ability, he was never promoted and on ceasing work for Tebbit after six enjoyable years, he became bored and frustrated. He was proud and delighted, however, to be elected Tory joint chairman of the APMIG, and derived great satisfaction from this role that strengthened his bond with vehicle manufacturing in his constituency. But when he was not involved with the group, he led an increasingly solitary existence. He seemed disenchanted with the general daily life of the Commons. A journalist who knew him well commented, 'He didn't seem hard or cynical enough for Parliament'. His generous tribute at my retirement party was still fresh in my mind. The SMMT's failure to re-register the APMIG, and its subsequent winding up, had undoubtedly been a severe blow to him.

As I was saying goodbye to my friends and clients at GCI-Sterling, I found my role in the tobacco industry strengthened and prolonged. My efforts at the 1993 party conference season had paid off. David Swan, as chief executive of the Tobacco Manufacturers' Association, wrote to say that he had been impressed by the attendance at functions and was convinced the industry must maintain its presence in future years. He thanked me with the words, 'Your ability to respond flexibly to events is exemplary'.

He renewed my contract the following month and expressed his delight, 'that our longstanding relationship is to continue'. He added, 'Your enormous contribution to the tobacco industry's parliamentary lobby has been recognised'.

Such a compliment was praise indeed. I had known and respected David since he had been switched from manager of an Imperial Tobacco factory in the North to a role in the public affairs department. He specialised in the increasingly important European Community area of activity. He had a sharp, incisive mind and a blunt, no-nonsense style. At our first business meeting, I decided that it would be a foolish consultant who tried to bullshit Mr Swan.

On the general subject of bullshit, I was concerned by a growing trend to misuse and misrepresent science to achieve particular political ends. In the late 1970s, anti-smoking campaigners, always looking for new allegations against the industry, started to complain about the danger of 'passive smoking'. They claimed that inhaling other people's smoke caused cancer and produced alarming figures of people alleged to have been affected.

It seemed to me that they were plucking statistics out of the air. I urged Imperial to challenge the figures and was assisted by politicians, especially in the Lords, who believed in providing evidence to support such claims. One such sceptic was the independent-minded peer Lord Stoddart of Swindon. A former power station clerical worker, he had been elected Labour MP for Swindon in 1970 but had lost the seat when an SDP candidate split the Labour vote in 1983. He had then been made a life peer and became involved with the Parliamentary and Scientific Committee. I had thought of suggesting to the P&S that it should hold a meeting on the misuse of science. But as I had always steered clear of involving the committee in the controversial problems of my tobacco industry client, I decided against that course.

Instead, I argued that the tobacco manufacturers should help finance a special one-day seminar on the problem. The proposal was adopted and Lord Stoddart agreed to host the occasion with two other peers – Lord Orr-

Ewing, a former middle-ranking Tory minister and chartered engineer, and Lord Monson, a crossbencher and hereditary peer, who was president of the Society for Individual Freedom. Dr James Le Fanu, medical correspondent of *The Daily Telegraph*, agreed to chair the meeting with two distinguished scientists as speakers - Dr Petr Skrabanek, Reader in Community Health at Trinity College, Dublin, a specialist in epidemiology and the sociology of medicine; and Dr Gio Gori, Director of the US Health Policy Centre, and head of a programme of basic studies for an independent assessment of health hazards and risks. Other industries were invited to participate such as nuclear energy, motor vehicles and dairy products. All of these had suffered from allegations of damage to the community and consumers, based on specious scientific claims.

Members of both Houses of Parliament were invited, together with the Press. I thought it did a useful job but it failed to stem the growth of junk science and misuse of statistics. In December 2008 there came a spectacular breakthrough in the battle to provide the nation with trustworthy statistics. Despite the efforts of a few of my parliamentary friends, civil servants had continued to mislead the public with phoney figures at the behest of their ministerial masters. They had got away with so much for so long when they at last pushed their luck too far.

The head of the UK Statistics Authority, Sir Michael Scholar, publicly rebuked 10 Downing Street and the Home Office for issuing 'selective' figures of knife crime, against the advice of his officials. After my own struggle to get accurate figures on smoking and health, I was heartened to read Sir Michael's words. He complained that figures on stabbings had not been properly checked and revealed, 'The statisticians who produced them, together with the National Statistician, tried unsuccessfully to prevent their premature, irregular and selective release'.

Indignantly he concluded, 'I hope you will agree that the publication of prematurely released and unchecked statistics is corrosive of public trust in official statistics'.

The Home Office had leaked information suggesting that progress had been made by the Government's *Tackling Knives Action Programme*, and had been supported by 10 Downing Street.

Sir Michael followed up his complaint by declaring soon after that selective leaking of data to support the Government's political position eroded confidence in official figures generally. He proposed that ministers and their advisers should be stripped of privileged access to official statistics before they were formally published. I gave a cheer when he added, 'What we ought to do is move to a system in which everybody gets the figures at the same time. That is when the politics should start'.

Simultaneously, the Press carried a report on January 3rd 2009 exposing another 'figures trick' by ministers. Once again the tobacco industry was the victim of misleading information from the anti-smoking camp in Whitehall. Health Secretary Alan Johnson announced that the display of cigarettes and tobacco in shops would be banned from 2011. He claimed that this draconian action was favoured by an 'overwhelming majority' of 96,000 responses to a six-month public consultation exercise. It was then revealed that only a handful of those respondents were individuals submitting their personal views. The majority – almost 70,000 – were views sent in by anti-smoking pressure groups funded by the Department of Health. The Government was funding bodies to lobby itself and its preferred position.

Just how much was being spent was revealed in August 2009. Figures based on private research showed that Whitehall and public sector agencies had paid out over £37 million in 2007/08 on lobbying and political campaigning. Research by the Taxpayers' Alliance found that in that period, £1.8 million went on health policy campaigns, including £191,000 paid to ASH. A spokesman declared, 'It is at best absurd for the Government to spend taxpayers' money promoting its own policies through third party groups' and called for a ban on the use of public money for such activities.

A further devastating blow to the reputation of Home Office crime statistics came in late April 2009. Louise Casey, the Home Secretary's crime and anti-social behaviour expert, publicly admitted, to the embarrassment of Home Secretary Jacqui Smith, the public did not trust the crime figures she had published. Miss Casey said confidence was so low that the public was no longer surprised if official statistics turned out to be false.

I always believed the tobacco industry should have demanded an independent inquiry into the statistics of the alleged annual total of smoking related deaths, which were used by Health Ministers and the anti-tobacco lobby.

In the world of respectable science, Sir Gerard Vaughan, with the active support of his bustling buddy Sir Trevor Skeet, had been elected unopposed as chairman of the P&S Committee in 1991. In his constituency he was to become known as 'The Silent Knight' due to his inactivity in the

Commons chamber. As chairman of the P&S, however, he was very active indeed. I did my best to support him. In particular, I devoted much time to the organisation of a conference on *The Implications and Consequences of Japan's Emerging Lead in Technology.* It was held in association with the Royal Society and was Vaughan's big idea for his period of chairmanship. It went well and Vaughan wrote to thank me for, 'Your tremendous effort and contribution to the conference'.

Despite Vaughan's pre-occupation with Japan, I saw China as the area of longer-term importance. I arranged for the committee to act as joint hosts with the Government to a delegation of five senior members of the Science and Technology Committee of the Chinese People's Political Consultative Conference. The committee also successfully intervened to persuade the Government to rethink its decision to close the Science and Technology section at the British Embassy in Washington DC. When Vaughan retired as chairman in 1994, he thanked me and my hard-working assistant secretary Annabel Lloyd, in the committee's annual report. 'The committee would not be where it is but for their continued enthusiasm and skills'.

With his words ringing in my ears I was not prepared for what happened next. At the age of sixty-four, I decided that I would only serve for two more years during which time I would help the new chairman and committee to appoint my successor. I told Vaughan that as I would have only one other client in that period – the tobacco industry – I would be able to give more time to the committee for no extra fee. While expressing regret that I was planning to retire so soon, he said he thought that I had the committee's interests at heart.

As usual, when it came to finding a Labour MP to take the chair I had a problem. Once again I suggested Tam Dalyell but Vaughan and other senior committee members made clear that such a proposal was not a runner. Despite Tam's interest in science and technology and his long membership of the committee he was still seen as a maverick. In view of the problem, Vaughan thought he should serve an extra year as chairman. I demurred as this would break the traditional alternating cycle and lead to protests from the minority group of Labour members. When he re-iterated his proposal I warned him that if he put his name forward I would feel obliged to resign as secretary – as I had threatened once previously in 1984. At this he retreated – but he was seriously displeased.

I decided to consult my friend Nick Brown, a Labour frontbench Treasury spokesman whom I had persuaded to take on the job of honorary treasurer of the committee. I knew Nick was not interested in taking on the chairmanship – and was, in any case, too busy. But he promised to help. In time he came up with a name – Mrs Anne Campbell, MP for Cambridge. A statistician and academic, she had entered the Commons in 1992 and, despite her lack of experience in Parliament, was prepared to take on the job. Although she was virtually unknown to them, the Tories agreed to support her nomination and she was elected as the second woman chair in the committee's history. Bright, attractive and in her early fifties, she quickly learned the ropes. What she did not reveal was that she did not intend to serve the normal three years.

In her first year, thanks to my reading of trade union literature, the committee was able to fulfil a useful watchdog role. I read in the journal of the MSF union, some of whose members worked in public sector research establishments, that as a result of the Government's Efficiency Unit's scrutiny, there were likely to be closures and job losses in that area. There had been warning of this review in a White Paper in May 1993, but the eventual announcement had been made with so little publicity that parliamentarians who were interested in the issue were unaware that it had begun. I phoned our new president, Lord Flowers. He admitted to having no knowledge of this development and asked me to draft a letter inviting Sir Peter Levene, the Prime Minister's Adviser on Efficiency and Effectiveness, to an urgent meeting of officers and other key members of the committee to discuss the situation.

Sir Peter accepted and heard the concern at the speed with which the review was being undertaken. As a result of our initiative, both the Lords and Commons Select Committees on Science and Technology held urgent enquiries into the review. Moreover, at a meeting of our committee, Sir Peter was left in no doubt that, while some change was necessary, his review was not the way to set about it. Our intervention saved important research work and jobs. One MP who was particularly pleased was Doug Hoyle who had been president of the MSF union and recently elected chairman of the Parliamentary Labour Party. Ennobled in 1997, he now sits in the House of Lords as Lord Hoyle of Warrington.

In May 1994, I received a letter from Anne Campbell. It said that having discussed the situation with Lord Flowers and Gerard Vaughan, they had agreed that it was not appropriate for the administrative secretary to continue beyond normal retirement age. I now understood why a Tory Whip had described Vaughan as 'untrustworthy' and why another had said he was 'two-faced'. He had agreed with my plan to serve for two more years, but behind my back he had made an issue of my age and the fact that I was also working for the tobacco industry.

I had revealed this when first appointed and had never concealed it. However, while to some MPs being a lobbyist was bad enough, to be one for the tobacco industry was beyond the pale for the majority. Anne Campbell was an active member of the anti-smoking brigade. Vaughan had got his revenge for my decision to block his attempt to serve as chairman for a fourth year. Anne Campbell was twitchy about professional lobbying. She added in her 'sacking' letter that the decision was in no way a reflection on my 'very good past work for the committee'. Nevertheless, without discussing it with me, she had drawn attention to the fact that Commons membership of the committee had declined during my term of office.

If she had asked me why, she would have discovered that there were two reasons for this: the first was that leading MP members of the committee, like Sir Ian Lloyd and Sir Trevor Skeet, thought I was doing such a good job that they asked me to form other more specialist committees on information technology, minerals and energy. These siphoned off MPs with special interests in such subjects who found that the Parliamentary and Scientific Committee could not cater sufficiently for their requirements. The second reason was that while Commons membership in 1978 stood at 123, this included a number of MPs who attended just once a year – for the free slap-up annual lunch at the Savoy Hotel.

In my opinion, such free-loading MPs were an expense the committee could do without. At the risk of losing them, I introduced a small membership fee for parliamentarians. Over twenty failed to pay. Good riddance, I thought. After the 1992 General Election, Commons numbers dipped to just below the magic one hundred - a drop I was about to deal with. Within two years of my departure, MP membership had fallen to seventy-two and slumped to forty-seven by 2003!

When Nick Brown heard about my early 'retirement' he was not best pleased. Some friends in the Labour Whips' Office were also annoyed. They told me over a drink that if they had any influence, Anne Campbell would never get a job in government. As it happened, she never did. Despite her excellent academic qualifications and ability, the only position she got was as a lowly parliamentary private secretary – an unpaid aide to a minister. I was allowed to remain as secretary until the end of April 1995 when I was given a very generous send-off and made a Life Member – a category I had introduced years before so that those who had served the committee well could stay in touch.

One of my last duties as administrative secretary, in February 1995, was to compile evidence for the P&S to submit to the Committee on Standards in Public Life. This was chaired by Lord Nolan and set up by Prime Minister John Major following a series of sleaze scandals involving MPs and some lobbyists. It was looking into the financing and operation of all-party committees that were linked to industries and areas such as science and technology. In the evidence, I described the P&S as a well-respected pressure group in the broadest sense that was financed entirely from membership subscriptions. I recalled that it had had only two administrative secretaries in its 56 years – Commander Powell and me. We were both professional parliamentary consultants - or lobbyists - serving a wide range of clients. I explained that this arrangement had worked well, as these secretaries played an important role in maintaining continuity and traditions. I added, however, that the committee's current chairman was proposing that my replacement should not be a lobbyist, nor have links with any professional lobbying organisation.

The committee's officers cleared my draft – although Mrs Campbell queried my description of the P&S as a pressure group. Lord Nolan's team read our evidence but did not call me.

When it came to appointing my successor, Mrs Campbell persuaded the officers to look for an ex-civil servant or academic. There were many applications for the post, a significant number being from those who had been made redundant. In my experience, retired second tier civil servants on short-term contracts are generally looking for a quiet time and are not inclined to take initiatives. Academics often lack management skills. It was perhaps not surprising that the committee's parliamentary membership slumped so quickly after my departure. Perhaps, too, it was poetic justice that in her sixty-fifth year the voters of Cambridge turned Mrs Campbell out of her Commons seat at the 2005 General Election. To give her credit, she had shown courage and integrity in voting against the Government's decision to invade Iraq.

The source of my greatest pride and pleasure on retiring was a letter I received from the committee's former president, Sir Ian Lloyd, whom I held in the highest regard. The former Tory MP, a driving force in the setting up of POST and the Parliamentary Information Technology Committee, wrote that it had always been a great pleasure to deal with me, adding:

'Even when we disagreed about some triviality or other – and that was rare – I always had the impression that you were acting in what you took to be the best interests of the Committee as a whole. Moreover, at no time did I ever receive the slightest impression that your opinions were politically inspired. That is always a tremendous achievement in any parliamentary organisation which is dedicated to an all-party influence on affairs... I think I can truthfully say that we made some progress together in the enlargement of the Committee's influence over the House, especially in the successful establishment of POST...

Well done thou good and faithful servant of Parliament!'

We were to meet for the last time in 2006 when the Parliamentary Information Technology Committee invited us both to attend a reception to mark its twenty-fifth anniversary. He kindly told me that he thought I should have received an honour for my work with the P&S Committee for setting up of the Parliamentary Office of Science and Technology. I was tempted to tell him that I had once had a small problem with MI5 but decided not to. It would have been too long a story...

Sir Ian, who in the previous few decades had done more than any other backbencher to assist science and technology to service the Commons, died the following year.

As for Sir Gerard Vaughan, he was to find himself in increasingly rough water. It was revealed that he had been lax in disclosing his commercial interests in the Commons Register between 1984 -1987. In 1995, aged seventy-two, he came under pressure from senior figures in the Tory Party to retire at the next general election. Since the previous one he had spoken in only ten debates in the Commons and his last contribution had been to support proposals to improve the pension scheme for MPs.

Meanwhile, in 1995, the membership of my Lords and Commons Pipe and Cigar Smokers Club was soaring towards one hundred. This so impressed one member, Lord Holmpatrick, that he asked me to establish a new all-party group – on meningitis, an illness that was causing growing concern and attracting much media attention. With the support of the National Meningitis Trust I quickly did so and, as this was important charity work, for no fee. I was soon arranging meetings for the Associate Parliamentary Group on Meningitis. Labour MP Sandra Osborne was elected chair, supported by Lord Holmpatrick and Liberal MP Mike Hancock as vice chairmen; Labour MP David Drew as honorary secretary; and Tory MP Caroline Spelman as honorary treasurer.

Meningitis bacteria live in the back of the nose and throat and a large proportion of the population were said to be carriers. A weakened immune system can give rise to infection. Research had uncovered that increased sexual activity among teenagers in the 1990s, with deep kissing and multiple partners did much to increase the risk of infection among fifteen-to-nineteen-year-olds. The introduction of the meningitis C vaccine led to a sharp drop in deaths among teenagers from about 2000 onwards.

It was an important subject but attendance at meetings in the Commons was disappointing. As I was anxious not to eat into the charity's funds, I advised the Trust not to offer hospitality to induce parliamentarians to attend. This had been a mistake. My error was highlighted when a rich pharmaceutical company that was marketing a cure for the illness hosted a drinks and food reception at the Commons. It attracted a full house of thirsty MPs. Clearly, I was getting naive in my old age. I decided to retire from the secretaryship of the group in May 2000, after my seventy-first birthday. To my embarrassment I had also discovered a conflict of interest. At one meeting of the group, the expert speaker alleged that smoking was a factor that exacerbated meningitis.

As the general election approached I decided that now I had time to spare, I would volunteer to work for the Labour Party, which I had re-joined. The choice of Blair as leader seemed to have been a good one in terms of the electorate, and he appeared to be well served by Peter Mandelson and his ex-journalist press secretary Alastair Campbell. Personally, having watched them at work during party conferences, I found them distinctly unlikeable arm-twisting operators, and I was sure that I would have clashed with them had I still been a political journalist. The man who seemed to me in most need of professional PR assistance was the bumbling, scarcely articulate, aggressive deputy leader John Prescott.

I wrote to offer my help and listed my experience. Months passed and I received no reply. This silence confirmed my opinion that Prescott needed help. As we moved into summer my thoughts turned from Prescott to Provence. With members of the Fountain Society we were due to travel to study water features in that lovely, sensual region, basing ourselves in Aix. Then, with two special friends from Kennington, Eileen Brooksbank and Roger Tydeman, we planned to drive to Ventimiglia for a tour of the famous English gardens of the French Riviera. Ever since Lord Brougham had put the coastal village of Cannes on the map in the 1830s, the English had been pouring down there, not least wealthy landscape gardeners attracted by the natural beauty of the area and the warm, balmy air. We planned to visit La Mortola first, perhaps the most famous of the English gardens, which was developed by the Hanbury family on a neglected promontory near Menton.

When we returned to our hotel in the evening I was handed a fax from my daughter Caroline informing me that a woman from Labour Party HQ had been trying to contact me. Prescott's office had passed my letter up the line. Presumably, he had decided that I could be of no personal help to him but could be of assistance to Tony Blair's team at Millbank. When I got back to London I returned the call and arranged to report for duty the following week.

In my letter to Prescott I had listed my experience as political consultant to a wide range of companies. This had aroused interest as they were preparing a business agenda to attract support from key figures in commerce and industry.

Labour's campaign headquarters was housed in the 30-storey Millbank Tower, facing the Thames about a quarter of a mile from the Houses of Parliament. The Party had taken a two-year lease on the ground and first floors to provide room for a campaign staff of some two hundred, and an auditorium for daily press conferences.

I had been told to report to the security desk on the ground floor for an appointment with a Tracey Allen, of the key campaigners' task force. I was sent up by lift to the first floor and held in a waiting area by a glass door through which people were passing using swipe cards. How different from the old relaxed days of Transport House, Labour's one-time HQ. Times had changed. I was about to be part of the most security conscious, efficient, controlled and high tech party election machine ever constructed in Britain.

Tracey emerged from the large room that was packed with desks, cabinets and computers. She was friendly and businesslike and introduced me to her team. Their main job was to cold call potential contacts in industry, commerce, science and so forth for inclusion on the Party's database. The aim was to have a contact in every sizeable organisation with whom the Party could deal, at least initially, to discover what such organisations wanted from a Labour Government. I was told to explain that even if an individual or company had some contact with Labour in the past, this fact had not necessarily been centrally filed.

The extent to which information had not been filed was suddenly revealed to me. I had taken with me an *Express* cutting from March 1992 headlined

'Labour's Friends in the City'. It described the role of the Labour Finance and Industry Group, revived in 1972 by Lord Gregson, former president of the P&S Committee and one of Labour's few industrial doyens. I had underlined the names of key members and was surprised that some of them were not on the database. These included my friend from the LSE, Welshman David Goldstone, wealthy chairman of Regalian Properties. I knew he had been close to Kinnock. The cutting was whisked away and presented to someone higher up while I wondered about other gaps in Labour's much lauded, sophisticated system. It was explained to me that much information from the Kinnock era had not been 'processed'.

I was told that when making contacts, I was to stress that to improve dialogue with industry, New Labour wanted to find out about the problems facing companies and other organisations. These would be taken into account in framing the policies to be implemented on assuming power.

I looked around at the other people on the floor. They were mostly young, recently graduated, or employed as MPs' researchers. All seemed enthusiastic and dedicated, and most of them were hoping for a government job when Labour won power. As someone on the wrong side of sixty-five I looked distinctly out of place. I felt old and, because I looked old, they treated me politely and with puzzled patience. When I told them that I was a part-time lobbyist for the tobacco industry, there was a look of disbelief – sometimes followed by a hoot of laughter.

Some of those in the room were monitoring the media. Others were part of the Rapid Rebuttal Unit, and, aided by a computer database, they pulled out facts and statements to counter claims made by rival parties. Yet more were employed in detailed work to support candidates fighting key marginal seats.

They told me that once the election started, there would be daily morning press conferences in the 240-seat auditorium on the ground floor. These would be controlled by Blair's spokesman Alastair Campbell and David Hill. The latter was an experienced and respected Labour Party press officer who, like the late John Smith, resembled a suburban bank manager. As editor of *Science in Parliament*, the journal of the P&S Committee, I enjoyed the privilege of a press pass for party conferences. As for the campaign supremo Peter Mandelson, I had come to the conclusion that with his record of failure in general elections, he would be desperate for victory and would try to persuade Blair to do anything to win votes. This surely was his last chance.

He had a parliamentary seat, having been foisted on the reluctant Hartlepool constituency party in 1992. This caused much annoyance to the previous MP, my disenchanted friend Ted Leadbitter, and his circle. But life as an Opposition MP representing a northeast constituency far from the bright lights of London was not Mandelson's idea of good living. The one-time Young Communist needed a big city stage.

To be fair to Mandelson, Blair had few fixed political opinions and was so frustrated by years in Opposition that by 1994 he was willing to say almost anything to win power. His impatience with his Party after its defeat in 1992 came oddly from the politician who had been a unilateralist and member of CND. Over a short period he also faced both ways on the great issue of Britain's role in Europe. Of course, unilateral disarmament was official Labour policy when Blair first stood for Parliament in a 1982 by-election in Beaconsfield, a safe Tory seat. After his defeat, he wrote to Michael Foot, who had campaigned for him, and described the unilateralist policy as 'realistic, radical and profoundly relevant'. I have also been told that he wrote a fulsome letter of admiration to Tony Benn.

Although I had committed myself to helping New Labour win, I was uneasy about the Party's manifesto. I asked Labour politician friends whether they, too, were worried that it was such a thin document. Those on the left of the Party wanted more proposals for change. Others, like Blair and Mandelson, clearly preferred to travel light. With bad memories of some past, overloaded manifestos their motto was 'the less baggage the better'. I was so keen to get the Tories out, I did not let the issue worry me too much.

In January 1997 in Westminster's smart Queen Elizabeth II Conference Centre, Blair and Gordon Brown launched a document called *Promoting Prosperity: A Business Agenda for Britain.* Published under the banner of the Institute for Public Policy Research, it was signed by business leaders, academics and the general secretary of the TUC, John Monks. One of the business signatories was George Simpson, managing director of GEC. I had got to know him when he was chief executive of Rover and had chaired meetings of the public affairs committee of the SMMT.

I attended the launch of Blair's industrial initiative and was reminded of those heady, far-off days of Harold Wilson, in the run-up to the 1964 Election. Wilson won the support of industrialists, businessmen and scientists with his promise to harness 'the white heat of technology' to the service of Britain. I hoped it would not end in the same bitter disappointment. Some hope!

Once the election campaign got underway, I spent most of my time phoning business contacts, following up leads and completing record sheets. On the industry front, for example, I recorded that the chairman of Ford of Britain was basically neutral – an improvement from the previous election when the chairman had been outspokenly anti-Labour. In the science sector, my friend Dr Maurice Goldsmith, head of the International Science Policy Foundation, approved of New Labour's policies for science, industry and education.

When a Party is out of office for too long, it is desperate for support and becomes easy prey for highly organised pressure groups. This had happened to Labour, out of office for eighteen years, having lost four general elections on the trot. The very professional pressure group, Action on Smoking and Health (ASH), was one of those bodies which had moved in on Labour. They got the Party to commit to supporting a ban on the advertising and sponsorship of tobacco products. In view of my support for New Labour, this was an embarrassment.

Early in 1996 reports were appearing in the press about the likelihood of a ban on tobacco advertising within a year of Labour winning the election. Such expectations were fuelled when Blair appointed Kevin Barron as Health Spokesman. Barron's own bill to ban advertising had previously been killed off in the Commons. He believed Labour would introduce a bill very similar to his of 1994 as a priority. A split had developed, however, between Labour's health and sports spokesmen. The former proposed extending the ban on advertising to restrictions on the £8 million a year sponsorship of sporting events by tobacco companies. Yet in September 1996, Shadow Sports Minister Tom Pendry endorsed a speech by Labour MP and athlete Kate Hoey – tipped by some to be Blair's Sports Minister – in which she said Labour would not seek to restrict tobacco sponsorship of sport. Said Pendry: 'That is our policy: Some sports depend on tobacco money to survive'.

In terms of a UK basic industry, the sponsorship of Formula One international motor racing was of great importance. This high tech business provided hundreds of good jobs, and helped to underpin Britain's motor manufacturing industry. Tom Pendry knew this and did his best to ensure that Formula One would be exempt from any general ban on sports sponsorship.

From my vantage point in the Millbank control centre, I was able to confirm that the election manifesto would commit a Labour Government to a ban on tobacco advertising and sponsorship. The industry was left to pray that it would not be a high priority.

I warned that in my opinion, New Labour was bound to win. From my years of covering general elections I had concluded that while the Party was well organised, this time the campaign would not be decisive. The public had decided that it was time for a change – just as Margaret Thatcher had been swept to power on a tide of opinion in 1979. When the inevitable happened some in the media, always quick to build up or destroy a personality, wrongly gave too much credit to spin merchants Alastair Campbell and Peter Mandelson. Blair would have won without them.

In expectation of Labour winning, I received an invitation from Labour's general secretary Tom Sawyer to join the victory rally at the Royal Festival Hall in the early hours after polling day. I decided I would be too tired that Friday morning and returned my ticket to Tracey to pass on to someone on the waiting list. As the results flowed in and Labour was shown to have won a landslide majority, I regretted that I had passed up the opportunity to attend an historic victory party.

When my colleagues at Millbank arrived at the office later that morning they were issued with passes for Downing Street. As they hurried along to Whitehall they were given flags to wave as Blair arrived to enter 10 Downing Street. Those with children had been encouraged to bring them. Mandelson's plan was to give the impression of families spontaneously pouring on to the streets, delirious with delight at New Labour's victory. My own delight was somewhat diminished when several people who had chosen to work for Robert Maxwell were included in Blair's Government.

Lord Donoughue, who had been taken on by Maxwell in 1988 as a City financial expert to run London and Bishopsgate Investments, became Parliamentary Secretary, Minister of Agriculture. In 1992, Labour's spokesman on City affairs, Mo Mowlam, had called on Donoughue to pay part of the large sum he had earned from Maxwell to the pensioners who had been robbed by the great fraudster. The call went unheeded.

Another former Maxwell employee, the tough Helen Liddell, MP for Airdrie and Shotts, was appointed Treasury Economic Secretary. She had sought employment by Maxwell in the 1980s when his reputation was well known, and became personnel director of his *Daily Record* and *Sunday Mail*. People I knew who had worked hard and effectively for Labour on the frontbench throughout the long years of Opposition had been passed over and left without jobs.

They included Tom Pendry, who had been a formidable Shadow spokesman on Sport and Tourism. He was to receive a peerage. Tom was justifiably shocked and angry not to be given a government post. Before entering Parliament the green young Blair had sought – and got – his help and advice. Indeed, if Tom had not helped him win Sedgefield in 1983, he might never have got to the Commons. Blair had an agreement with his more politically experienced wife, Cherie, that if she won a seat before he did, he would end his parliamentary ambition and devote his time to the law and the family. In the light of Blair's record as Prime Minister, many people must wish that Tom had not been so helpful.

Faced with the New Labour Government's pledge to ban tobacco advertising and sponsorship, the manufacturers agreed to try to mobilise trade unions with members in the industry to lobby against the commitment. They were encouraged by my successful efforts, over some twenty-five years, to involve the unions in the battle against anti-smoking legislation and so protect precious well-paid jobs.

David Swan informed me of the industry's decision to help set up and fund what would become the Tobacco Workers' Alliance (TWA). This organisation would encompass the four major unions: Manufacturing, Science and Finance (MSF); Transport and General Workers (TGW); General and Municipal (GMB) and Engineers (AUEW), all of which counted tobacco industry workers among their members. I was delighted when he added that the industry would like me to be the middleman between the new union group and the tobacco manufacturers. A meeting with relevant union representatives was soon held at a London hotel and as we introduced ourselves, I think it helped that I could say I was a Labour Party member.

I was impressed by the calibre of the union people from factories as far afield as Bristol, Nottingham, Southampton, Belfast, Liverpool, Cardiff, the Northeast and Scotland. I was particularly impressed by the chair of the TWA, the business-like Mrs Brenda Warrington of MSF. We had had met previously at Labour Party conference functions. I was confident that we had formed a formidable pressure group to argue the case for protecting some of the best jobs in British manufacturing industry.

There had been further changes at Imperial Tobacco, my oldest client, in the year before the election. The swashbuckling Lord Hanson, who had built up one of the largest industrial conglomerates in the world by a series of spectacular takeovers, made known that he was about to break it up.

Imperial Tobacco would be one of four new companies to be floated. No other sector in Hanson's empire had made money like Imperial - possibly the best purchase he had ever made. With brands such as Embassy, Superkings and Regal (of Regal Reg fame), Imperial had about forty two per cent of the market. It was expected to overtake Gallaher, owned by American Brands, by the end of the year.

The plan was to continue to run the company's manufacturing facilities in Bristol, which produced some 320 million cigars a year, and Nottingham, where a large factory rolled out the cigarettes. Hanson broke up his empire, then announced in September 1996 that he would retire as chairman of the group that bore his name within a year. He had kindly allowed me to continue as Imperial's parliamentary adviser after I had done my best to help block his takeover bid of Imperial Group, so I wished him a happy retirement. I still related more closely to Imperial and former members of its public affairs team than to any other members of the TMA. Peter Middleton, whom I knew from Imperial, was an ebullient ex light infantry officer. As he was known to organise good parties, I decided to hand over the secretaryship of the ever-growing Lords and Commons Pipe and Cigar Smokers Club to him.

As well as national No Smoking Day and Raleigh Day functions, I had added a popular annual cigar-tasting dinner. Three Tory earls and four future members of the Blair Government joined over thirty parliamentarians at the first of these dinners. By the time I handed over to Peter Middleton the club counted eight earls and two viscounts in its eighty-strong membership. Among them were some colourful and doughty campaigners for smokers' rights, such as Ralph Harris the lively pipe-smoking economist who had been a great influence on Margaret Thatcher. The first life peer to be appointed by her, he took the title, Lord Harris of High Cross. He was chairman of FOREST, the body set up to champion the freedom to smoke, and his natural exuberance, sense of fun and skill as a speaker played a big role in its success.

The club's first female member was another lively, sociable character – Baroness Trumpington, a Tory ex-minister who served in the famous Naval Intelligence unit at Bletchley Park in World War II. Female membership doubled when Baroness Betty Boothroyd, the former Labour Speaker of the Commons, signed up. Betty was the first woman ever to be elected Speaker and a popular addition to our membership. To my personal delight I was made an honorary member of the club on handing the secretaryship over to Peter Middleton and so was entitled to attend all its functions. A few years later Lord Mason followed my example and retired as club convenor. He was succeeded by Lord Wakeham, a former Tory Cabinet minister and at various times, leader of both the House of Commons and House of Lords.

The General Election had also brought about another change in the tobacco industry's battle line. As Tory MP for Luton North, John Carlisle had been one of the industry's most active supporters in the Commons but he resigned his seat to become the TMA's spokesman. He replaced battled-scarred Clive Turner who, having kept his cool in face of often vile abuse from anti-smoking fanatics, had decided to retire with honour from the field.

With New Labour in power, Public Health Minister Tessa Jowell lost no time in re-affirming the Party's intention to ban tobacco advertising and sponsorship. Then, in the autumn, the Bernie Eccestone affair exploded. It rocked the inexperienced Cabinet – while tobacco industry chiefs watched in bewildered amazement. On October 16th Ecclestone and other motor sport leaders had visited Downing Street to ask the PM to change policy on cigarette sponsorship and advertising. Nine months earlier Ecclestone had made a £1 million donation to the Labour Party, desperately in need of funds in the run-up to the General Election. The donation, claimed Ecclestone, had been sought by Blair's own chief of staff Jonathan Powell – an allegation later denied by Powell.

Powell was at the 10 Downing Street meeting when Ecclestone and the other motor racing chiefs warned Blair of the serious effect of an EU directive banning tobacco advertising and sponsorship. But rather than argue for a complete exemption for their sport, they proposed a phased international reduction. Blair ignored this sensible approach, and the next day ordered changes in Government policy to protect the position of the sport, which led to the exemption of Formula One from the proposed ban.

The anti-smoking brigade was furious when the exemption was announced in November and as the media began to follow up rumours of an Ecclestone donation, an even bigger storm broke. At first there were attempts to deny it. To end the row Blair appeared on television to apologise for the mess and to express the hope that the country still thought he was a 'pretty straight sort of guy'. The donation was paid back – but the concern lingered on. My friends in the tobacco industry, who had been treated like lepers by many Labour politicians, saw it as poetic justice that cigarette sponsorship had caused the New Labour Government its first major embarrassment.

As a result of the TV interview, the boyish-looking Prime Minister succeeded in his damage limitation exercise. In doing so, however, Blair was encouraged to believe he could charm his way out of anything. Helped by spin, smoke and mirrors, the Artful Dodger got away with a lot. Meanwhile Bernie Ecclestone's tobacco industry friends were amazed to learn that Blair had not been asked for complete exemption for motor sport. What sort of idiots had taken over Whitehall?

At a landmark meeting of EU Health ministers in Brussels on 4th December 1997, it was agreed that tobacco advertising and sponsorship would be banned in European Union states. After a long, frenetic day of horse-trading, it was announced that advertising would end in four years; most sponsorship in five; and all tobacco support for sports events by October 2006. That gave Formula One motor racing nine more racing seasons before its association with the industry ended.

Claiming that such a ban would be meaningless unless it applied to the whole EU, the Blair Government had said it would await the pending EU Directive. Germany, however, warned that it would challenge the proposed directive in the European Court of Justice because it was intended as a health matter – and health issues were outside the legal competence of the EU. The Commission, in fact, had based its dodgy directive on the clauses in the EU treaties dealing with the extension of the single market. As the Court's Advocate General was to point out in June 2000, the Directive was clearly about public health not trade, and its intent was the very opposite of opening markets. It should be declared null and void.

Faced with disarray and delay on the EU front, Blair's Government changed its mind and in 1999 announced that it would bring in a UK ban two years' ahead of the proposed Brussels' timetable.

Meanwhile, through the Tobacco Workers' Alliance, Whitehall was under steady pressure from major trade unions opposed to the ban. Within four months of its formation the TWA had made its views known to over one hundred constituency and union-related MPs through face-to-face meetings, correspondence and factory visits. It had collected thousands of signatures on a petition and submitted a well-reasoned response to a Government consultation document. It had, in fact, succeeded in raising the issue of jobs – previously ignored in the debate about smoking. At my suggestion, a letter signed by the General Secretaries of the MSF, TGWU, GMB and AUEW had been sent to Health Secretary Frank Dobson. It requested an urgent meeting to discuss the effect of the proposals on employment. Dobson – sacked in 1999 – found excuses for delaying such a confrontation.

The highly respected former Labour Chief Whip Derek Foster MP added to the pressure. While chairing a TWA meeting in the Commons, he declared, 'We hope the Government will take the problem of unemployed tobacco workers as seriously as the problem of other unemployed workers. Unemployment is a social evil that damages peoples' health. Every redundancy notice should by law have a health warning appended'.

Foster, MP for Bishop Auckland, was an Oxford graduate and a fan of brass bands. He also happened to be chairman of the Commons Select Committee on Employment so his views carried weight. Nevertheless, the Government introduced the promised bill but it had not passed all its stages before Blair called the 2001 General Election. To the delight of my tobacco industry friends, no anti-tobacco bill was included in the Queen's Speech for the opening of the new Parliament.

By 2002 – five years after the anti-smoking lobby had expected a bill to be introduced as a matter of priority – no legislation to ban advertising and sponsorship had reached the Statute Book. Then, in another tactical turn, the Government made known that it would support a private member's bill introduced into the Lords by Liberal Democrat peer Lord Clement Jones. It was based on the Government's previous bill and the timing of its second reading debate in the Lords was not convenient for many friends of the tobacco industry in the Upper House. It passed that crucial stage and went on to the Commons. There the Tory Party voted against the second reading, arguing that it would have been better to have a mix of public health campaigning, some restrictions on advertising and a tough tax policy. Despite such opposition, the bill passed its final stage in the Commons.

The Government had adopted the measure the previous March, but with typical bungling its passage had been delayed for three months after the tobacco industry pointed out ministers had to notify the European Commission of the bill's existence. There was further delay when the German Government sought clarification of several of the bill's clauses from the Commons. With the memory of the Bernie Ecclestone affair still fresh, Formula One motor racing would not be affected by the ban until 2006.

Ministers plucked figures from the air, and predicted the ban would save three thousand lives a year and reduce NHS bills by £340million. Tory health spokesmen argued that a clear link between advertising and smoking numbers had not been proved. No sooner was the bill on the Statute Book than the British Medical Association called for laws to ban smoking in public places. It claimed that one thousand people died every year because of passive smoking.

In 1999, the smuggling of tobacco products into Britain had become so serious that Chancellor Gordon Brown appointed Martin Taylor to carry out an independent evaluation. He concluded that the illegal trade would stop only when tobacco taxes were cut to the same as other European states, but this was not in line with Mr. Brown's thinking. Brown refused to publish his report and slapped a hefty 25 pence tax increase on a packet of cigarettes in his March 2002 Budget.

Mr Taylor revealed that half of all cigarettes smoked in the north of England were contraband. He also found that smoking among young people was on the increase because they could afford the cheap smuggled cigarettes. His warnings were underlined within a year by a report that was confirmed by the Office of National Statistics. It said that smoking was on the increase for the first time in twenty-five years.

To the embarrassment of Gordon Brown, the media reported that the main cause was the tax he had levied on cigarettes. This had created a £4 billion a year black market in smuggled packs. The Government was losing billions of pounds in revenue as a result. Anti-smoking organisations accused some tobacco companies of supplying the smugglers with their products in the first place – a charge hotly denied by the industry. Whatever the truth, there is no doubt that smuggling was exacerbated by Chancellor Brown's short-sighted tax policy.

Brown's tax rise had been a disappointment to trade unionists within the tobacco industry. I had helped to prepare a brief in which the TWA's pre-Budget deputation to the Treasury, led by Brenda Warrington, warned that an increase would lead to more smuggling and a loss of jobs and revenue. A well-supported Commons early day motion that I had drafted made the same points. I found the blind stupidity of the Chancellor unbelievable. His stated aim in raising tax on tobacco was to reduce smoking for health reasons. In fact, despite strong and persistent warnings, he succeeded in bringing about the first increase in smoking for twenty-five years. Already deeply disillusioned with Blair, I began to have serious doubts about the capability of Mr Brown.

After ten years in the job, the straight talking, no-nonsense David Swan retired as TMA Chief Executive in January 2002 to my regret. He was replaced by a man whose experience and style were very different. Tim Lord had worked overseas for BAT for ten years – first as president of the company in Venezuela and then at board level in India. Eight months after taking over he declared regretfully, 'The present Government has a great mistrust of the tobacco industry and refuses even to talk to us'.

There were good reasons why it should have talked. Tobacco taxation was higher in the UK than anywhere else in the world. This created opportunities for organised criminals to profit from smuggling cheap and often inferior brands, or from the production of counterfeits. One third of all cigarettes in the UK in 2002 evaded UK duty – as well as seventy per cent of rolling tobacco. Despite all the anti-smoking propaganda, there remained 15 million smokers in the UK who consumed 79 billion cigarettes each year.

Also in 2002 there came a change in the make-up of the TWA. It was reduced to three unions when the AUEW merged with MSF to form the AMICUS union. Roger Lyons of MSF and Sir Ken Jackson of the engineers became joint general secretaries of the new organisation – Britain's second largest union. Sir Ken retired when he lost a subsequent union election, but Lyons stayed on for a few more years, and became president of the TUC in 2004. Of all the union leaders, he was the most steadily supportive of the tobacco industry and active in its defence.

MPs were sent a TWA newsletter which warned that the EU ban on high tar tobacco exports would lead to the loss of thousands of British jobs unless a directive drawn up by Brussels bureaucrats was amended. A ban on exports of cigarettes with a tar content of more than 10mg, planned to start in 2003, would lead to the closure of a Southampton-based BAT factory that manufactured privately for export. Further likely closures included Rothmans in Darlington, Gallaher in Northern Ireland and big job losses at Imperial Tobacco, Nottingham.

In September 2002 the tobacco companies suffered another setback. The Advocate General of the EU's highest court rejected arguments by Imperial Tobacco and BAT Ltd aimed at overturning the new regulations on cigarette manufacturing and marketing. He also backed new laws that banned the use of terms such as 'light' and 'mild' to describe brands. Perhaps smokers would have paid more heed to the warnings about tobacco's harmful effects if scientists had done more to earn public trust.

Sir Paul Nurse, FRS, (director general science) of Cancer Research UK, addressed the P&S annual Savoy lunch in April 2002 and cited an example of how scientists' efforts to link tobacco and cancer could be frustrated by their sometimes 'arrogant' approach. He recalled that when the distinguished medical scientist Richard Peto visited China, which had a serious smoking problem, he assumed the Chinese would take his word for it that there was a link to cancer. The Chinese leaders, however, would not believe what he said as it had not been proved in their country – and until it was they were not prepared to take action. 'We need to earn public trust', warned Sir Paul.

CHAPTER NINE

The Fat Lady Sings

In February 2003, a cigarette advert featured a fat lady singing. It signalled that manufacturers had accepted defeat over the Government's ban on the advertising and promotion of their controversial products. The portly diva was seen on posters advertising the Silk Cut brand across the country and was part of a final spending spree by tobacco companies before the curtain came down on February 14th. This had been a £30 million a year industry. The fat lady had sung and it was indeed all over.

The Government claimed the ban would eventually cut deaths caused by smoking by three thousand a year. It had taken New Labour six years to win the battle – and it was not to be the last. In the financial year 1997-98 in which New Labour came to power, diseases allegedly caused by smoking had cost the National Health Service about £1.7 billion. Revenue from tobacco taxation had produced some £10 billion for the Government. There was also the financial benefit derived from cigarette consumption – and noted privately by Whitehall years before – that as smokers tended to die younger, there was a big saving on care for the elderly and state pensions.

Speaking for the TMA, chief executive Tim Lord said that it was with a degree of nostalgia that the tobacco industry 'says goodbye to the last tobacco advertisement, ending a long, creative and at times controversial era. We have always maintained that tobacco advertising is about brand choice, not an encouragement to smoke'.

Buoyed up by their victory on the advertising front, the anti-smoking crusaders stepped up their demands for a ban on smoking in public places. Preparations were in hand for the last big set-piece battle with the tobacco manufacturers and their workforce. On National No Smoking Day in March 2004, I was present as members of the Lords and Commons Pipe and Cigar Smokers' Club staged their most successful public light-up in defiance of political correctness. Pictures of such flamboyant characters as Lord Belhaven and Stenton, Lord Mason of Barnsley and Lord Harris of High Cross puffing their pipes in New Palace Yard, Westminster, appeared in five national newspapers. Club convenor Lord Mason explained that members were defending the right to light up where they wished.

Then, as some of my tobacco industry friends were becoming despondent at the growing support for a ban on smoking in public places, who should speak out against it but Health Secretary John Reid himself. At a Labour Party event in June, Mr Reid, who had smoked sixty a day before giving up eighteen months earlier, opposed prohibition by arguing that it was better to use education to get people to quit. The stocky Glaswegian and former Communist claimed that cigarettes might be one of the few forms of enjoyment available to the poor, and criticised 'the learned middle class' for being obsessed with banning smoking. 'I don't think the worst problem in our sink estates is by any means smoking', he told his audience. It was as though Rommel had crossed the lines to join Montgomery on the eve of Alamein.

In view of trade union thinking on smoking in public places and the effect of smoke in the workplace, the TWA's role became vital. In autumn 2003, Brenda Warrington's dedicated team had been heartened when the relevant TUC official, Owen Tudor, told a union conference that the TUC advocated common sense and negotiation on the issue. It was not against smokers. The ever-helpful Roger Lyons, MSF/AMICUS general secretary, had written to TUC general secretary elect Brendan Barber. Lyons called for a meeting of trade union general secretaries whose members would be affected by a ban, before the TUC General Council made a decision. The meeting was never held.

Following the 2005 General Election, the Blair Government launched a consultation exercise on the issue. Barber, influenced by anti-smoking propaganda, issued a statement on behalf of the TUC urging ministers to resist vested interest lobbying and seize the opportunity to ban smoking in all workplaces, including pubs and clubs. He did not seem to recognise that some who had a vested interest were members of leading trade unions – a vested interest in protecting their jobs in the tobacco industry. The TUC conference, however, on the initiative of the Musicians' Union whose members disliked performing in smoke-filled rooms, endorsed the call for a ban. The trade union front had been broken. Within the TWA only MSF/AMICUS of the three unions in membership, continued to stand firm.

Nevertheless, within the Government there were divisions on the detail of a ban. This situation was highlighted when, on the eve of a Commons vote on the issue, the disastrous Health Secretary Patricia Hewitt performed a public U-turn in less than twelve hours. On a radio programme in the morning she conceded that there was a strong case for allowing private clubs to allow smoking as they were like people's homes. In the Commons debate on the issue that afternoon she said the arguments were finely balanced on exempting clubs. But at the end of the debate, the dithering woman joined Prime Minister Blair, Chancellor Gordon Brown and ten other Cabinet members in voting for a complete ban. Former Health Minister John Reid and five other Cabinet members voted against it. On the February evening in 2006 the Commons voted by 384 votes to 184 – an overwhelming majority of 200 – to ban smoking in pubs, clubs, restaurants and workplaces by July the following year. Only private homes, hospitals, prisons, care homes and hotel bedrooms were exempted. A typical anomaly of the muddled measure was that if someone were sent to jail for continually breaking the smoking ban, once in prison they would be allowed to light up and puff away.

It was recalled that at the General Election the previous year, Labour proposed that non-food pubs and private clubs should be exempted, although smoking would not be permitted in the bar area. Despite that manifesto pledge, after the election many Labour MPs demanded tougher action. In a leading article, *The Daily Telegraph* described the Commons decision as, 'perhaps the most Draconian infringement of personal liberty yet imposed by this Government'. If that Government had possessed integrity and the courage to wait another year or two, the introduction of a newly manufactured air conditioning system, already successfully tested in the St. Stephen's Tavern across the road from Parliament, would have made the ban in pubs unnecessary. Right up to the ban, well-informed, independent journalists, such as Christopher Booker, continued to point to the lack of scientific evidence that passive smoking caused cancer. Many well-funded studies over the previous twenty years failed to prove decisively and by strict epidemiological standards that such a link existed. Even Sir Richard Doll, an important pioneer in research into the health dangers of smoking, commented in 2001 that 'the effect of other people's smoking in my presence is so small it doesn't worry me'.

By December 2007, pub sales slumped by over seven per cent because of the ban. Worst hit were the traditional working men's clubs and pubs, according to a survey of 2,708 licensees. The onslaught, however, provided me with the pleasure of meeting the artist David Hockney. With pressure building for a ban on smoking in public places, I suggested to the Tobacco Manufacturers' Association in 2004 that it should encourage FOREST to revive its fringe meetings at the annual party conferences. FOREST organised a meeting at Labour's Brighton Conference the following year and invited Hockney, a dedicated smoker, to be on the platform. It was the most successful pro-smoking meeting ever held at such a conference and Hockney delighted the packed audience with his blunt Yorkshire views on the activities of the anti-smoking brigade.

I was due to celebrate my seventy-sixth birthday in January 2006, so I had given notice to the TMA that I would be retiring as their consultant. For thirty-four years I had been the leading political adviser to the tobacco industry and I did not wish to hang on to the point where it would have to take the initiative to end the relationship. I had warned Imperial Tobacco at the outset that I did not foresee us winning the war against the anti-smoking lobby (although no government would be so foolish as to ban smoking completely). But we would win enough battles to seriously delay their victory and so enable the company to diversify into other, hopefully profitable, products.

To mark my retirement, Brenda Warrington and other leading members of the TWA gave me a very enjoyable farewell lunch in a smart restaurant in Buckingham Gate. The AMICUS Union was about to merge again – this time with the mighty Transport and General Workers Union and they were looking for a name for this new giant of the Labour movement. As Amicus had continued to grow and grow, I suggested 'Topsy'. It won a laugh but the name eventually chosen was UNITE.

Having rejoined the Labour Party after Kinnock stepped down as leader, I resigned again over Blair's decision to join the invasion of Iraq with brain-numb Bush, and swore never to re-join again. I was appalled not only by the decision but by the number of Labour MPs prepared to support the act of aggression. During my time back in the Party, I became a Labour governor of a local Kennington school for pupils with special needs. The Shelley School was a well-run establishment with a dedicated staff led by an inspiring headmistress. Soon after I became a governor, however, Lambeth Council added to the problems of running such a school by an ill-thought out scheme to move it to a different location. So much of the headmistress's valuable time was taken up by bureaucracy that she resigned in despair.

Another problem overshadowing us was the effect of the Government's *inclusion* policy that forced thousands of special needs children to attend mainstream schools. Councils were using the policy to close special schools which were expensive to run. At the Shelly School some of the pupils were very severely disabled and I sympathised with the parents of less disabled children who would have preferred to see them transferred to a mainstream establishment.

However, I knew how much personal attention was needed by such children and I believed that it was better for all that they should be educated in an environment designed for their needs. In time, Baroness Warnock, the leading expert on education and disability, came over to this opinion. Initially, she helped to launch the inclusive approach but renounced it in her book *Included or Excluded*. She wrote she was convinced that there were some children, particularly those with autism, Asperger's Syndrome, attention disorders and behavioural difficulties, who were failed in mainstream schools. She asserted that no adaptation could turn a school into an environment in which such children could learn. A special school might be the only place where a fragile child would learn skills that could be of benefit to them.

As a special school governor I had to confess that I found it difficult to judge what educational progress was being made by some of the disabled children, even with all the specialist attention they were receiving. Soon after the headmistress resigned I followed suit, having lost my eligibility to sit as a Labour governor on quitting the Party. I noted with interest some years later that Ruth Kelly, the Communities Minister, opted out of State provision to send her dyslexic son to an expensive private school.

When it came to proving a point about the ability of a disabled person to lead a normal life, the extraordinary Tony Van den Bergh was a great example. In 1998 I had joined the Association of Retired People over Fifty (ARP / O50) and let them know that I would be happy to help the organisation campaign on age discrimination and other issues. Their lively public affairs director Don Steele asked me if I knew Tony van den Bergh.

In fact, I had known Tony since my days as political editor of the *Daily Sketch*. His politically active daughter Peta was working for the Transport and General Workers' Union at Transport House in Smith Square. In the run up to the 1970 General Election, she was helping the Labour Party which was housed in the same building. The grandson of one of the Dutch founders of Unilever, Tony was at that time a writer and broadcaster. Previously he had headed the personnel department of tobacco company Godfrey Phillips, and had then gone on to help set up the anti-smoking organisation ASH, which was to give me so much trouble.

An exuberant bon viveur, he lived life to the full – and suffered some consequences. I visited him in hospital when he was in for a hip replacement. Typically, when he went in for a fourth such operation in 1987, he broadcast a running commentary on it that became the award-winning TV documentary *Treat Me Gently*.

At the age of eighty-two he decided to drive an electric mobility scooter from London to Dover and thence by Hovercraft to Ostend, to raise funds for the Lifespan Trust. He wanted to demonstrate that older people can enjoy active and adventurous lives despite disability. The operation was being supported by ARP / O50 and he and Don Steele asked me to assist with the public relations and drum up support from politicians. The scooter was legally entitled to travel on pavements, footpaths, cycle tracks and all public roads except motorways, and had two speeds of four and eight mph. Tony estimated, therefore, that he should be able to cover the distance in five days at a speed averaging four to five mph. *Operation Scooter to Dover* received the support of politicians and leading public figures such as junior Transport Minister Glenda Jackson, Shadow Health Minister Anne Widdecombe and former Trade Union leaders Jack Jones and Ron Todd.

On Monday June 7th 1999, Tony, disabled by arthritis and hobbling on his sticks, boarded his scooter on Parliament Green to set out on his ninety-mile drive to the coast. Among those there to see him off was my close friend Lord Alf Morris, the first Minister for the Disabled. We sheltered under trees as a summer storm broke and rain poured down. With water streaming off his waterproof jacket and down his short grey beard, the indefatigable Tony gave us a broad smile and a wave and set off for Dover. On arriving at Ostend as planned he was welcomed by the Mayor and a civic reception. He told the press that he wanted to dispel the media image of old people as 'cackling idiots' in their second childhood who sat around in a circle singing long-forgotten songs. We met a few times after his extraordinary achievement and as we sank our glasses of white wine I realised that *Operation Scooter* had been more exhausting than he expected. Early in May 2000 I learned from Peta that he had died. He was 83.

During the run-up to the British-American invasion of Iraq in 2003, the lack of reliable information from within the country became all too apparent. The root of the problem was to be highlighted that year by my close friend and one time colleague Corinne Souza, the daughter of a former senior British spy in Baghdad. Following a nerve-wracking time in the 1960s, and fearful for the safety of his family, Corinne's father informed his Secret Intelligence Service bosses at MI6 in London that he wanted to leave Iraq for good and live in Britain. Once based in London, he became a fierce internal critic of SIS conduct, its lack of knowledge of the Middle East and poor language skills, and became the target of attacks from senior colleagues who foolishly ignored his advice.

A businessman with diplomatic rank equivalent to First Secretary, he had unrivalled knowledge of Iraq, had been responsible for recruiting Iraqi and Kurdish operators, and had specialised in countering Arab terrorism. In her book *Baghdad's Spy* published in 2003, Corinne alleges that despite his high operational skills, he was driven out of the SIS by the incompetence, appalling personnel management and racism of many of its staff. She believes that this is why Britain has been unable to replace people like him or nurture a select cadre of Arabic specialists – with the result that British intelligence in the Middle East disintegrated to the point where it was unable to assist the CIA in the run-up to the terrorist onslaught on September 11[th.]

Lawrence de Souza was born in Baghdad in 1921 of a half-Kurdish, half-Iraqi mother and an Indian father. He then married an English woman. Proud to have British citizenship, he worked as a spy for Britain's secret service for some twenty years from the late 1950s during the deteriorating situation in the Middle East. When he and his family moved to London to escape an increasingly dangerous situation in Iraq, he continued to work for the SIS. Towards the end of his career, however, he was not allowed to resign when he wanted to, and was persistently harassed by members of MI6. In 1978, having opted for a retirement pension – an inconvenient arrangement for MI6 – he was put under enormous pressure to change his mind. When he resisted, pressure was then put on his wife to persuade him to change his mind.

Members of spies' families are expected to do their bit in the espionage game. Corinne's father had feared that the SIS would expect her to be helpful. When they discovered that she was in fact employed by the leading parliamentary consultancy, Charles Barker Watney & Powell his fears were realised. Soon after she had joined my team she was contacted by the intelligence service in 1980 who were interested in her political information work for our clients. They were also interested in her contacts with MPs such as members of the All-Party Motor Industry Group – especially Labour MPs. She refused to be drawn into their net but their pressure and harassment became so unbearable that she decided to resign her job. She had been doing excellent work for me and I was deeply dismayed when she gave six months notice in 1985. The reasons she gave were the pay and conditions. I was not to learn the real reason for her departure until some years later.

Eventually, following the death of her father and continued harassment of her mother by the SIS, Corinne turned to me for help. She had evidence of serious incompetence by the SIS on a major issue together with facts about the treatment suffered by her parents. She asked me to meet her in 1993 and for the first time, I learned of her family involvement with the world of espionage.

She decided to bring her evidence to the attention of a senior Conservative politician and asked me to suggest an appropriate former minister and member of the Privy Council who might be interested in taking up her case. I recommended Lord Colnbrook – my old friend from Imperial Tobacco consultancy days who, as Humphrey Atkins MP, had honourably resigned as Deputy Foreign Secretary over the Falklands mess. I offered to write to Humphrey to ask him to see Corinne, and soon after he invited us to meet him in the Lords.

Although he refused to air her complaints in public by tabling parliamentary questions, he raised them directly with Downing Street and, as a result of his high level intervention, Corinne received a qualified apology on the harassment issue. It came in a letter from Downing Street dated 13th April 1994. It stated, 'SIS wish to apologise for the distress they seem to have caused Miss Souza's mother. This had certainly not been their intention…' On other matters Corinne did not receive satisfaction. Unable to bring SIS staff members to justice, she exposed them collectively in her book.

As Corinne was preparing to launch her exposé of the incompetence and appalling behaviour of certain civil servants, I began to hear growing complaints about the army of special advisers drafted into Whitehall by Blair and his team at 10 Downing Street. By 2002, senior mandarins were describing the development as a threat to the long-established, hallowed impartiality of the civil service. Among those voicing public concern was former Cabinet Secretary Lord Armstrong, who complained that some special advisers had gone beyond advising ministers and had sought to control or direct civil servants. This had happened when my one-time neighbour in Dulwich, Sir Robin Butler, was Cabinet Secretary and in a strong position to protest.

In particular there had been a big turn-out of Whitehall press officers, a growth of spin-doctors and a consequent loss of confidence by the media. Within a year of taking office, the Blair/Campbell regime had sacked at least seven department directors of information who, it was suspected, would bridle against New Labour's particular brand of political censorship.

Blair, like Wilson, had won his first general election on a wave of good will after an even longer period of Conservative rule, which had ended in a mire of sleaze and mismanagement. Yet within a few years his relationship with the media had deteriorated badly, and his spin machine and the firm tactics of his Rottweiler press secretary Alastair Campbell had seriously undermined the confidence of truth-seeking reporters. His disastrous decision to join *crusader* Bush in the unjustified invasion of Iraq and his development of the 'dodgy dossier' finally put an end to whatever remained of the original love affair with sections of the media.

My last personal memory of Campbell is from Michael Foot's 90th birthday party at the Gay Hussar in July 2003. As I left the crowded restaurant, I saw Campbell standing outside in the street, a scowl on his surly face as he bad-mouthed some recusant reporter. The party was a great success and I met many old friends in the crowd, including Ian Aitken and Geoffrey Goodman who had helped to organise the event, which was generously funded by the Transport and General Workers' Union.

Over the years I had met Geoffrey regularly at the annual October reunions to mark the death of the *News Chronicle*. He had become one of the most highly respected and foremost commentators on Labour affairs since the 1950s, and was one of Michael's closest friends. At the forty-second reunion in 2002 which was attended by some thirty former members of the *Chronicle*'s staff, someone recounted how, on returning from holiday, he discovered that he had been burgled and his Second World War medals stolen. I chipped in to say that when I had been burgled by MI5, the thief had left my father's medals but stolen his gold watch. On hearing this Geoffrey revealed that he, too, had been burgled by MI5 in the mid 1970s. He had been very close to the Wilson set-up at 10 Downing Street and when he told the Prime Minister's private secretary Marcia Williams about the break-in, she told him that he was just one of a crowd. She revealed that in just over a year following Wilson's return to Downing Street in 1974, thirteen people working closely for him had been burgled - presumably by MI5.

When Michael Martin, MP for Glasgow Springburn, former metal worker and player of the Highland pipes, accepted my invitation to be Labour joint chairman of the unofficial All-Party Committee for the Tobacco Industry, I did not foresee that he would eventually be elected Speaker of the House of Commons. Although at times annoyed by decisions of the manufacturers, he was a helpful chairman of the group and took necessary action to try to protect jobs in the industry. At party conferences he supported industry functions.

As a senior Commons chairman and the most experienced on the Labour side, he clearly had to be seen as a possible future Speaker and when he was elected in 2000 I wrote to congratulate him. Labour's Betty Boothroyd had retired from the chair and there seemed to be Tory resentment that the convention of alternating this prestigious post between the main parties had been broken. Perhaps some were also unhappy that he was the first Roman Catholic to fill the position since the Reformation. New Labour's younger MPs, however, were all for breaking cobwebbed tradition and were delighted when working class Michael refused to wear the wig and breeches that had been the ritual garb of the Speaker. I thought he had got off to a good start, comparing well with other Speakers I had known. Even when accusations were made that he was not sufficiently impartial and tended to favour the Labour benches, I did not regard it as too serious. After all, when Betty Boothroyd succeeded the admirable Bernard Weatherill as Speaker, she had been subjected to a whispering campaign by Tory MPs who alleged she was biased against them. What I did not like was the way in which some parliamentary reporters sniggered at Michael's working class background, with one snobbish sketch writer nicknaming him *Gorbals Mick.*

As complaints grew about his alleged hyper-sensitivity and difficulties in dealing with his staff, I was unhappy to learn that he had hired the costly libel law firm Carter-Ruck to deal with media accusations. By October 2007, these legal battles were to cost the public purse over £21,000. Then came the fuss over his expenses.

It was disclosed that over a six year period, he had been allowed to claim £75,000 over six years on his constituency home in Glasgow, despite having no mortgage and living rent free in the Grace and Favour Speaker's apartment in the Houses of Parliament. It also emerged that he claimed £7,500 a year for using his home as an office. The press demanded his resignation.

Coupled with growing evidence that some MPs had been seriously abusing the parliamentary expenses allowance system, this scenario added to the growing lack of public respect for the Commons as an institution. Members of Parliament were even increasingly held in lower esteem than journalists – or lobbyists! The fact that in some cases Commons rules had not been broken when MPs claimed thousands of pounds for properties that they had already paid for fuelled demands for drastic reforms of the whole system.

That system had started to go rotten when Harold Wilson was Prime Minister. Surprise, surprise! During one of the spells of economic crisis that marked his bumpy years in Downing Street, he was afraid to increase MPs salaries to levels to which they were entitled, because he was trying to hold down wages nationally. To wriggle out of the jam, Cabinet minister Edward Short was instructed to produce a new package of expenses for MPs to claim as a means of buying them off. This parcel of perks became known as *Short Money* and as the years went by, it became not so much short as generous.

Although MPs salaries have continued to be too low, their pensions are also seen as generous by a large sector of the public.

Having spent some fifty years of my life in and around the Houses of Parliament I have been saddened by the public's loss of respect for our parliamentary institution and its members. As Prime Minister, Tony Blair added to the problem. He was not a 'House of Commons man'. His attendance was poor, he rarely bothered to turn up to vote, and he diminished the role of MPs by a number of reforms and manoeuvres.

Critical of Blair's off-hand treatment of the Commons, I was pleased when Baroness Boothroyd, the retired Speaker, launched a scathing attack on his attitude to standards and Parliament. The vivacious Betty enjoyed a drink and a smoke and had joined the Lords and Commons Pipe and Cigar Smokers' Club. She has good dress sense and has always been well turned out when attending club functions. Sitting as a crossbencher in the Lords, I agreed with the views she expressed in a television interview:

'I would like to think we had made progress on our institutions but sadly there has been a lot of spin, a lot of sleaze, which I hoped when the Blair Government came in would be cleaned up. That has not been the case and the House of Commons is not treated with the respect it should be. It's sad to say that the Prime Minister comes to the House of Commons only once a week to answer questions. He's never seen in there. I doubt whether he takes part in debates there. I feel Parliament is not being treated as a proper debating area where the leaders of our country are seen at the Dispatch Box'.

Blair of course, had changed the Prime Minister's Question Time from the traditional two slots a week slots to just one. Betty must have been pleased when, soon after her attack, he retired from 10 Downing Street to embark on his role as a peace envoy to the Middle East. Soon after leaving Downing Street in a trail of Iraqi and British blood, Blair spoke publicly of the importance of faith – a subject that according to the Church of England's leaders had been seriously neglected during his time in office. A church report accused his administration of failing society and lacking a moral vision for the country.

I recalled how much time I had put in to help get this man into Downing Street and I became seriously worried about my judgement.

CHAPTER TEN
Deaths and Disillusion

Baroness Thatcher, relaxed and wearing a tasteful turquoise suit, smiled as she moved towards me in the small crowded room where we had gathered to launch Alfred Sherman's last book – and, unwittingly, to witness her last meeting with her one-time guru. As she stopped to chat I recalled how I had encouraged Alfred, some thirty years before, to join the Keith Joseph think-tank which was to set her on the path to power. She said what a good move that had been and we agreed that Alfred was brilliant when it came to developing and articulating new ideas designed to make a breakthrough, often ruthlessly, on some policy front. We agreed, too, with smiles, that he was no diplomat – no gift to public relations. They had fallen out over policy when she had been at 10 Downing Street for a few years and had not spoken for a long time.

His new book *Paradoxes of Power* was not designed to heal the breach as it concluded that her administrations of the 1980s were, for the most part, merely an interlude that had left the post-war consensus largely unchanged. We were, in Alfred's opinion, back to where we started. By 1990 he argued, Margaret Thatcher had come to represent a new status quo. Problems which had vexed the country when she had bid for the leadership remained… it was like the old days of 'stop-go' but the booms seemed to be getting shorter and the busts longer and deeper.

It was a warm evening in July 2005 and we had met, appropriately, at the Centre for Policy Studies in Westminster. There were thirty people present, among them an old friend of Alfred's and mine from LSE days, Neville Beale, Sir John Hoskyns, a former Downing Street adviser, and Professor Kenneth Minogue. Neville had met Alfred again in the 1970s and was surprised to discover that he was a Tory councillor for Chelsea's Earls Court ward. As chairman of the local Tory Party, Neville was asked by the Council leader not to re-adopt Alfred as a candidate. One of his sins: 'excessive criticism' of his fellow councillors. This censorious habit was to cause irritation in due course at the very highest level of government.

In a preface to the book, Lord Tebbit wrote that Alfred was frequently frustrated by what he regarded as a lack of courage and conviction by politicians. But although critics attacked him for being too materialistic, Tebbit stressed that Alfred was aware that free market capitalism was merely a tool, not an objective. Lady Thatcher, ignoring her doctor's advice to desist from public speaking, paid a short tribute to Alfred, saying, 'We could never have defeated Socialism if it had not been for him'.

I wanted Alfred to sign my copy of his book before leaving the party. He looked exhausted, slumped in a chair, and could barely write his signature. As his attentive Portuguese second wife administered to him, he seemed about to be sick and then, to my alarm, slipped to the floor. I feared he was dying. But he survived until the end of August the following year. He was eighty-six. I attended his funeral at Mortlake Crematorium and to my surprise was one of only twenty-one people in the chapel. *The Times* had devoted a whole page to his obituary in recognition of his importance.

Yet up to the day of his funeral Margaret Thatcher had sent no message of sympathy to his widow and was not represented at the final ceremony. Neville Beale was there together with another graduate from the LSE. In front of the coffin was draped the colourful standard of the International Brigade Memorial Trust. The Trust's secretary recalled Alfred's courage. As a seventeen year old, he had fought with the Brigade in the Spanish Civil War before he was captured and held for seven months in atrocious conditions in a Fascist prison camp. He survived his hellhole with stoicism and dignity before being released in an exchange of prisoners and returned to England. Throughout his subsequent life he would sing – on appropriate occasions – Spanish revolutionary songs.

In October 2006 we assembled again in the Centre for Policy Studies for a memorial meeting. Sir John Hoskyns recalled meeting Alfred in 1975 when the CPS was only eighteen months old and said the Centre would never have started without him. He described Alfred as a formidable thinker and an extraordinary political phenomenon and recalled some of his aphorisms, 'One true enemy is worth a hundred false friends'; 'A university education advances all one's attributes including one's stupidity'.

Recalling privately my schoolboy ambition to be an 'eminence grise', I consoled myself with the thought that although I had not earned the soubriquet, I had helped Alfred into that role – and no one could dispute his claim to that title.

I had expected to see one of my favourite people at the meeting – Ralph Harris, Lord Harris of High Cross. I had been told he planned to be there and was disappointed when the jovial pipe-smoking economist did not appear. It was announced next day that he had died of a heart attack. Two great, but very different, free marketeers had died within two months.

Ralph was sadly missed in March the following year when the Lords and Commons Pipe and Cigar Smokers Club met on National No Smoking Day to enjoy a puff in public and put up two fingers to the increasingly successful and intolerant anti-smoking brigade. Ralph, in his deerstalker hat, had always been a favourite subject for the media cameramen, who swarmed around on these occasions. This year there were more than ever, for it was to be the last occasion on which members of the twenty-year-old club would be able to light up in public. On July 1st the ban on smoking in public places was due to come into force.

National No Smoking Day ended with a reception for MPs and peers hosted by the Tobacco Workers' Alliance in a Commons dining room. There I learned that after ten years of activity, the trade union pressure group to preserve jobs was to be disbanded after October's Labour Party Conference. I heard the news from Brenda Warrington who had done a first class job as TWA chair for the past decade.

There was one more blow to come. When I talked to John Cummings, the former miner Labour MP for Easington, who for years had sponsored the TWA's Commons receptions, I learned that he planned to retire at the next general election. I had known him before he entered Parliament in 1987 for, as a local councillor, he had travelled to London to attend my launch of the Coalfield Communities Campaign. He introduced me to his young research assistant who was studying, as I had, International Relations at the LSE. I was flattered when John described me to the young man as the 'best and nicest' lobbyist in Parliament.

Like other final acts that day, it was the last function to be hosted in the Commons by the TWA. They were leaving the field of battle with drums beating and flags flying. I was proud to have been associated with them and had greatly enjoyed their comradeship. One of the senior Labour MPs who found time to look in on the reception was Nick Brown, a staunch supporter of the fight to save the jobs of tobacco workers. A series of young men had operated as campaign secretary of the Alliance.

A particularly successful one was Gary Follis, whom I introduced to Nick and who eventually went to work for him as a special advisor on his return to Government in the Whips' Office in 2007.

At the end of July 2007, four weeks after the ban was introduced on smoking in public places, a publican wrote to *The Daily Telegraph*. He recalled that the Government had told the nation that once the smoking ban was in force, 'People would flock to our pubs, trade would be well above normal and food sales would go through the roof'. Ruefully he added, 'I think that somewhere along the line somebody has forgotten to tell the non-smokers. Where are they? We geared up with extra staff, revamped the menu, did a paint job, but no extra trade... Average British pub takings are twenty-two per cent down since July 1st. I have been told of five closing down within ten miles of me'.

Sales of cigarettes fell by over eleven per cent in July 2007 compared with the previous year. Some twenty-eight per cent more people gave up smoking that month than in July 2006. By February 2009 adult smokers in England were down to twenty-one per cent.

Hit by the smoking ban and higher taxes on drink, some forty pubs were closing every week by January 2009. By August the weekly closure rate had climbed to fifty-two, bringing the annual rate to 2377 with a loss of 24,000 jobs in the sector. Together with the closure of many post offices, this trend was leaving village communities with no centre of social life and activity. Meanwhile, people who had enjoyed their visits to 'the local' were confined to their homes with cans of lager, their cigarette smoke inhaled by their children as they watched TV together.

As I had warned the brewers twenty-five years before, with their work against the tobacco industry largely complete, the professional health lobbyists now turned their attention to alcohol. If the drinks industry had seen tobacco as a buffer zone and had helped to protect it, their turn in the firing line might have been delayed. By July 2007 the Government's Chief Medical Officer Sir Liam Donaldson was recommending that tax on alcohol should be increased significantly to discourage drunkenness. He declared, 'As with tobacco, price works in reducing alcohol consumption. Tobacco is a good example of a health problem that is in hand'.

He also suggested that drinks companies should be banned from sponsoring sporting and other events to break any association between alcohol and physical fitness or glamour. It had worked with tobacco, he added.

In March 2009 the Commons Select Committee on Health accused the Government of wasting billions of pounds on un-researched initiatives that were 'little more than propaganda'. Huge sums had been squandered on 'ineffective and possibly damaging campaigns aimed at moulding our lifestyles without even basic calculations being made about the hoped for benefits'. In the same month, the Advertising Standards Authority went further by ruling that a Health Department anti-smoking advert was so extreme it could frighten young children by suggesting their parents could die imminently if they smoked.

Yet another friend had died – Lord (Jack) Weatherill. Friends and admirers of the respected former Speaker packed Westminster Abbey for his memorial service on a cold, sunny day in October 2007. As I sat surrounded by Tory parliamentarians, former MPs and their spouses, my memory led me back to conversations and incidents involving him over some forty years. I recalled how, as Deputy Chief Whip, he had been called out in March 1979 to identify the parliamentary pass beside the shattered, unrecognisable body of Airey Neave, assassinated by an IRA bomb as he drove from the Commons car park. Jack told me he was aghast when faced with this appalling task. I saw Margaret Thatcher in the congregation and recalled that she had not wanted him to have the Speaker's post. Jack, after his retirement, had joked that he was, 'Not the choice of the cardinals and had been put in by a peasants' revolt'.

Looking back at his time in the Commons, he would lament that it had lost its traditional role and relevance. In his view, this was largely because of the growth of the select committee system that took an increasing number of MPs away from the chamber. The problem was to become worse under the Blair Government with its deliberate policy of bypassing that arena. He was part of the negotiations over Blair's plans for reform of the House of Lords and played an important role in the arrangement that gave ninety-two hereditary peers the right to continue to sit and speak in the Upper House.

My recollections ended as the service in the Abbey began and a priest paid tribute to Jack's humanity, integrity, strength of character, modesty and charm. There were many other tributes too. I looked at Baroness Thatcher and wondered whether she would admit to making a mistake when she tried to block Jack's election to the Speaker's chair.

My previous visit to the Abbey had been to attend the service for Sir Edward Heath, who died in July 2005. I had been allocated a good seat and thought that Baroness Thatcher looked unusually spry as she walked in to bid a final farewell to her old adversary who some claimed had been in a perpetual sulk since she defeated him for the Tory leadership decades earlier. The description 'Renaissance Man' is often misused when people talk of someone gifted in several fields. However, I have long believed that it rightly applied to Heath.

He not only reached the peak in politics, but was an accomplished musician, a leading international yachtsman, a collector and connoisseur of art, a successful wartime soldier with an on-going interest in military affairs and a City operator who built up a considerable fortune with the help of well placed friends: quite a record for the son of a Broadstairs builder. Moreover, he had courage and integrity.

I was spending an increasing amount of time at memorial services and funerals and was beginning to feel my age when Alf Morris popped up again to give me something useful to do. Active as ever in the defence of disabled people, his Lordship had launched an independent inquiry into the scandal of the supply of contaminated blood to haemophilia patients by the National Health Service during the 1970s and 1980s.

By 2009, nearly 2000 people exposed to HIV and hepatitis C by such bad blood and blood products had died since being infected in what has been described as, 'The worst treatment disaster in the history of the NHS'. Some supplies had even been purchased cheaply from American companies who bought the blood from drug addict donors, inmates of US prisons and prostitutes riddled with disease.

The Haemophilia Society first called for a public inquiry in 1988 but this justifiable demand had been resisted by successive governments. On the advice of civil servants, ministers had chosen instead to hold in-house Health Department inquiries into narrowly defined aspects of the scandal. Only officials were involved and there was no opportunity for infected patients, the dependents of those who had died, or even former ministers to give evidence. As president of the All-Party Parliamentary Group on Haemophilia, Lord Morris decided that the only way forward was to hold a privately funded independent inquiry in public. This would ensure that the voices of those most affected would be heard at last – after twenty years of Whitehall obstruction.

The well-respected former Labour Solicitor General, Lord Archer of Sandwell, agreed to chair the inquiry and shortly before the first sitting in April Alf asked me to advise on publicity. I produced a press release that drew attention to the many MPs of all parties who were supporting Alf's initiative that aimed to shame the Government for failing to hold an official inquiry.

On the eve of the opening of the inquiry, it was revealed that thousands of haemophiliacs had developed HIV and hepatitis C from contaminated blood because warnings to the Government about the risks had been ignored. The BBC *Newsnight* programme said it had obtained a letter from the head of Britain's public health surveillance centre. In it, he warned the Health Department about the risk of AIDS from Factor Eight, the clotting agent used to help haemophiliacs. The 1983 letter had called for a ban on US blood – but successive governments since then had claimed wrongly that not enough was known about the dangers of Factor Eight to justify stopping treatment.

As I attended sittings of the inquiry, it became clear from the evidence that, at a crucial time, one man responsible for not getting to grips with the blood supply problem and infected US imports was someone I knew well – Dr. Gerard Vaughan. He had let me down over my retirement from the secretaryship of the Parliamentary and Scientific Committee. Now he appeared to have let down thousands over the issue of the use of infected blood. Vaughan had been Minister of State for Health from 1979 to 1982. Lord Jenkin of Roding, who as Patrick Jenkin had been Secretary of State for Health from 1979-81, told the inquiry that he had left day-to-day administration to Vaughan. Since Vaughan was a doctor, he knew a lot more about the medical aspects than himself. Moreover, as Vaughan was knowledgeable about blood supplies he, Jenkin, was happy to delegate to him the day-to-day conduct of affairs on the subject – provided he kept Jenkin in touch with anything important. Every month he received a report on the problem of infected blood and when necessary spoke with Vaughan to ensure he was happy to continue to deal with it – and was doing so satisfactorily.

Jenkin got the impression that the department wanted to ensure that the Blood Transfusion Service (BTS) could be relied upon again as there had been a shadow hanging over it. He was told the BTS was not self-sufficient and that it had to buy blood products from other sources, including the USA. But he was not told from where in North America it was coming. He assumed it was a reliable source. While the Secretary of State was responsible for issuing licenses for blood products to be sold or administered, he was in the hands of expert committees. Considerable medical expertise was necessary to make a judgment and Jenkin said Vaughan might very well have had some understanding of the subject - but he himself did not.

Long after leaving the Government, Jenkin was horrified to learn of the extent of the contamination. He decided to look back at department papers to find out if there was any evidence to support claims for compensation from infected people. He was told that all files relating to contaminated blood products had been destroyed as the department had settled HIV cases, and compensation had been paid. Compensation, however, had not been paid to people suffering from hepatitis C, and it was admitted later to Jenkin that it had been a mistake to destroy the files. Later still, some of the 'destroyed' files were found in the department.

In fact, it emerged that between 1979-81, the department was aware that the Transfusion Service had bought infected, contaminated blood products from the USA and that this had been given to patients, many of them haemophiliacs.

It appears that Vaughan was in a position to know this, and as a minister directly involved, failed to raise the alarm with his Secretary of State. What is not known for sure is whether Vaughan was told that some of the blood was taken from prisoners in US jails or bought from intravenous drug users with HIV and hepatitis C. It is now known that because the alarm was raised so late, more than 4,500 people with haemophilia were infected with hepatitis C through NHS contaminated blood products, and of these more than 1,200 were infected with HIV.

There was an impressive media turn out for the July sitting of the inquiry where the star witness was Lord David Owen. As a doctor and junior Health Minister from 1974-76 he had taken a great interest in the supply of blood. I was impressed by his dedication and felt that if his recommendations had been implemented the issue of 'bad blood' would not have arisen.

The question was raised of why the Ombudsman, who investigated cases of maladministration, had been unwilling to hold an inquiry into the scandal. It emerged that he had argued that the problem was not one of maladministration but that it had arisen from a political, ministerial decision. Officials of the mismanaged Department of Health had made known that no representative from the Ministry would give evidence to the Archer inquiry since it believed the investigation was unnecessary.

As Blair's period in office was drawing to a close, my feelings about him were summed up by Sir Alastair Graham, chairman of the Government's

Committee on Standards in Public life. He had made a number of justified criticisms of ministers' behaviour and Blair had intervened to ensure that Sir Alastair's tenure of office, due to end in April 2007, would not be extended. In March, Sir Alastair launched a scathing attack on the mired Blair administration and declared that it would be as strongly identified with the loss of public trust as John Major's was with sleaze. He asserted, 'The public certainly feel let down over the period. The most fundamental thing is that Blair has betrayed himself. He set such a high bar for people to judge him and has fallen well below the standards he set for himself'.

Elected on a wave of public anger over allegations of Tory corruption and sleaze, Blair solemnly pledged that he would never let Labour politicians behave in a manner that even appeared not to comply with the highest ethical standards. But in the early days of his administration, he had been caught up in the affair of the Ecclestone donation and Formula One tobacco sponsorship.

Blair's image during his premiership had not been improved by the activities of his once inventive image-maker Peter Mandelson. Blair felt he owed him a debt for selling New Labour to the voting public like some new washing powder that gets things *Whiter than White*. Whatever the reason, Blair certainly gave Mandelson an extraordinary number of second chances. He took him back into the Government twice in a short time after scandals had forced him to resign.

Sir Christopher Kelly replaced Sir Alastair Graham as chairman of the Committee on Standards in Public Life. In a press interview, Sir Christopher admitted that the state of affairs that had greeted him was 'surprising'. He was well aware of how difficult it would be to rebuild trust in politicians after such episodes as cash for honours, and the dodgy dossier of the Iraq war. His advice to MPs in January 2008 was, 'The way to earn trust is to be straightforward and honest'.

Within a few weeks the public was to be angered and appalled by revelations of the abuse and misuse of their expense allowances by *honourable* Members of Parliament. Was Sir Christopher talking to the deaf?

As my lobbying days were over, I watched with interest from the sidelines as the old issue of registration of clients raised its head above the parapet once more. It was October 2007, thirty years since John Addey and his allies had clashed with the Public Relations Consultants' Association on the issue when I had argued that the registration of lobbyists and their clients should take priority. Now some MPs were condemning a new code of principles produced by the Association of Professional Political Consultants. This would allow lobbyists to keep secret their client lists. By proposing that they should not be required to keep a public register of clients, the Association was seeking to end an existing system under the profession's self-regulation code. It suggested that organisations should instead always be clear and precise about their identity and any body they represented.

For some MPs, this did not go far enough and they insisted that permanent and complete openness about all clients was essential. Gill Morris, Alf's daughter, who had taken over some of my clients when I retired from GCI London, had been elected chair of the Association. She ran a successful and respected business, and argued that the principles in the new code provided a good foundation. They included an undertaking to, 'Never offer financial or other inducement' to holders of public office. Others argued, as had Addey, that clients were entitled to keep their identities private.

The dispute flared as MPs on the Commons Public Administration Committee were preparing to launch yet another investigation into lobbying. Soon the sums paid to a few parliamentarians from unprincipled lobbyists would look paltry compared to what many more were receiving under the disgraceful system of parliamentary expenses. Following evidence of abuse of the arrangement under which MPs could claim money to pay mortgages on homes in their constituencies or in London, the Commons Speaker was obliged to release claims made by Labour Cabinet ministers and leading Tories.

The sickening extent to which Britain's taxpayers had been funding the homes and living expenses of MPs was finally exposed in May 2008, after months of attempts to block publication of the figures. Under the lax but legal allowances system which parliamentarians had set up for themselves, some had milked the Additional Costs Allowance of up to £22,000 a year to spend on maintaining a second home.

I was reminded of Harold Wilson's ill-considered and devious initiative to boost expenses in lieu of a justified pay rise when Sir Christopher Kelly, chairman of Parliament's Committee on Standards in Public Life, warned MPs in April 2008 that, 'Expenses should never be regarded as a substitute for pay'. His committee declared that MPs had to be seen to lead by example and observed that the public would not be satisfied with the review of the expenses system being carried out by Commons Speaker Michael Martin. Sir Christopher was quoted as saying that he could think of no similar example of self-interested individuals investigating their own allowances. He wanted an independent inquiry.

As I listened to Prime Minister Gordon Brown address the 2007 Labour Party Conference mostly about his background and personal beliefs, I was convinced that he was about to go to the country to seek an endorsement of his tenancy of 10 Downing Street. He had not faced the normal Party leadership election, or the test of a general election. He knew, however, that most voters had been glad to see the back of the Blairs. Many thought he had done a good job as Chancellor, providing a steady economy with low interest rates and rising property values. He must have been encouraged to believe that he could win an autumn election and another five years in power. He seemed to have made a good start as Prime Minister.

Suddenly, there were doubts in Downing Street. To my surprise he decided he could not risk asking the electorate for a vote of confidence. I was reminded of Callaghan's mistake in 1978 when he decided to postpone facing the voters. Soon, like Callaghan, Brown was up to his neck in troubles.

By the spring of 2008 he was engulfed in a bitter political row over his ill-judged decision to abolish the 10p tax band in his last Budget as Chancellor the previous year. The stated aim of his tax policy was to help the poorest in society, yet, by abolishing the 10p tax rate, he had added to the financial burdens of many on the lowest incomes. There was cause for serious doubt about his ability to think through the consequences of his tax proposal.

Then I recalled his handling of the tobacco tax and I told myself that we should not be surprised. Despite clear warnings from independent experts, Chancellor Brown slapped a twenty-five per cent tax increase on cigarettes – thus boosting the influx of cheap, smuggled tobacco products from abroad and leading to an increase in smoking. His stated aim had been to reduce smoking for health reasons. Instead, he ignored expert advice and brought about the first increase in the habit for twenty-five years. He not only had a blind eye. He had a blind spot intellectually.

Stubbornly he and his obedient Treasury ministers defended the 10p tax band decision until faced with a real threat of defeat in the Commons. But they did not move fast enough to avert a massive defeat in the May local elections when Labour recorded its lowest share of the vote for forty years. Greater disasters, not only for Brown, but for Britain, lay ahead.

Nearly twenty years after I had been employed as a lobbyist by the Ford Motor Company to assist it in its successful bid to buy Jaguar, news broke that it had decided to sell the famous British marque. It was also reported that it was selling Land Rover, which I had failed to help General Motors buy in the 1980s and which Ford had purchased in 2000. Production of the two iconic brands had been a serious financial burden to the company, which had lost over £6 billion in 2006. I recalled how Ford had ambitious plans to use a revived Jaguar to compete with Germany's BMW and Mercedes-Benz. Despite its management skills and experience, it had failed. As rumours spread of the proposed sell-off, the trade union I had worked with on the tobacco front spoke out in alarm at the possibility of an asset stripping private equity company becoming the buyer. The union, renamed Unite, had many members working at the two plants.

Tony Woodley, joint general secretary, warned that if the only chance was the private equity option, then there should be some form of direct government intervention in the interest of jobs and the British economy. He need not have worried. In March 2008 India's Tata Group bought Jaguar and Land Rover in a £1 billion plus deal that was quickly endorsed by the trade unions as it secured some 18,000 jobs. The sale had ended two decades of Ford ownership of British luxury brands. Ford made known that it intended to concentrate in future on its traditional operations in the USA. Another wheel had turned full circle.

By November 2008 another past American client, General Motors, was seen to be in serious trouble. GM shares fell to a 65-year low after the company admitted it may run out of money by the end of the year. Union boss Tony Woodley said that the collapse of GM would be catastrophic with an immediate impact on its Vauxhall plants in Britain that employed some 5000 workers.

Early in 2008, some thirty years after I had assisted the Police Federation as their political consultant to win a major new pay deal, they were once again locked in battle with a Labour Government. Home Secretary Jacqui Smith had refused to approve the full 2.5 % pay rise recommended by the Police Arbitration Tribunal. Her counter-proposal of 1.9 %, which would have meant a loss of £250 a head, on average, had been branded a breach of faith by the police who insisted that she should have abided by the recognised arbitration procedure. Once again it was highlighted that, unlike other public employees, the police were prohibited from taking industrial action, joining a trade union or belonging to a political party. And once again, the police talked of the need to consider strike action if they were to be treated so unfairly by government. As before, the Tory Party supported the police force, describing it as the victim of a betrayal of trust.

Labour had failed to learn the lesson over police pay and law and order that it lost in 1979, and thirty years later found itself in an even worse situation. The Police Federation's annual conference took place in May 2008. Representatives of the 140,000 rank and file officers in England and Wales voted overwhelmingly to support a change in the law to allow them to strike. Their leaders complained bitterly that relations with the Government had reached an all-time low, and a ballot revealed that eighty-six per cent of officers wanted the right to take industrial action – a right they had lost in 1919 under the Police Act. Since that time they had been in a different situation from other public sector workers – and generally had been treated accordingly. That was until the dispute with the Callaghan Government in 1978, and the Brown Government's decision to break the agreed formula for handling pay claims in 2007.

When the over-promoted, inexperienced Home Secretary attended the conference next day, she was ridiculed and insulted. She had a much tougher time than Callaghan's Home Secretary, Merlyn Rees, when I had helped to organise the *stony silence* protest at the Federation's Scarborough conference.

In one vital area the police were in a weaker position than in 1979 – and in facing up to them the Government was well aware of their Achilles' heel. Over the past few decades, the police had gradually lost the respect and support of the public. The problem was accurately summed up in September 2008 by the president of the Police Superintendents' Association Ian Johnston. He publicly admitted that all too often police officers disappointed the people they were in business to serve. He complained that they were 'rude and uncivil' and had to learn to provide a better service.

He was echoing my personal experience in Kennington over some twenty-five years, when he said, 'There are too many occasions when police stations are not open, when we don't answer the phone and when, having recorded an offence, we don't go back to keep people up-to-date on what we are doing. Over half the complaints against the police are about rudeness and incivility and about lack of service. We need to pay attention to that… National poll after national poll says that despite our record on crime levels, confidence is decreasing'.

That lack of confidence was deterring decent people from getting involved when they witnessed a crime.

The Government, of course, carried a large share of the blame for this situation. The Blair administration with its reliance on targets, had over-loaded the police with report writing. Bogged down with paperwork, Dixon of Dock Green could no longer find time to do his job on the beat. Despite a defensive Government claim that it had cut red tape, in July 2009 Home Office figures revealed that police time spent on paperwork was increasing. By September, according to official figures, the rate at which the police solved violent crimes had fallen to forty-seven per cent, the lowest ever. A Police Federation spokesman noted that police were, 'Tied up with bureaucracy'. The detection rate in 1997 when New Labour took power was seventy-eight per cent. Morale had slumped and had been damaged further by the Government's clumsy handling of the police pay award.

By April 2009, however, the police had fallen even lower in public esteem. Footage of officers handling demonstrations around the Bank of England during the G20 Conference revealed the use of unnecessary force. Protestors had used their mobile phone cameras to record the evidence. I was dismayed by TV images of brutality by officers and suspected that the largely law-abiding British public would be less inclined to support the police or their rightful pay claim.

The chairman of the Independent Police Complaints Commission (IPCC), Nick Hardwick, took note of the growing outcry. On April 19th he publicly criticised police behaviour, expressed 'serious concerns' about the supervision of officers and called for a national debate about tactics used in maintaining public order. In a breach of the rules, officers policing demonstrations had covered up their identification numbers to avoid being reported. He described this practise as 'unacceptable' and reminded them that they were 'servants, not masters' of the public.

It seemed to me that if Laura Norda were to be an important issue at the coming General Election it would be muddied by evidence of police brute force in attempting to restore order on the streets. It struck me, too, that if the video-phone technology had been available during the battles between police and striking coal miners twenty-five years earlier, perhaps there would have been a greater public outcry about a disproportionate response to the desperate men demonstrating to protect their livelihoods.

In a police force once admired by the public as the thin blue line between themselves and disorder, the bullyboy ethos had grown. And it seemed to me that New Labour had done little or nothing to discourage it.

As Miss Smith was holding down the pay of her police force, the public was outraged to learn in March 2009 that Britain's Home Secretary had been availing herself of the second home allowance. This was within the rules of the Commons, allowing MPs from distant constituencies to stay in London.

With the prospect of serious defeats in local and European Parliament elections in June, Gordon Brown bowed belatedly to mounting public fury over the expenses scandal that involved so many ministers and Labour and Tory backbenchers. But instead of working with the Tory and Lib Dem Party leaders to produce a cross-party formula, he played politics with the issue and desperately tried to win credit for taking action by coming up with his own plan. To the astonishment of MPs on all sides, he proposed replacing the abused second home allowance with a daily attendance allowance for MPs. Within a week, overwhelming opposition to that ill-conceived plan forced him to drop it. Instead, it was agreed that the Committee on Standards in Public Life should tackle the second homes problem as part of its wide-ranging inquiry into MPs expenses. Bewildered MPs then voted for a clutch of interim measures including abolition of the unnecessary second home allowance for London MPs.

In due course Jacqui Smith, having departed from her position as Home Secretary in a Cabinet reshuffle, suffered the humiliation of having to apologise to the Commons. Parliament's Standards and Privileges Committee chastised her in October 2009 for wrongly designating the room she occupied in her sister's London house as her principal residence. In view of her ministerial battle with the Police Federation, it seemed poetic justice that her police guards' logbooks, when she was Home Secretary, proved she had spent less time at the London address than she had claimed.

To distract public attention from the ministers' abuse of expenses, Damian McBride, the Prime Minister's head of strategy and planning at 10 Downing Street, prepared a vicious smear campaign against leading Tories and their wives. Using an official 10 Downing Street e-mail address, he sent drafts of his proposed slurs to Labour blogger Derek Draper, one-time aide to Peter Mandelson. But before the false allegations could be posted on the web, the e-mails fell into the hands of an independent political blogger who exposed the ugly plot and forced McBride to resign in disgrace. Some decent Labour politicians were appalled that Gordon Brown could have employed someone so amoral and unscrupulous as his right hand man, and they spoke out in horror. My old friend Tam Dalyell, living in retirement in Scotland, described 10 Downing Street as 'a vipers' nest' and asked, 'How do you employ a man like McBride in the first place?'

As I read his words I recalled that when I first became involved with the Labour Party as a schoolboy in 1945, it was led by a truly honourable and decent politician – Clement Attlee. What must the saintly Clem be saying as he looks down from his stained glass window at the disgusting mess festering at the very heart of New Labour?

Not that a smear campaign emanating from a Labour leader's office was a new phenomenon. Around 1960, Hugh Gaitskell, a reckless womaniser, had encouraged his aide John Harris to spread damaging allegations about the sex life of Harold Wilson, his challenger for the leadership. The difference was that the smear tactics of Gaitskell and his office viper Harris were not revealed by the press. Moreover, sexy Hugh never reached 10 Downing Street.

Events turned out badly for another of my once-esteemed former clients – BAA. With hindsight it should have been forced to give up at least one of its English airports when it was privatised by the Thatcher Government in 1987, a process in which I assisted. Mrs Thatcher, of course, wanted no unessential complications to the sell-off at that time. But up to then it had enjoyed a reputation for competent management and satisfactory service.

Around 1990 when travelling by air I was proud to wear the BAA tie presented to me by the company for my work as its political consultant. By 2005 I would have risked being lynched by angry, tormented passengers if I had worn it at a London area BAA airport. By 2007 I swore that in future I would try to avoid the agony of flying from Heathrow or Gatwick. BAA had been bought by a Spanish consortium in 2006, and I could not believe that service at any of its seven airports in England and Scotland would be improved by that development. I did not foresee how much worse its record would become, culminating in the catastrophic opening of its new Terminal 5 at Heathrow in 2008.

'BAA is one of Britain's most arrogant, complacent and customer-unfriendly businesses', wrote journalist Jeff Randall, adding, 'It's a showcase for the disbenefits of immunity from competition'.

Unfortunately for the bosses of BAA, the Government's Competition Commission agreed. In August 2008, it recommended the break-up of BAA's monopoly in a report welcomed by travellers, politicians and most airlines. It said BAA should be made to sell three of its seven airports – Gatwick and Stansted in the London area and either Glasgow or Edinburgh in Scotland. 'These changes should deal with many of the problems which the travelling public have faced for many years from lost luggage, long queues and delays', declared the Commission, adding: 'One of the main reasons for privatising BAA as a single entity was for investment in new capacity. But in terms of runway capacity, this has not happened'.

It went on to blame BAA for being unresponsive to the needs of airlines and a lack of initiative over expanding runway capacity. Instead it had invested in more and more moneymaking shops. That rang a bell for me. I recalled my personal disappointment following privatisation and the retirement of BAA chairman Sir Norman Payne. I discovered that for the new management, the first aim was to expand the shopping area rather than improve comfort and service for economy class passengers like me.

Sea Containers, another proud old client, bit the dust. Under the leadership of flamboyant tycoon James Sherwood, the transport conglomerate had owned such glamorous assets as the Orient Express. It had gone bankrupt in October 2006. The once confident, adventurous Sherwood had left his debt-ridden company earlier that year. By August 2008, the directors were offering creditors shares in a new, restructured company to be named Sea Co. Ltd.

It had been exhilarating to be a consultant to Sherwood, who had spent some forty years building up his business and I had always felt a tingle of excitement on entering his ostentatious headquarters, adorned by large golden balls, overlooking The Thames.

In August 2008, twenty-five years after my suggestion for a grass roots corner shop campaigning organisation had produced the nation-wide Tobacco Alliance of small retailers, it announced that in the face of the Government's latest threats to sales it was re-branding as the Tobacco Retailers' Alliance. In May, ministers announced a consultation programme on proposals to ban the display of tobacco in shops and a ban on packs of ten cigarettes, claiming that the low price made them attractive and accessible to children. In its summer newsletter the Alliance complained that to prepare a shop for a display ban would be costly and sales would be lost when customers did not realise that cigarettes were sold there. Potential customers would also tend to go to larger outlets where they could be sure their favourite brand would be stocked.

Small tobacconists were facing an unprecedented threat to their business and the Alliance explained that to rally them to fight for their existence, the organisation's name would include the word 'retailers'. This change of name by my brainchild and the Government's proposed ban on tobacco displays in shops gave a great boost to membership of the Tobacco Retailers' Alliance - 10,000 independent retailers joined the organisation in the twelve months to August 2009.

The corner shops had played an important role in combating the campaigns of the anti-smoking lobby and justified Imperial Tobacco's faith in my suggestion and in then persuading the whole manufacturing industry to set up the Alliance. It struck me that in a roundabout way, Imperial could benefit from a display ban in such shops because, coupled with the ban on advertising, it would make it virtually impossible now for new competitors to enter the market.

As for the continued persecution of the tobacco industry by anti-smoking ministers, I have wondered about the effect on Labour's support at a general election if thousands of beleaguered but popular small corner shops urged customers to vote for one of the other parties?

While the public has lost confidence in MPs, politicians have lost confidence in Whitehall. There has been a growing grumble for some years about the incompetence and lack of management skills of too many civil servants. The problem was recognised in 2006 by Sir Gus O'Donnell, the Cabinet Secretary and head of the Civil Service, when he set in motion a series of capability reviews of departments. He said, 'We have to improve management at the top, through rigorous performance management and intervention where necessary. We must listen to what those who use public services are saying to us. We have to improve our own capability and skills…'

The failure of the Civil Service cannot be put down to a shortage of staff. In 2007 over half a million people were employed by the Service and its agencies. About two thirds resign before normal retirement age, suggesting that many get fed up – and this points to bad management and poor leadership. There is also evidence of a lack of pride, courage and integrity at the top level where officials have failed to stand up against the growing habit of ministers to recruit special advisers from outside the Service. Has any top civil servant resigned in protest at the undermining of the traditional role of the Civil Service? The mandarins hang on to maximise their generous pensions and add to their collection of gaudy honours.

Further evidence of a lack of standards and conflicts of interest in the top ranks of the Civil Service was revealed in February 2009. For years I was surprised at seeing senior officials enjoying the costly hospitality of leading businessmen at venues such as the Royal Opera House, Ascot and Twickenham. In my opinion, they should have declined such corporate hospitality from private companies who were seeking Government contracts or other favours. Eventually, under pressure, Whitehall had reluctantly been obliged to reveal the extent of the 'freebies' enjoyed by the mandarins.

Much of my own negative experience of the Civil Service has involved the Foreign Office. In 2007, a Commons Select Committee launched a scathing attack on its style of operating, and at about the same time a former ambassador asked pointedly whether Britons abroad could any longer expect the protection of their embassy. He warned that British embassies were of little use to Britons abroad. My own experience in journeying overseas in the 1970s and 80s with groups of parliamentarians leads me to endorse his judgement. From Washington to Helsinki, I saw MPs and peers let down by embassy officials. In my business dealings with some former ambassadors I found them lazy and lacking initiative - although often likeable at a social level.

'Honourable' is a word that has been much used and abused in Parliament. It has lost its meaning to such an extent that it should be dropped as a prefix for MPs. Way back in 1965 James Callaghan threw a glaring light on the conduct of some MPs. As Chancellor of the Exchequer, he revealed his contempt for their behaviour in an unusually frank speech as his Finance Bill was being debated in Parliament. He declared bitterly, 'I do not think of them as the Honourable member for X or Y or Z constituency. I look at them and say investment trusts, capital speculators or "that is the fellow who is the Stock Exchange man who makes a profit on Gilt Edge". I have almost forgotten their constituencies, but I shall never forget their interests'. Despite his words the situation was to deteriorate. Regretfully, Callaghan himself later became associated with some shady financial operators.

By 2008, after Tory and Labour sleaze, cash for honours, the abuse of expenses, the dodgy donations and the cynical breaking of election manifesto pledges, there was an audible public snigger when MPs referred to each other as 'honourable members'. Having worked in and around the Palace of

Westminster for some fifty years I believe standards have fallen steadily.

Since the Second World War, there has been a big change in the type of people sitting on the green leather benches. In the 1930s, the Tory Party was largely dominated by retired Service officers, county landowners, lawyers and the type of businessmen who could take time off to attend to national business in the Commons. Over a third on the Labour benches were sponsored by trade unions, having spent most of their lives in manual work in the mines, railways and similar occupations or as union officials. They had already enjoyed satisfying, worthwhile careers before entering Parliament. They had gone there not to earn good salaries topped up with expenses perks, followed by plum pensions, but in a spirit of service.

That pre-war picture was still largely in place when I joined the Parliamentary Press Gallery in 1957. Standards, however, were beginning to slip and Downing Street was involved in the decline. As events developed, what struck me was the stark contrast between the high standards of public life during the Attlee Government after the war, and what I saw happening in the 1960s, 70s and onwards. I recalled how, as a Labour-supporting student, I read with dismay the rare case of Attlee's junior Trade Minister John Belcher. He was disgraced and driven from office because of his involvement with a dubious East European businessman. The affair was nothing compared with the scandal of John Poulson whose web of corruption entangled top Tory Reginald Maudling and Labour local government bigwigs such as Andrew Cunningham and T. Dan Smith. At a higher level, ministers were lying to Parliament over the Suez war collusion, and Prime Minister Macmillan encouraged Cabinet members to brazen out scandals - as in the case of Colonial Secretary Lennox-Boyd and the Hola camp killings.

Nostalgically some old Tory knights of the shires recalled to me the days when members of the Government 'took the honourable course' and resigned. They would refer in particular to gentlemanly Sir Thomas Dugdale who quit as Agriculture Minister in 1954 over the Crichel Down affair. This concerned serious mismanagement in the handing back of farmland requisitioned by the military during the war. Dugdale was lauded as a man of honour who took responsibility for mistakes made by others.

October 3rd 2008 is one of those dates that will stick in my mind: the day on which a good political friend received the job in government he should have got the previous year; and the day on which a parliamentary friend I had known longer than any other died peacefully in hospital, rich in well deserved honours. I wrote to Nick Brown to congratulate him on becoming Gordon Brown's Chief Whip, and added that the Prime Minister was lucky to have someone so loyal and experienced in that key post. On becoming Premier in 2007 Brown had, in my view, unwisely appointed Blairite Geoff Hoon as Chief Whip with Nick as deputy. I wrote, as well, to Grace Thomson to express sincere condolences at the death of her husband George – the Rt. Hon. The Lord Thomson of Monifieth, Knight of the Thistle, whom I was pleased to describe as one of the most popular and respected parliamentarians at Westminster.

For me the highpoint of our long relationship was when George was appointed an EEC Commissioner by Prime Minister Edward Heath in 1973 and asked me to be his public relations officer with a seat in his cabinet. My decision to decline his flattering offer was certainly the most difficult and important in my professional career.

With George's death, I was the last surviving member of the editorial team that had relaunched *Forward* as a Gaitskellite weekly journal in 1956. He had been deputy editor under Francis Williams, who had been the first to die. Brainy columnist Douglas Jay died next, followed by John Harris, who had been assistant editor before becoming aide to Hugh Gaitksell. George's link with *Forward* went back to 1946 when, demobilised from the RAF, he had become assistant editor of what was then a weekly Scottish Labour journal. He took over as editor in 1948 and as a Labour moderate, he had the tricky task of trying to balance his position with the more extreme left wing views of his readers in the Scottish Labour movement. Perhaps that background enabled him to sympathise with my position when I was political editor of *Reynolds News*.

In 1952 he entered Parliament as MP for Dundee East and in time *Forward* moved south to London. Apart from our early journalistic partnership I discovered that we had some other experiences in common. As young men, we had both been influenced by the old Etonian Labour intellectual John Strachey - me by his writings, and George because Strachey was MP for a neighbouring Dundee seat. We were both also interested in Commonwealth and colonial affairs and worked in our spare time for the Fabian Colonial Bureau.

In the run-up to Gordon Brown's autumn Government reshuffle, Nick Brown's name had been much to the fore in the Press as Labour MPs, plotting to force the unpopular Prime Minister to resign, tried to rally others to the rebel cause. In the hothouse atmosphere of Labour's annual conference in Manchester, rumours spread of the imminent reshuffle. Nick was tipped to return to the post of Chief Whip which he had held when Tony Blair formed his first Government in 1997. The rumour alarmed the anti-Brown faction as Nick was said to be feared by many MPs for his 'ruthless' approach to party discipline.

A Government source was quoted as saying, 'A lot of people are scared of Nick. Making him Chief Whip wouldn't be popular but it would be bloody effective'.

There had been another appointment in the reshuffle, however, that must have stuck in Nick's throat and which prompted me to add in my letter of congratulations, 'I do hope the Prince of Darkness does not let the team down for a third time'.

To everyone's amazement Gordon Brown had brought back into the Cabinet as Business Minister the man twice driven from government office by scandals – the Rt. Hon. Peter Mandelson! After his last departure from the Cabinet, his close friend and protector, Tony Blair, had got him the post of European Trade Commissioner. Gordon Brown had enticed him from this plush Euro post and now, soon to be made a peer, he was grinning cockily from newspaper front pages, his reptilian eyes as cold as ever as he quipped, 'Third time lucky'. I thought it would be a relief for Chief Whip Nick that the man he so disliked would be in the Lords and not the Commons.

We had lunched together over the years and had often shared our uncomplimentary views on Mandelson, the Sultan of Spin. Nick's loathing of the man reflected that of his boss Gordon Brown whose decision to bring him back into the Cabinet was clearly that of a desperate man. It was a move that aimed to block attempts by senior discontented Blairites to oust him from 10 Downing Street.

The day after he took his seat in the Lords, Mandelson sat a few rows behind me at George's funeral service in Kennington. He had chosen the flamboyantly long title of Baron Mandelson of Foy in the county of Herefordshire and of Hartlepool in the county of Durham. He was a close friend and former consultancy business associate of one of George's sons-in-law, Roger Liddle. George's daughter Caroline, married to Liddle, holds a top position at the BBC.

In the midst of leading Liberal Democrats such as Lord Bill Rodgers and Baroness Shirley Williams, Mandelson smiled smugly and looked at ease. With his Party trailing the Tories in the polls and a general election due within a couple of years, Gordon Brown desperately needed a friendly media. Yet he had brought back a politician loathed and distrusted by many leading journalists. News of his surprise return was greeted with an excited 'tally ho' by the press. The tone was set by David Randall in the *Independent on Sunday* who whooped, 'A new Peter Mandelson hunting season is underway'.

Within twenty-four hours of his appointment, the first of a new series of Mandelson embarrassments for the Government emerged. The Tory Shadow Chancellor, the young and inexperienced George Osborne, revealed that Mandelson had 'dripped pure poison' about Gordon Brown. This had taken place during a private chat in a taverna while on holiday in August on the Greek island of Corfu. Mandy, of course, strongly denied criticising the Prime Minister. What a start to the new job that was supposed to close the great divide between the Blairites and the Brown brigade.

Publication of the report of the inquiry into the use of bad blood by the NHS had been delayed several times. As I waited for its release, I received a phone call in December 2008 from a Colonel Terence English of the Royal British Legion (RBL). He said that Alf Morris had suggested he should ask me to help with an imminent press release. I agreed to meet him at the Army and Navy Club, St. James', in the belief that the RBL had some interest in the bad blood scandal. As soon as we sat down to talk I realised we were talking about different inquiries – and different reports. Trim and businesslike, Colonel English needed urgent help in another major scandal – the Government's failure to deal with the damaging effect on the health of British servicemen of what had become known as Gulf War syndrome.

It soon emerged that we were only a few days away from a major breakthrough for yet another of Alf's crusades. This was a fifteen-year battle to win fair treatment for British troops who had served with US soldiers in the 1991 Gulf War and, as a result, had suffered from a range of illnesses. Over the years the tight-fisted, callous Ministry of Defence had stubbornly rejected claims that these illnesses were connected with service in the Gulf. The MoD refused to accept liability for something it argued could not be described as a 'syndrome'. While still in the Commons, Alf had become honorary parliamentary adviser to the Royal British Legion in 1989, and in 1994 he was a founder member of the Legion's Inter-Parliamentary Gulf War Group. Together with a small group of dedicated MPs, Tam Dalyell among them, he had put severe pressure on defence ministers to shame the Tory Government into investigating the unexplained illnesses among Gulf War veterans. To Alf's dismay, the new Labour Government continued to play for time on the issue of compensation for the sick ex-servicemen. The Blair Government had rejected a call from the RBL for a public inquiry and by 2002 legal notice of intention to claim compensation had been lodged on behalf of nearly 2,000 veterans. In the USA, the Department of Defence faced a far bigger problem. The US had deployed 700,000 troops in the Gulf compared to Britain's 50,000 and a Congressional Committee of Inquiry into Gulf War Illnesses had been set up.

In recognition of his campaigning work on the issue in Britain, Alf was invited by the US Congress to sit on the inquiry committee - a unique but well earned honour. Faced with the UK Government's continued refusal to hold an inquiry, Alf, now in the Lords as Lord Morris of Manchester, decided to set up an independent public inquiry. This was a forerunner of the one he established to investigate the NHS bad blood scandal. Lord Lloyd of Berwick, a former senior High Court Judge, agreed to chair it for no remuneration. It would: 'Investigate the circumstances that have led to the ill-health and, in some cases death, of over 5000 British troops following deployment in the Gulf'. The Ministry of Defence - uncaring and irritated by the initiative - refused to attend the hearings.

In his report, Lord Lloyd destroyed the Ministry's case for inaction and concluded that sick Gulf War veterans were entitled to an admission by the Government that they were ill because of their service in the Gulf.

As I sat with Colonel English in his club on November 13th 2008, I learned that a landmark report from the US Congress' Research Advisory Committee was due to be published the following Monday. The development was very 'hush-hush' as a leak in London of the American report would be embarrassing. Alf had told the Colonel that I might be able to assist by alerting contacts in the media, although there must be no advance publication. The RBL had taken the risk, however, of issuing an embargoed news release at the weekend. It could have led to a leak in the Sunday press of the US report – but the embargo was unbroken.

I was invited to attend a press conference in the House of Lords on the Monday to coincide with the publication of the report. It was to be chaired by Lord Craig of Radley, who was Chief of Defence Staff during the first Gulf conflict. Alf was absent as he had been invited to Washington for the launch of the American report but he had drawn attention to the fact that US spending on research into the problem exceeded £260 million compared with £8.5 million in Britain. That was why the report's findings were so important.

After making 'alert' phone calls to some newspapers and the Press Association that morning, I arrived for the press conference and was introduced to the gentlemanly Lord Craig as BBC staff set up their cameras. He spoke simply and to the point. The American report confirmed the views of veterans that their illnesses were indeed triggered during their service in the first Gulf War. It cited 'strong and consistent' evidence that two neurotoxins were to blame – one in pills given to protect troops from the effects of nerve agents, the other a pesticide much used during deployment.

Lord Craig welcomed the report and asserted that it should lead to improved research and treatment in the U.K. Recognition of the full extent of the illnesses suffered by veterans – and the obligation owed to them - was long overdue. They were victims of war as much as anyone struck by a bullet or shell. Moreover, medical treatments for their conditions were needed, '…to protect current and future military personnel at similar risk'.

He criticised the Government for sheltering behind an alleged lack of medical evidence for the illnesses so many had suffered, and called on it to accept the American findings and deal promptly with those veterans who were suffering. Soon after I learned that others who had suffered for decades from callous neglect by Whitehall – the thousands of haemophiliacs infected by contaminated blood provided by the NHS – were at last to learn the results of Lord Archer's independent public inquiry into the scandal.

Alf Morris, who had set up the inquiry two years before, confirmed to me that its report would be published on Monday 23rd February. He asked me to help the inquiry's secretary Vijay Mehan to produce a news release and to advise on dealing with the media. It was to be the most successful media relations operation in my public affairs career.

Press and broadcasting organisations had been alerted a few weeks in advance by reports that the Government was obstructing the inquiry. It was withholding over thirty documents required by Lord Archer, some on the grounds of commercial interest. In the week before publication, Vijay was bullied by some sectors of the media. They threatened not to report the inquiry's findings unless they were given advance interviews with Lord

Archer or his team and advance copies of the report. I advised him not to give way. I assured him that all the media would have to cover the report on publication day as it was too important to ignore. Vijay stood firm and I was proved right. There were a few helpful 'curtain raiser' reports which included sympathetic items on the BBC's *Today* programme at 7 and 8 a.m. on the day of release. But no one broke the embargo on the hard news.

There followed a packed news conference at 10 a.m. in a room at the Commons with many of those present clutching copies of my news release. It had clearly struck the right alarmist note. The Archer report's findings were featured on every news bulletin broadcast throughout the day, ending with sympathetically handled interviews by Jeremy Paxman on *Newsnight*.

The report got widespread coverage in the papers and in a leading article *The Daily Telegraph* wrote, 'There could scarcely be a more appalling failure of the public health system than the fate inflicted upon thousands of haemophiliacs who relied upon the NHS for their supplies of blood, only to discover later that they were contaminated'.

The refusal over the years of any government to conduct a formal inquiry was described as 'extraordinary' and it urged the Brown Government to address the report's proposed improvement in compensation for the victims and their carers.

As part of a detailed two-page spread in *The Times*, Libby Purves commented, 'It is a story from the realms of nightmare'. Dealing with the disgraceful fact that the NHS had imported a blood product from America collected from people at high risk of HIV and hepatitis C, such as paid intravenous drug users and prisoners, she noted that haemophiliacs treated with this in the 1970s and 1980s had, 'Lived with anxiety and misery ever since'.

The report concluded that a full public inquiry should have been held much earlier. Procrastination in becoming supply self-sufficient had had disastrous consequences. Had this been achieved sooner, the scale of the catastrophe would have been significantly reduced. It added that commercial priorities should never again override the interests of public health. The situation had been compounded by the failure of some doctors to tell patients that they had contracted HIV.

Lord Archer's team decided not to point the finger of blame at individuals, to the disappointment of those wanting scalps. It was clear, however, that both the Labour Government of Callaghan in the 1970s and, even more so, the Thatcher Government in about 1982, had missed opportunities to prevent the tragedy.

Chris James, chief executive of the Haemophilia Society, with whom I had been dealing, welcomed the report and said that many of his members would have liked an apology from Whitehall, but added, hopefully, that it would come in the form of action '...*that the Government now takes*'. He was delighted with the media coverage for the report which I had helped to get, and, if sympathetic blanket coverage could influence a government to act, hopefully we had succeeded.

At a small dinner party at the Houses of Parliament a few weeks later, Alf Morris thanked me in front of Lord Archer and other guests. He said he had never experienced anything like the coverage we had achieved. I replied that I had never before had the privilege of being involved with a cause more worthy of such wide and deep public publicity.

Despite the media's support for the call for urgent action, the Government did very little in the months that followed. In October, a disappointed Alf told me he had decided to introduce a private member's bill in the Lords to implement the recommendations. With his determination and experience in getting such bills on to the Statute Book, I felt confident his measure would become law.

We were sitting together at the 70th anniversary lunch of the Parliamentary and Scientific Committee, presided over by Lord Jenkin of Roding who had given helpful evidence to the Archer inquiry. In his speech to over a hundred guests, Lord Jenkin drew attention to my presence and there was applause when he recalled my service as secretary to the committee. It was nice to be remembered.

Entitled the *Contaminated Blood (Support for Infected and Bereaved Persons)* bill, Alf's measure was published in November and passed speedily and unamended through the Upper House. It faced its vital second reading debate in the Commons on February 5th 2010. To win support, I drafted news releases for the Haemophilia Society, one of which warned that MPs who tried to block the bill would be named and shamed in their constituencies in the run-up to the General Election. The warning went unheeded. A woman junior Government Whip blocked the measure, seriously delaying the second reading debate until February 26th. Gordon Brown and his ministers had arrogantly ignored the media's support for the Archer Report and Government Whips continued to block the bill when it came up for consideration on private members' business days.

As the Government maintained its position, Alf warned in a BBC radio interview that the issue, and his measure, would not go away. To me, Gordon Brown's determination to prevent the 'fair deal' bill becoming law and callous refusal to compensate victims and bereaved families made a mockery of his much-publicised General Election slogan, 'A future fair for all'.

Over the course of the Gulf War and bad blood scandals, governments and many ministers had come and gone - continuity had been provided by officials. Surely it was time to change the system to ensure that the guilty men of Whitehall could no longer expect a job for life. By coincidence, the previous week a report by the cross-party think tank Reform had argued that it was time that individual officials were held personally accountable for policy decisions and blunders. Lamenting that Britain's once highly esteemed Civil Service was 'all but immune to scrutiny', it argued that the rules that made it virtually impossible to sack incompetent officials should be scrapped. I hoped that the report would cause alarm bells to ring in the cloistered corridors of power.

The make-up of the Commons membership with which I had been working continued to change. By the early 1980s it was very different from the late 1950s when I first worked at Westminster. The largest group on the Tory benches in the 1950s was made up of businessmen, with 156 directors, financiers, executives and consultants. There remained in the 1980s a strong trade union link on the Labour side, but union research workers and junior officials had replaced heavy industry workers. There had been a marked increase in those who had worked as researchers for MPs, ministers and shadow ministers, or for research organisations. The law was well represented in the Chamber by a hundred barristers and twenty solicitors and former polytechnic lecturers and journalists were also there in number. To add to the problem of lack of experience in business management and manufacturing industry, the average age of MPs was much lower than in the 1950s. The era of the full-time professional politician had arrived.

The Commons had too many people who had done little else but politics in their lives. Unlike MPs of the earlier period, especially on the Tory benches, they were financially dependent on their parliamentary salaries and expenses. In the wake of Margaret Thatcher's first two general election victories there had been a surge of young Tory MPs who viewed Parliament primarily as a means of earning a good living – especially if they could augment their salaries with fees as parliamentary advisers to industry and lobbying firms.

Eventually, in November 2008, a Cabinet minister complained publicly that voters were being turned off politics by career politicians who had no experience of 'real life'. The Communities Secretary Hazel Blears pointed out that politics was being dominated by an elite whose careers had been spent in political jobs. Too many MPs and ministers had little or no wider experience.

Miss Blears, a solicitor before entering Parliament at the age of forty-one, declared, 'There is a trend towards politics being seen as a career rather than a call to public service. Increasingly we have seen a transmission belt from university activist, MP's researcher, think-tank staffer, special adviser, MP and ultimately to the front bench'. Surveying the scene on both sides of the Commons, she concluded that it was deeply unhealthy for the political class to be drawn from a narrowing social base and range of experience. Miss Blears' straight-talking did not make her popular with government colleagues, and her own Cabinet career ended in 2009 following her involvement in the parliamentary expenses scandal.

In mid-November 2008 there came evidence that MPs at last were getting the message that the public regarded them as a closed community, and out of touch with issues affecting the man-in-the-street. They decided to set up a Speaker's Conference to conduct a yearlong inquiry into how to make the Commons more representative of the nation, and more relevant to its needs.

As 2009 and my eightieth birthday loomed, I found myself saying, 'This is where I came in…' - a repeat of the 1929 stock market crash in the early autumn of 2008 and a monumental international credit crisis bringing down financial institutions on both sides of the Atlantic. Was another Great Depression just around the corner? The hunt was on for the guilty men. Were the spivs of the world of finance to blame – the hedge fund wide boys, or those who gambled with other people's money from the luxurious executive headquarters of the big banks?

I was reminded of the career of the American city crook whose activities led to the destruction of Valin Pollen, the soaring PR company, soon after I had joined it in January 1989. His apparently sound business had been bought by money-rich VP which then discovered that it owed huge sums in unpaid taxes to the US Government for which it had become liable. Gordon Gekko, the most ruthless wheeler-dealer on celluloid Wall Street, had been partly based on him. And his most memorable line? 'Greed works'. Well this time greed had destroyed the confidence of investors. Fuelled by the cheap money policies of the US and British Governments, that greed had finally toppled the bankers' house of cards. As Chancellor for a decade, Gordon Brown had preached the need for prudence and claimed credit for ending boom and bust. In the end, he had presided over one of the biggest bust-ups of all times.

The financial crisis had a result that must have had Alfred Sherman spinning in his grave. In the mid-1970s, Alfred had famously declared 'Keynes is dead!' My old friend had led the revolt against the 'law' of economist John Maynard Keynes that governments could spend their way out of a recession. Influenced by Alfred, Margaret Thatcher had discarded Keynesian pump-priming as a solution for economic ills and plumped for free market, monetarist solutions. Now, after some thirty years, the discredited Keynes, whose policies had been blamed for stagflation, was miraculously enjoying a second coming.

Chancellor of the Exchequer Alistair Darling, faced with the worst slump since the Great Depression, declared, 'Much of what Keynes wrote still makes sense'. Riding a wave of state intervention which had brought about the nationalisation of crisis-hit banks, he spelt out his proposals to use taxpayers' money to spend the way out of recession with a series of major capital projects. The type of state investment advocated by Keynes in the 1930s – and implemented by Roosevelt in the USA with his New Deal – was again in fashion. Despite my admiration for Alfred Sherman's intellect, I had always retained a great respect for the towering intelligence of Keynes. I pondered on who would be proved right in the long run – Alfred's free marketeers or the Keynesians.

Then I remembered that Keynes had famously said, 'In the long run, we are all dead'.

As Britain sank into its first recession for sixteen years and the banking system came closer to collapse than at any time in nine decades, the Government showed its contempt for Parliament when it announced in October 2008 that MPs would get their longest Christmas break since records began. Apart from a few protests from Opposition MPs, the Commons – broken-backed and lacking both pride and a proper sense of its democratic role – accepted the insulting hand-out of a twenty-four day holiday. Unemployment was soaring, people were losing their homes and businesses and pensioners were being squeezed but MPs gladly set about planning what to do with their extra week off.

Not that many of them were taking the opportunity to debate Britain's role in the international financial crisis when it was presented to them in the Commons. A banking bill before Parliament at that time provided an ideal opening for MPs to discuss the reasons for the appalling collapse of so many ill-managed, greedy financial institutions. The prospects for Britain in the short-term looked very bad. It had smaller savings and greater personal debt than any other country. Yet only seventeen MPs turned up for the debate which collapsed early for lack of speakers when it could have gone on for hours. A relatively new MP, Charles Walker (Con. Broxbourne) asked in dismay, 'What is the point of Parliament? Is it purely a supine lapdog?'

Well, yes, Mr Walker, sadly I must tell you that is what it has become. Having supported an unlawful invasion of Iraq, the Commons had then allowed a guilty Government to attack hallowed civil liberties on spurious grounds of national security. Now its response to a financial and economic crisis was row after row of empty seats in the Commons chamber. The days when my old friend Leslie Hale and his coven of 'midnight hags' had kept Tory ministers up all night by exploiting Commons procedures had long since passed. Too many backbenchers today think their democratic role is fulfilled by joining in a yah-boo chorus at Question Time once a week. Few of them have bothered to master Parliament's more intricate procedures. In my time in the Press Gallery, it was not uncommon to be kept on duty until well past 2 a.m. as Opposition masters of procedure kept the House sitting, wearing down ministers. Today the emphasis is on working family friendly hours and maximising expense claims.

Exasperated by growing evidence of the Government's incompetence, I asked Tory MP contacts why Her Majesty's Opposition was not forcing votes of no confidence in the Commons. I recalled the old days when Opposition parties would have gone for individual ministers for monumental failures such as we had witnessed at Defence, Health and the Home Office by tabling Commons motions to reduce their salaries. To my dismay, the Tories replied that the Government was supported by such a large and supine Parliamentary Labour Party that it would survive with a large majority. There would be nothing to gain. I disagreed. Trying to hide my impatience, I explained that a full-scale Commons debate preceding the vote – assuming the Opposition was capable of deploying a good case – would be bad publicity for the Government and would further undermine public support for it. Moreover, if angry constituents challenged Labour MPs about such scandals as poor equipment for our troops in Iraq and Afghanistan, they would not be able to disclaim personal responsibility if they had supported guilty ministers with their votes in the Commons.

According to research by the Committee on Standards in Public Life published in November 2008, public respect for politicians had slumped and barely one in five voters trusted Government ministers to tell the truth. A poll of 2,312 people revealed that forty-one per cent of voters thought standards had fallen, a sharp rise from thirty per cent in 2006. A mere thirty-three per cent thought people in public life who were found guilty of wrongdoing would be punished.

Sir Christopher Kelly, the committee's chairman and Westminster sleaze watchdog, accused MPs of a sense of entitlement to over-generous expenses that had left the public increasingly cynical.

Within two weeks of the MPs' holiday announcement, the European Commission warned that the impending recession would hit Britain harder than leading nations on the Continent. It forecast that unemployment would rise by twenty-five per cent in 2009, the economy would contract by one per cent and the budget deficit would soar. It told Gordon Brown that he would be presiding over one of Europe's highest rates of public debt by 2010, while Britain's economy was shrinking.

Faced with this monumental financial crisis the Government revealed its counter-measures to the Commons on November 24th. It emerged that borrowing would leave the nation facing a higher level of debt than when the Government called in the International Monetary Fund to bail Britain out in the late 1970s. Still vivid in my mind was the scene I witnessed as the punch-drunk Chancellor Denis Healey recalled from the airport en route to the IMF, addressed a rebellious Labour Party Conference in a bid to win its support.

On November, the lordly Mandelson gave leaders of what remained of Britain's car industry an hour to argue the case for an urgent infusion of funds to prevent more vehicle manufacturers collapsing and throwing thousands of people out of work. Paul Everitt, chief executive of my one time proud client the SMMT, said later they had emphasised to the Business Secretary the need to address liquidity and restore demand. That very day Jaguar and Land Rover had been forced to announce further job cuts.

There was an urgent need for Government action. Yet the hard-pressed industry had to wait another eight weeks, with the economic crisis worsening, before Mandelson produced his rescue plan. I feared it was too little too late. In 2007, before the recession, the UK had produced more vehicles and engines than ever before. The motor industry had shrunk since the days I had advised it on lobbying but it had become more efficient, employed nearly a million people and exported three quarters of its output. In December 2008, car sales had halved compared to the same period the previous year. By February 2009, production of new cars had fallen by some sixty per cent.

In despair, the SMMT decided not to hold its international motor show that I had proudly attended years before with leading members of the All-Party Motor Industry Group. By the end of February another of my old clients, the car and aircraft manufacturers GKN, warned it would shed 2,400 jobs in 2009, following a cut of 3,450 the previous year. I recalled the days when, at the height of its success, I had regularly visited its plush HQ in St. James's to report on political developments affecting its business. Then, in March, the plight of Vauxhall Motors became especially serious. Its American owner, General Motors, was in deep financial difficulties and could not rule out a bankruptcy filing as it embarked on a drastic and urgent restructuring operation.

I was interested to read a report that Mandelson, while visiting factories in the northeast, had been shown work on the development of the electric car. Nearly thirty years earlier, the possibilities of such vehicles had been brought to my notice by Lord Ironside, an active member of the Parliamentary and Scientific Committee. The major car manufacturers, however, had shown little interest in their potential. In 1990, I had helped persuade my client the SMMT to produce a 'green' policy document *The Motor Vehicle and the Environment*, and I noted that the possible production of an environmentally friendly electric car did not receive a mention.

To protect the vested interests of member motor companies, the Society's slim 15-page booklet had struck a very cautious note. In March 2009, however, Mandelson, master of smoke and mirrors, wanted to divert public attention from the mammoth problems of the motor industry and the economy as a whole. As a result, by early April the media were encouraged to report that the Prime Minister aimed to make Britain a world leader in the production and export of electric cars and hybrid petro-electric vehicles. The plan was to introduce them 'en masse' across Britain, and to open talks with power industry firms to provide roadside power points to recharge batteries.

I could not believe that motorists were unrealistic enough to be bowled over by Gordon Brown's dream of an imminent electric revolution - a dream in part inspired by the hope of winning 'green' votes in coming elections. Moreover, experts who had driven electric cars were quick to point out snags that I had heard of over the years: their expense, limited speed and range, problems of recharging batteries and their own environmental damage. I could not believe that, having ignored the motor industry for over a decade and then crippled it with the recession he helped to create, Mr Brown thought he could get off the politico-economic hook with this gimmick.

Within days, however, Transport Secretary Geoff Hoon rushed out a statement announcing that motorists would receive a grant of up to £5,000 towards an electric car from 2011. The subsidy, made necessary by the high cost of the 'green' vehicles, would be available for five years in a bid to help Britain become 'a world leader in low-carbon transport'. A national network of battery recharging points would need to be in place to keep the short-range vehicles on the road. I foresaw a new challenge for Britain's bored young vandals: how many unguarded power points could they put out of action in a night? More frustration loomed ahead for the long-suffering motorist.

I felt happy, however, for my old P&S Committee friend Lord Ironside. He had campaigned for decades on behalf of the electric car and from 1976-83 had been president of the Electric Vehicle Association of Great Britain. Some MPs who earned consultancy fees from oil companies regarded him as a tiresome crank. Now his dream was coming true. I recalled also that way back in 1981, the Select Committee on Science and Technology under the chairmanship of my friend Lord Gregson, had urged government to invest more in developing electric vehicles.

In the delayed Budget statement on April 22nd 2009, Chancellor Darling unveiled another scheme to offset the steep decline in car sales. To encourage new car sales, up to 300,000 motorists would be given £2,000 each to scrap their existing vehicles that were at least ten years old. The hard-pressed industry would have to put in half the money for the £600 million scheme that would run until March 2010.

Mandelson had noticed that similar schemes had been successful on the Continent.

But while Mandelson involved himself in headline grabbing initiatives and meddled in other matters, Britain's ailing automotive industry waited in vain for the much-needed loans he had promised six months before. Then came a critical Commons report. It justified the effort that many of us had put into seeking a constructive parliamentary bi-partisan approach to the industry's problems through such initiatives as the All-Party Motor Industry Group. The Commons Business and Enterprise Select Committee completed an in-depth inquiry in July by declaring its profound disappointment with the Automotive Assistance Programme unveiled half a year back by Mandelson. The All-Party Select Committee noted that not a single penny had been advanced through the scheme and said that an urgent, coherent strategy was needed across tax, environmental targets and support measures. In July, the scrappage scheme did lead to the first car sales rise for fifteen months – up by two per cent. But light van sales fell by a third and analysts supported the MPs, warning that the industry needed much more and wider support.

As for the Budget as a whole, with no evident sign of guilt or shame, Darling unveiled the biggest rise in Government borrowing since World War Two. He admitted that the national debt would double to around £1.2 trillion in the future and that the budget would not be in balance again until at least 2018. Swingeing new taxes included a top rate of 50% for people earning more than £150,000 a year - another breach of his Party's 2005 election manifesto.

For some commentators, New Labour had finally broken with middle Britain. The successful Blair-Brown-Mandelson formula that had won the vital support of the middle classes by holding down taxes had been thrown overboard. In a desperate bid to rally the tribal support of Labour's critical paymasters, the trade unions, Brown had declared class war. Mandelson had returned to government in time to witness the death of the New Labour experiment that had won my support in the mid 1990s. Stained by innocent Iraqi blood, by sleaze, lies and appalling mismanagement, it had failed abysmally to wash 'Whiter than White'. The financial crisis was certainly one of international dimensions, but why did Britain have the biggest budget deficit in the developed world? Why did it have the highest level of personal debt?

Industrial giants who had once paid me for information and advice were being toppled by greedy financiers and incompetent politicians in Britain and America. One of the companies to go out of business in July 2009 was Barkers Group Limited, incorporating what was left of Charles Barker, the firm that had employed me for twelve years. As part of the Barkers services group, it had gone into administration just three years short of its 200th anniversary. Since 1812, it had been a trail-blazing company in advertising, top-level consultancy, public relations and the dissemination of parliamentary and political information. I had worked for it twice as long as for any other firm in my bumpy career and I consoled myself with the thought that the Butler curse had not played a part in its demise.

With manufacturing generally hard hit by the recession, I was dismayed to learn in mid-February 2010 that Teesside, industrial heart of my Cleveland County, was suffering more than most areas. The Corus steelworks at Redcar, near Middlesbrough, employing a workforce of 1,600 was being closed by its Indian parent company, Tata Steel, which had failed over ten months to sell it off. Gordon Brown tried to make up for his previous lack of interest by last minute attempts to sell the plant. Too late: what a contrast to his costly efforts on behalf of the high-living whiz kids of the financial sector. I pictured the deep despair in the Teesside trade union clubs and pubs that I had known so well, first as a local journalist and then as director of the campaign to set up the County of Cleveland. For numerous reasons, Teesside would always have a place in my heart.

The country's grave situation should have rung alarm bells for MPs, especially those on the Labour benches. In the era of the full-time professional politician, holding on to a seat in Parliament was essential to maintaining one's living standards. What other jobs provided such a short working week, long holidays, perks, expenses and subsidised pension? So they had lost the respect of an increasingly disenchanted and cynical public. As they approached the General Election year, the reaction of many in Parliament seemed to be 'So what?!' Like the Government, they were out of touch with the people they were meant to serve.

But within the walls of their costly mock gothic palace by the Thames – the best club in Britain – a time bomb had been ticking. In May 2009 it exploded with revelations in *The Daily Telegraph* of the monumental scale of the expenses racket that shocked even a seasoned old Parliament watcher like me. The newspaper had got hold of the full details of MPs' expense claims, and in particular allowances for second homes. MPs, led by the Speaker, had hoped to conceal these from the public.

Day after day for some weeks, ministers, shadow ministers and backbenchers of all parties were named and shamed by the media for their abuse of the rotten system. As the first instalments of the great exposé covered the front pages, some thick-skinned MPs called for *The Telegraph* to be investigated and prosecuted over the leak. Then came an extraordinary scene in the Commons chamber involving my local Labour MP Kate Hoey, highly regarded for her integrity and independence. When she rose to suggest that calling in the police would be a waste of money, the rattled Speaker rounded on her in red-faced fury with a bitter personal attack that stunned all who witnessed it. Clearly, he had lost it.

Demands grew for his immediate resignation over his handling of the expenses scandal. A week later, following a dramatic confrontation in the Commons with MPs demanding he should go, he became the first Speaker to be forced out of office for three hundred years. I had known him from his time as a successful and popular joint chairman of the All-Party Tobacco Industry Group. However, I had been wrong in my belief that this working class Scot from a Glasgow slum would be a modernising and reforming Speaker. Instead, soon after taking on the prestigious role of Britain's First Commoner, he had clashed with staff, and attracted adverse criticism over his personal expenses and of his chairmanship. He had finally been brought down by his failure - as administrative head of the Commons fees office - to deal with the abuse of allowances by MPs, and by his attempts to prevent publication of the facts and figures.

As for Kate Hoey, I was delighted that she had come out of the shambles so well. Over the previous few months I had been in contact with her on behalf of a local school headmaster who had been badly treated by the Lambeth education authority. Although he was recovering from cancer, it had exhibited a callous disregard for his poor health and fine teaching record. Typically, Kate Hoey had tried to ensure that he was treated with fairness and humanity.

With the successful launch and wide media coverage of Lord Archer's report on the NHS bad blood scandal, I began, at the age of eighty, to seriously contemplate the prospect of hanging up my boots. Then a newspaper report startled me into second thoughts. Appalled by what I read, I decided I had to offer my services to the Gurkha veterans of the British army who were campaigning against an outrageous Government decision to ban them from living in Britain. As an Indian Army Officer Cadet of seventeen, I had hoped to join a Gurkha regiment. But it was

September 1946 and the day after I joined the India Cadet Company at the Guards' Depot Caterham, it was announced that no more British soldiers would be sent to India for commissioning. Britain was to start withdrawal from the subcontinent, which would soon be submerged in a welter of blood from bitter racial conflict. As I waited months for a selection board commission in the British Army, my platoon was commanded by Gurkha regiment officers for whom I had great respect.

I recalled that experience as I read that one of my favourite actresses, the lovely, feisty Joanna Lumley, whose father had served with the Gurkhas, was supporting the be-medalled veterans seeking the right to live in Britain, the country for whom they had fought. The High Court had declared that it was unlawful of ministers to prevent Gurkhas who had served in the British Army before 1997 from living in Britain. The Home Secretary Jacqui Smith responded by issuing fresh criteria but the bar was set so high that only a few hundred would qualify.

I added my voice to the national uproar but before I could offer to help the Gurkhas' campaign, Parliament, within days, sprang into action. At last in tune with the public mood, it passed a motion tabled by the Liberal Democrats with support from the Tories and Labour rebels. It called on the Government to scrap the immigration rules that were designed to prevent the Gurkhas from living in the country they had served so loyally and well.

Not since 1978, in the last year of Callaghan's premiership, had an Opposition, aided by governing Party rebels, defeated an Administration – the issue then stemming from the Ford Motor Company's breach of an unworkable incomes policy which had led to the SMMT asking me to set up the All-Party Motor Industry Group. As with Callaghan, Gordon Brown had now been humiliated. He did a reluctant U-turn. All Gurkha veterans with at least four years service were granted the right to live in Britain. Decency and democracy had triumphed. I hoped it was not just a one off - that we would not have to wait another three decades before the Commons took up arms once more against an overweening, out of touch, failing executive.

Meanwhile, lobbying was once again in the news – in the worst possible way. The results of Parliament's failure to apply watertight rules of conduct for 'honourable' members had been highlighted dramatically in January 2009. The Commons watchdog Public Administration Committee had opened the New Year by drawing attention to an increase in the number of New Labour former ministers who were using insider knowledge to gain jobs with lobbying and other firms. It criticised the revolving door that allowed them to move freely and quickly from Whitehall into highly paid jobs where they could profit from former government contacts. Stricter regulation was called for.

The public was then stunned by a serious case of sleaze in the House of Lords which some had naively assumed to be above such scandals. Faced with closer scrutiny in the Commons, some unscrupulous lobbyists had switched more of their activities to the Lords where it was easier to defeat the Government – and where some peers were prepared to influence law-making for fat fees. I had suspected that a number were on the payroll of lobbying firms since the 1970s – and, of course, for a short time Lord Cullen had drawn a small fee from my company for giving advice. The lid was taken off the can of worms by a *Sunday Times* investigation. Reporters posing as lobbyists approached ten peers and pretended to seek help in amending legislation in favour of a Chinese client. Four - all Labour, including two former ministers – offered to help.

A day after the Commons had turfed out Speaker Martin the Upper House voted for a six-month suspension of two of the erring peers – Lord Truscott and Lord Taylor of Blackburn. It was the first time in over three hundred years that such a penalty had been imposed. The other two, Lord Moonie and Lord Snape, cleared of serious wrongdoing, were ordered to apologise to the House.

Soon after this, other peers faced allegations and inquiries, including in some cases police investigations. I had to agree with *The Sunday Times* that the prefix 'noble' to address members of the House of Lords was often as inappropriate as 'honourable member' for those who sat in the Commons.

Many peers were members of the Lords and Commons Pipe and Cigar Smokers' Club and at its convivial meetings, a tobacco industry spokesman would give an update on the latest government threat to its operations. It was left to individual members to decide, however, whether they should take any counter-action in Parliament on behalf of smokers. The most that pro-tobacco parliamentarians received from the industry – unless they were registered paid advisers – were occasional lunches and dinners or outings to sporting or cultural events. Many, often unscrupulous, enemies would have delighted in a tobacco industry scandal, but I ensured that my client was never placed in a potentially embarrassing situation arising from its dealings with parliamentarians. And so it was with all my clients.

The extent to which some lobbyists had used MPs to hire Commons dining rooms for clients' functions aimed at seeking to influence government decisions was revealed in official records released on February 4th 2010. At least forty MPs had reserved such rooms for outside organisations in recent years.

On entering the world of public affairs consultancy, I did not hesitate to say my range of services included 'lobbying'. I did not know then that the word was virtually banned in the public relations profession, as it was believed to have disreputable connotations. A small number of PR specialists were active lobbyists but preferred to describe themselves as 'parliamentary consultants'.

By my open style and with the success of my early campaigns – despite criticism and opposition from leading members of the public relations profession – I was successful in getting the word 'lobbying' accepted and the activity recognised as an honourable part of the democratic process. There were disreputable PR operators involved in underhand lobbying and in paying MPs to help them, but I argued that there was no reason to blame the well-established practise of lobbying itself. Within a few years hypocrisy was swept away. By the late 1970s, my erstwhile critic, the Public Relations Consultants' Association decided that the word was acceptable after all. Respected bodies, such as my client, the influential Confederation of British Industry, were happy to use it publicly to describe their operations in and around Parliament.

It was depressing, therefore, that things slid backwards in the 1990s. Once again, the word 'lobbying' started to become synonymous in the media with corruption thanks to the activities of a few cowboy consultants and greedy parliamentarians willing to accept cash to influence decisions.

Successive governments have been too lax in tackling this corruption – a problem which, when coupled with the glaring abuse of the parliamentary expenses system, has led to the growth of public disillusionment with politics and politicians. Alarmingly, it has produced a situation that could strengthen the hand of those extremists on the far left or far right who would destroy Britain's democratic institutions if given the opportunity.

A damning *Daily Telegraph* headline on February 5th 2010 seemed to me to sum up the appalling situation: 'This rotten Parliament'. It topped the revelation that 381 MPs – more than half the Commons – had been found guilty of over-claiming on their parliamentary expenses. Sir Thomas Legg, an independent auditor appointed to carry out an in-depth inquiry, had reported that many more MPs had abused the flawed system than the 'few bad apples' blamed originally. His review accused them of putting personal gain before protecting public money. More than £1 million would have to be repaid.

The Crown Prosecution Service announced next day that thirteen separate charges of theft by false accounting had been brought against three Labour MPs and one Tory peer in relation to their expenses. The fact that the dishonesty of so many parliamentarians had been exposed was deeply depressing. The most serious result of the scandals, however, was the untold damage to Parliament and our system of democracy.

Since my days as a schoolboy studying the British constitution, I had regarded our Parliament with pride and reverence. The day I entered the Parliamentary Press Gallery in 1957 as a political correspondent of the respected liberal *News Chronicle* was one of the proudest in my life. The thought of the public losing faith in Parliament as an institution saddened me.

Following the 2009 scandal of the 'cash for changing legislation' link between a few peers and lobbyists, Sir Christopher Kelly, chairman of the Committee on Standards in Public Life, demanded urgent action to stop peers from abusing their privileged positions. He called for a new investigatory body and '…appropriate sanctions – suspensions, expulsions and so on depending on the severity of the offence'.

Tory leader David Cameron, searching around for his daily headline subject in the run-up to the General Election, caught up with the problem of corrupt lobbyists on February 8th 2010. Solemnly he promised to take steps to curb the industry. His aim, to ensure that attempts by business to seek influence on government policy did not become the 'next big political scandal'. In particular, he pledged to stop recently serving former ministers from operating on behalf of lobbying firms.

A month after Cameron's pledge, fresh allegations against three former Labour Government Cabinet ministers accused of apparently offering help to lobbyists prompted Gordon Brown to make known that his election manifesto would promise to introduce a new 'statutory register' of lobbyists and their clients. Former ministers would be barred from lobbying for a year after leaving office. After so many years of inaction were we about to see some reform at last?

In my opinion, anyone found guilty of seeking to corrupt a parliamentarian should face a long prison sentence and corrupt parliamentarians should be sentenced to an even longer spell in jail. Given such overdue action perhaps it will become respectable once more to call oneself a lobbyist.

One thing, however, is crystal clear. In the light of the great expenses scandal of 2009, unless Britain's voters elect truly *honourable members*, our MPs can do far more damage to the reputation of Parliament than a legion of law-breaking lobbyists.

BIBLIOGRAPHY

John Campbell, *Margaret Thatcher*, Jonathan Cape 2003

Susan Crosland, *Tony Crosland*, Jonathan Cape 1982

Joe Haines, *Glimmers of Twilight*, Politico's Publishing 2003

Morrison Halcrow, *Keith Joseph*, Macmillan 1989

Mark Hollingsworth, *MPs for Hire*, Bloomsbury Publishing 1991

John Junor, *Listening for a Midnight Train*, Pan Books & Chapmans 1990

Derek Kinrade, *Alf Morris, People's Parliamentarian*, National Information Forum 2007

David Marquand, *Britain since 1918: the Strange Career of British Democracy*, Weidenfeld & Nicolson 2008

Alf Morris & Arthur Butler, *No Feet to Drag*, Sidgwick & Jackson 1972

David Owen, *Time to Declare*, Penguin Books 1992

Robert Peston, *Who Runs Britain?*, Hodder & Stoughton 2008

David Powell, *The Power Game*, Duckworth 1993

David Powell, *Counter Revolution: The Tesco Story*, Grafton Books 1991

Christopher Powell & Arthur Butler, T*he Parliamentary and Scientific Committee*, Croom Helm 1979

Robin Ramsay, *Politics & Paranoia*, Picnic Publishing 2008

Alfred Sherman, *Paradoxes of Power*, Imprint Academic 2005

Peter Shore, *Leading the Left*, Weidenfeld & Nicolson 1993

Corinne Souza, *So You Want to be a Lobbyist?*, Politico's Publishing 1998

Corinne Souza, *Baghdad's Spy*, Mainstream Publishing 2003

Peter Taylor, *Smoke Ring: The Politics of Tobacco*, Bodley Head 1984

Margaret Thatcher, *The Path to Power*, HarperCollins 1995

Baroness Warnock, *Included or Excluded*, Routledge 2006

Peter Wright, *Spycatcher*, Viking Penguin Inc. 1987

Hugo Young, *One of Us*, Macmillan London 1989

NOTES

1. The author worked at various times from 1971 to 2009 as a consultant on parliamentary affairs and public relations for the following organisations: Allied Lyons, BAA, British Road Federation, British Sugar Corporation, Cardiff City Council, Cement & Concrete Association, Channel Expressway, Cleveland County, Coalfield Communities Campaign, Confederation of British Industry, Corporation of the City of London , Engineering Council, Essex County Council, Europe - American Conference, Euroroute, Ford of Britain, GKN, General Motors, Grand Metropolitan Estates, Haemophilia Society, Isle of Wight Authorities, Imperial Group, Imperial Tobacco, Institute of Directors, Institute of Professional Civil Servants, Law Society, Logos, Luton Borough Council, Marubeni Corporation, Motorola, Pembrokeshire County Council, Plymouth City Council, Police Federation, Public Relations Consultants Assoc., Roads Campaign Council, Royal Automobile Club, Rothmans UK, Royal Insurance, Sea Containers, Science in Parliament, Society of Motor Manufacturers and Traders, Standard Telephones & Cables, Surrey County Council, Tesco, Teesside County Borough, Tobacco Advisory Council, Tobacco Manufacturers' Association, Tobacco Workers' Alliance, Tyne-Wear Metropolitan Authority, Ultramar, Woking U.D.C., World Union of Free Romanians, Yorkshire Water

2. The author served as administrative secretary for the following bodies at various times over the same period: All-Party Roads Study Group, All-Party Motor Industry Group (founder secretary), All-Party Minerals Group (founder secretary), All-Party Tobacco Industry Group – not registered (founder secretary), Associate Parliamentary Group on Meningitis (founder secretary), Lords & Commons Pipe and Cigar Smokers Club (founder secretary), Parliamentary Information Technology Committee (founder secretary), Parliamentary and Scientific Committee

262

INDEX